FREEDOM OF EXPRESSION ACROSS BORDERS

FREEDOM OF EXPRESSION ACROSS BORDERS

Communication, Culture, and Language

EDITED BY

Sachiyo M. Shearman, Linda G. Kean,
Mary Tucker-McLaughlin, and Władysław Witalisz

PUBLISHED BY ECU ACADEMIC LIBRARY SERVICES

Suggested citation: Shearman, S. M., Kean, L. G.,
Tucker-McLaughlin, M., Witalisz, W. (2023). Freedom
of Expression Across Borders: Communication, Culture,
and Language. Greenville, NC: ECU Academic Library
Services.
DOI: https://doi.org/10.5149/9781469677958_Shearman

ISBN 978-1-4696-7794-1 (paperback)
ISBN 978-1-4696-7795-8 (open access ebook)

Published by ECU Academic Library Services
Distributed by the University of North Carolina Press
www.uncpress.org

CONTENTS

This book examines how freedom of expression can be defined, shared, acted on, and responded to globally. Scholarly contributions come from a variety of disciplines including communication, literature, linguistics, translation, journalism, cultural studies, art, and other humanities and social science perspectives.

In designing this volume, the editors collected works on freedom of expression and communication, culture and identity from a broad swath of viewpoints. This compilation addresses ideas such as language and translation and their impacts on expression, mass media, and its ability to create and restrict freedom of expression, humor, and political satire, and the impact of expression of thought in the classroom and around the globe.

Essays included in the volume were presented at the Across Borders IX Conference—Freedom of Expression: Communication, Identity, and Culture on May 16 - 19, 2022, co-organized and cosponsored by East Carolina University College of Fine Arts and Communication, Jagiellonian University ID.UJ Excellence Initiative Programme, and State University of Applied Sciences in Krosno.

All essays included in this edited book went through the blind peer review process. The editors would like to thank the contributions of the following esteemed reviewers, Władysław Cholpicki (Jagiellonian University), Cindy Elmore (East Carolina University), Todd Fraley (East Carolina University), Monika Goghen (Jagiellonian University), Christopher Gullen (Westfield State University), Erika Johnson (East Carolina University), Elżbieta Mańczak-Wohlfeld (Jagiellonian University), Mariusz Marczak (Jagiellonian University), Brian Massey (East Carolina University), Aysel Morin (East Carolina University), Adrienne Muldrow (East Carolina University), Maria Piotrowska (Jagiellonian University), Keith Richards (East Carolina University), Eric Shouse (East Carolina University), Borim Song (East Carolina University), Jessica Teague (East Carolina University), and Deborah Thomson (East Carolina University). These scholars representing various fields reviewed and provided valuable comments on the manuscripts of this book.

The editors would also like to thank Justin Tyler King for designing the book cover. He is a graduate student in the School of Arts and Design in the College of Fine Arts and Communication at East Carolina University. Last but not least, we would like to thank John McLeod (The University of North Carolina Press), Samuel Dalzell (The University of North Carolina Press), and Joseph Thomas (East Carolina University Academic Library services) for their support in making this book's publication possible.

The Editors

WŁADYSŁAW WITALISZ | Jagiellonian University

"He who destroys a good Booke kills reason itself"

John Milton, Elon Musk, and the Question of Freedom of Expression (By Way of Introduction)

Abstract

John Milton's "Speech for the Liberty of Unlicenc'd Printing" delivered to the Parliament of England in 1644 reflects the intellectual's impassioned opposition to the same Parliament's Ordinance for the Regulating of Printing. Published as a pamphlet and distributed freely in defiance of the binding censorship laws, the work is, to this day, considered an important voice in building awareness of and support for freedom of expression as a civil right. Milton's humanist and religious education equipped him with ample argumentation against censorship from Greek and Roman history as well as the history of the Church. His republican, antiroyalist understanding of the state made him adapt ancient philosophical ideas of liberty to a political discourse that foreshadows the letter and spirit of the Bill of Rights of 1689, a landmark act that defines basic civil rights for the new parliamentary monarchy of William of Orange. The essay looks at Milton's argument in the context of what is known about censorship and the freedom of printing in 17th-century England and posits its validity in current debates on the need to control the internet and modern means of expression. Elon Musk's tweets on the subject are referred to as popular reverberations of the current debate on the subject.

Keywords: Milton, Musk, censorship, freedom

The debate on the concept of the individual's freedom to voice their views and opinions is as old as the human faculty of speech. The emergence of writing, which separated the temporary act of expression from the message that lasts and communicates itself repeatedly to new readers, made the issue even more problematic and led to various codifications of what could be said or set in writing and where. The dispute between those who defend and those who desire to control free speech turned from a purely ethical to a political argument and has informed major concepts of human social and public organization to this day.[1] In the broadest of terms, it has always been a dispute between liberty and authority laying claims to the power of information that the changing communication technologies offered. Every new technological invention that allowed an individual act of expression to be shared, become public, and finally go global (writing, printing, telegraph, telephone, radio, television, internet, mobile phone, social media), brought the issue of freedom of speech to the forefront of intellectual debate. The emergence of the digital society, with practically unrestricted spread and circulation of information, burdens our times with the need to consider and possibly regulate the impact of the accessibility of the digital message on our social and political reality.

We are today in a historical and civilizational moment somewhat similar to Early Modern Europe, a time when printing (invented only a few decades earlier) was becoming widely available and affordable. The statistics of early book production still look impressive today. Lucien Febvre and Henri-Jean Martin (1976) estimate that by the end of the 16th century some 200 million volumes of books had been published in Western Europe. The effects of Gutenberg's invention are seen as revolutionary because it completely changed the ways in which information and knowledge were distributed. Gilmore (1952) states that the invention of printing brought about "the most radical transformation in the conditions of intellectual life in the history of western civilisation" (p. 186). Sixteenth-century Europe quickly learned to use the printing press as an effective tool in public debate. Thanks to the efficacy of printing, both conservative propaganda and subversive criticism could quickly reach growing numbers of readers—literacy was on the rise as a result of the availability of books—and turn them into political supporters or opponents.

Unlike other trades and businesses with medieval roots, which had their rules and practices defined by the guilds, printing and publishing remained unregulated in Europe until the second half of the 16th century and is seen by economic historians as a significant contribution to the growing competitiveness of the emerging capitalist markets. Many new fortunes were made on the proliferating printing companies in major European cities. The growing number of printing houses was likely to also bring the idea of competitiveness to the content of the printed texts. Jeremiah Dittmar and Skipper Seabold (2019) argue in an interesting survey of the German publishing market of the 16th century that, in more competitive markets, one could encounter a greater diffusion of innovative, radical, socially daring content:

> [W]e find that competition among printers promoted the spread of business-practise ideas that drove individual achievement and local growth. Competition in printing also mattered for the diffusion of revolutionary re-ligious ideas. In an environment in which political freedom, representation, and voice were severely restricted, economic competition among printers promoted the diffusion of religious and political ideas that drove institu-tional change during the Protestant Reformation. (Dittmar & Seabold, 2019, p. 49)

The authors quote examples of printers who published Luther's work and papal denunciations of Luther within the same year (Dittmar & Seabold, 2019, p. 10).

The new technology of book production, ushering a new ideology of com-munication, came to England in 1476 with William Caxton setting up his printing press at the Almonry House of Westminster Abbey, not far from Fleet Street (Blake, 1991).[2] Soon, London became a thriving center of the printing and publishing industry, and the English learned to employ the press in their religious and political disputes. The early Tudors treated the press as an in-strument of royal policy, while the opposition, as long as censorship allowed it, used it to criticize and denounce royal decrees and decisions. D. M. Loades (1964, p. 29) notes that during the reign of Mary (1553–1558) "the opposition press was more vigorous and prolific than the official and contributed substan-tially to the insecurity and unpopularity of her government." Mary's act grant-ing the Royal Charter to the Company of Stationers in 1557 was an attempt to exert greater control over the printing industry and to exercise a stronger censoring grip over the content of the publications. Through the charter, the company received a monopoly over printing and bookselling in London and the rest of the kingdom and established a prepublication licensing system meant as a censorship net. The wardens of the company were additionally given the authority to "seize, take, hold, burn" books that had been published without the company's license and "imprison or commit to jail" any person printing books against the company's rules or expressing seditious or heretical opinions (Bently & Kretschmer, "Stationers' Charter").[3] The Stationers' Register continued to serve as a censoring instrument for the government, on the one hand, and as a copyright safeguard for the printers and publishers, on the other, throughout the Elizabethan, Jacobean, and Stuart times.

The contemporary debate between liberty and authority in information distribution must primarily be concerned with the spread of the digital technology of communication. Our times' parallel to the impact and the challenges of the printing press is obviously the career of social media and how they influenced our government of information. Printing took more than 100 years to change the face of public and political debate in Europe. In our digital world, the revolution happened in no more than 30 years. While the benefits and the dangers resulting from the applications of the new communication technologies are much greater than those we faced 500 years ago, the questions we are asking appear essentially the same: about limits of freedom and our responsibility for the word. To probe this apparent historical parallel further, I propose to look at the ideas of two important proponents—each in his own way—of the cause of liberty, living and making an influence in these two distant revolutionary periods of human history: John Milton and Elon Musk. However incongruous this pair may appear, each speaks definitively on the issue and positions himself decisively as a champion of free speech.

John Milton (born 1608) grew up intellectually in the midst of a heated debate between liberty and authority, which the Renaissance experienced more vehemently than any earlier period in human history. Milton's devotion to classical republicanism (see Rahe, 2004, pp. 243–275), which questioned the divine right of kings as the essence of social and political structures, was additionally informed by a much wider and specifically Miltonian attitude of intellectual liberty and endorsement of free will. "Reason is but choosing," Milton declares in *Areopagitica* (1644/1932, p. 25), a polemical pamphlet addressed to the English Parliament in 1644 and later published as a booklet. In it, Milton daringly criticizes censorship and the government's licensing of printing. Rereading this almost 400-year-old argument for the "Liberty of Unlicensed Printing" today, in the context of the current debate on the control of the internet, shows that the ages of dialectics of the freedom of expression have not brought us closer to conclusions and that the questions asked by the Early Modern man, only recently empowered by the potential of printing, are still our questions.

Milton's England, especially London, saw a proliferation of printing presses. The popular print culture grew rapidly and completely changed the political, moral, and intellectual debate of the times, making it more accessible for the populace and more intensive. No wonder that this outburst of printed expression was viewed with suspicion by patriarchal institutions of power and that licensing and censorship laws were strengthened.

Today we are again asking ourselves questions that Milton and his contemporaries asked about the benefits and the ills of free unrestrained access of each and every individual to a medium of expression that carries much farther than any other medium has ever carried before. It is especially intriguing to look at Milton's *Areopagitica* in the context of the opinions recently expressed by Elon Musk. Musk's purchase of Twitter and his handling of its privacy and control policies made headlines around the world and added fuel to the censorship discussion that is underway on the internet. The world's favorite billionaire calls himself "a free speech absolutist" and proposes, very much like Milton, to remove existing restrictions and controls.

And like all his other projects, he sees his Twitter mission as a global and universal issue. "This is a battle for the future of civilization," Musk tweeted in November 2022, after he announced the release of the Twitter Files, internal company documents revealing former censorship practices. "If free speech is lost even in America, tyranny is all that lies ahead" (Musk, cited in Kang, 2022). Yet Elon Musk is not John Milton. His call for freedom lacks Milton's intellectual background, his humanist perspective, and his moral concern. In addition, Musk may be driven by completely different motivations. A *Guardian* headline reacting to Musk's plans to buy Twitter warns, "Elon Musk wants to own Twitter to protect his 'freedom,' not everyone else's" (Reich, 2022).

Milton's concern for the right to free expression was the result of his classical education and his adherence to republican political philosophy, which opposed any form of controlling tyranny (including the democratic tyranny of the majority) and taught individual civic virtue and responsibility. His Puritan faith, urging him to confront the original, unmediated, and unadulterated text of the Bible, additionally taught him to value access to the word as spoken or written by its author. Milton interprets book censorship in Protestant England to be a remnant of old Catholic practices—he refers to the Inquisition and its suppression of reformation writing—by which the Prelates of the Church of England were still maimed and which should be removed together with other papist impurities.

Areopagitica was written by Milton in a particular political context of the early years of the English Civil War. It was his response to Parliament's Ordinance for the Regulating of Printing, also known as the Licencing Order of 1643. The parliamentary order practically reinstituted the stringent royal censorship measures of the Star Chamber Decree Concerning Printing of 1637, which the same Parliament had annulled in 1641 by abolishing the ill-reputed Court of Star Chamber.[4] After two years of relative freedom, the English printing market was again to be regulated and controlled, this time by the parliamentary side. The Puritans soon came to understand the political power resulting from the control of the printed word—the Licencing Order now gave to Parliament the authority that the Stuart kings used to have over printing. Milton's impassioned reaction against the order is no surprise since the act spoke against the primary ideals of tolerance and individual freedom cherished by the antiroyalists. In addition, Milton himself had just suffered from the effects of the new censorship laws: the first of his tracts on divorce was not granted the right to be printed and was published without a license and the author's name.[5] *Areopagitica* would also be published without a license in 1644 and with no indication of the publisher.

Areopagitica offers a well-informed historical overview in which Milton praises the liberal approach of the ancients to publication policies and criticizes the Catholic Church, especially the Pope and the Inquisition, for their arbitrariness and overstrictness in granting their *imprimatur* for publication. He advises his contemporaries to follow the ancient tradition and repeats after the ancients that to understand and embrace truth one must be allowed to learn all of its shades. The process of arriving at a true conviction about a problem is, therefore, dialectical, admitting different views and allowing the expression of opposing opinions.

Milton's argument in the *Areopagitica* revolves around two basic concepts—freedom and truth—and proposes that the search for truth and its expression should not be restricted in any way. Milton's unconditional obligation to follow truth results primarily from his essentially Puritan motivation for the search for Biblical truth and for true religion: "Truth indeed came once into the world with her divine Master" (Milton, 1644/1932, p. 43), and the mission of man is to seek it and purify it of misconceptions and misinterpretations. It is not impossible, Milton argues, that truth "may have more shapes than one" (Milton, 1644/1932, p. 53). He explains that the search for truth is an ongoing process effected by men sharing the findings of their quest, however imperfect and straying they may be. "[T]he scanning of error [is necessary] to the confirmation of truth" (Milton, 1644/1932, p. 19), the author argues to refute his own objection positing the danger of reading about vice and falsehood. Milton's rhetorical appeal to the Puritan-dominated Parliament is intentionally encased in the language of current religious and moral discourse, but his perspective becomes much wider, scholarly, and humanist, when he warns that bans and restrictions on the freedom of printing will lead

> to the discouragement of all learning, and the stop of Truth, not only by disexercising and blunting our abilities in what we know already, but by hindering and cropping the discovery that might be yet further made both in religious and civil Wisdom. (Milton, 1644/1932, p. 5)

Elon Musk hits a similar universalist tone in his tweet on the "battle for the future of civilization," though his concern is more about the political effects of censorship ("tyranny is all that lies ahead") than the progress of scholarly debate (see Reich, 2022).

Milton's most quoted line in his defense of free printing is the famous trope that almost anthropomorphizes the book as a living creature that can be killed, for "he who destroys a good Booke, kills reason itself, kills the Image of God as it were in the eye" (Milton, 1644/1932, p. 6). Such a metaphor could be coined only by a writer who understands the nature of the creative process and himself experienced the rapport between the author and his text. Milton the poet knows that "Books are not absolutely dead things, but doe contain a potencie of life in them to be as active as that soule was whose progeny they are; nay, they do preserve as in a violl the purest efficacie and extraction of that living intellect that bred them" (Milton, 1644/1932, p. 5).[6] Milton's failure to receive the license to publish his divorce tracts, inspired by the author's own experience and interest, may have influenced this rhetorical device.[7]

While Milton admonishes the abandoning of all prepublication censorship, he is far from being a free speech absolutist. There are books that do not deserve the attention of readers and should therefore be destroyed, he proposes. The measure of a good book for Milton is certainly not its artistic quality, but the truth it contains, truth that is opposed to what is untrue, not accepted, or believed to be true. Milton seems to be excluding from the true picture of the world what today we call fake news, falsehood, fabrication, unverifiable information. He names two particular examples of untruth that degrade a book: libel or personal slander, and because of his strong religious convictions, blasphemy. Libel and blasphemy, he argues, must not be tolerated and against them "the fire and the executioner will be the timeliest and the most effectuall remedy, that man's prevention can use" (Milton, 1644/1932, p. 57). Although libel laws still function in our systems to protect individuals from the damage that words can do to their reputation, blasphemy (from the Greek βλασφημέω), impious or profane speaking of God or sacred things, has disappeared from most state laws and has been replaced with the much more subjective concept of offense against religious feelings. For 17th-century Puritans, all Catholic writing was blasphemy. Milton bluntly denounces the publication and distribution of Catholic authors who promote "Popery and open superstition, which as it extirpats all religions and civill supremacies, so itself should be extirpat, provided first that all charitable and compassionat means be us'd to win and regain the weak and misled" (Milton, 1644/1932, p. 54).

Notwithstanding the fact that he questioned the need for censorship, only five years after writing his defense of the freedom of printing, Milton himself became a censor for *Mercurius Politicus,* an important Commonwealth newspaper of the 1650s.[8] One wonders if he then judged himself against his own opinion about licensers in *Areopagitica,* where he offers them no flattery (Milton, 1644/1932, pp. 31–32). Milton assumes that the licenser would hardly ever be a man of better judgment or greater ability than the author himself and believes that the censors will not judge books by their intrinsic merit. They would rather approve the publication of those books that suit the temper of the reading public and that are in harmony with the views and opinions already current and popular in the country.

Milton's argument about the correlation between popular reading preferences and the choices of the censor or the licenser immediately reminds us of the contemporary phenomenon of information bubbles, which the media create and sustain for their own financial benefit and often for the sake of political gains of the powers supporting them. Internet search engine filters, content-recommendation machines that track users' most frequent choices, or the ideologically crafted social media messages we decide to follow are the modern "censors" that flatter our reading preferences and separate us from what we do not like to hear. Only these cybercensors, these algorithms defining and restricting our access to information, are much more effective and much more dangerous than the undereducated individuals Milton referred to.

Milton openly calls censorship a form of tyranny and argues that it deprives people of the necessary intellectual exercise of reviewing their beliefs in order to reassure or redefine themselves. All kinds of beliefs, including religious beliefs, he says, must constantly be kept under review; people should be encouraged to develop within themselves the spirit of enquiry and an attitude of questioning. "Where there is much desire to learn, there of necessity will be much arguing, much writing, many opinions; for opinion in good men is but knowledge in the making" (Milton, 1644/1932, p. 46). Milton's optimist vision of human potential allows him to see this continuous reviewing and questioning as progress toward truth and reason, which he understands in religious terms: "[T]here must be many schisms and many dissections made in the quarry and in the timber, ere the house of God can be built" (Milton, 1644/1932. p. 47). A similar vision of intellectual openness and human progress, coupled with the more modern understanding of human rights, has informed many later attempts at defining and securing the freedom of speech, including the First Amendment to the American Constitution, which bravely introduced some Miltonian ideas into politics and law.

If today we recognize Milton's then controversial opinions as an important contribution to the political and legal discourse on freedom, why are we less willing to embrace Elon Musk's call for the absolute freedom of Twitter? After all, we all stand up for the freedom of speech, the freedom of expression, the freedom of publication, and Musk, at least on the surface, seems to be saying what Milton wrote almost 400 years ago. Some of our concerns arise from the difference between Milton's and Musk's understanding of freedom. The concept of absolute or radical freedom that Musk invokes in his tweets was unknown to 17th-century thinkers and may be traced no further than to 20th-century French existentialists (see Natanson, 1951, pp. 364–380). Milton understands the term freedom in the humanist and the moral sense, which can be most readily clarified by referring to another of his tracts, *Defensio Secunda*, written in 1654, where we read, "Know that to be free is the same thing as to be pious, to be wise, to be temperate and just, to be frugal and abstinent, and lastly, to be magnanimous and brave" (Hughes, 1957, p. 837). Freedom is placed among virtues that define the basis of human integrity and human moral liberty. This freedom is a freedom from necessity, an act of free volition of which intelligent creatures are capable. The idea is further developed in *Paradise Lost* where freedom becomes a moral choice. Milton's description of the newly created Adam and Eve contains the intriguing concept of "filial freedom":

Two of far nobler shape erect and tall,
Godlike erect, with native Honour clad

In naked Majestie seemd Lords of all,
And worthie seemd, for in thir looks Divine
The image of thir glorious Maker shon,
Truth, Wisdome, Sanctitude severe and pure,
Severe, but in true filial freedom plac't;
Whence true autoritie in men....
(Milton, 1654/1957, Book IV, lines 288–295)

Milton's definition of man is a theological one and identifies human freedom (the faculty of moral choice) with man being created in the image of God. Adam and Eve are Godlike erect and in them the image of their glorious maker shines. In the context of *Areopagitica* and *Defensio Secunda*, "filial freedom" can be read also as the stoic, but also Puritan, virtue of temperance. Filial freedom is not absolute freedom, it is the freedom given to the child by a caring father, a freedom that has boundaries, and yet a freedom that gives authority rooted in the child's responsibility for the uses of freedom. It is a freedom that is curbed by choice for a higher good. No filial responsibility can be found in Musk's revelations about his plans. He is as free as his fortune allows him to be. In an article in the *New York Times*, Mike Isaac and Lauren Hirsch propose that "by taking the company private, Mr. Musk could work on the service out of sight of the prying eyes of investors, regulators, and others" (2022).

There is no single law regulating online privacy and online freedom in the United States, but we need to remember that Twitter is a global company transgressing political borders and functioning in a variety of legal contexts. In the face of the digital revolution, whose impact is much more powerful than Gutenberg's invention, the debate concerning the freedom and the safety of internet users is gaining momentum and will have to lead to legal codifications. The European Union is probably closer to a unified understanding of the problem than any other political power. Europe has been reviewing the laws of its members concerning the regulation of the internet for some time, but even though the review has not been completed, the Digital Services Act (DSA) was published in 2022 in a joint effort of the European Council and the European Parliament. The act is called "An agreement for a transparent and safe online environment" and is proudly proclaimed the world's first in the field of digital regulation. The preamble of the act announces that it follows the principle that what is illegal offline must also be illegal online. It aims to protect the digital space against the spread of illegal content and to ensure the protection of the fundamental rights of users (that is authors). The *European*

Law Monitor ("What's happening regarding the Digital Services Act?," 2022), the official information portal of the European Parliament, summarizes the major implications of the act as follows:

> The DSA introduces an obligation for very large digital platforms and services to analyse systemic risks they create and to carry out risk reduction analysis. This analysis must be carried out every year and will enable continuous monitoring aimed at reducing risks associated with:
>
> - dissemination of illegal content;
> - adverse effects on fundamental rights
> - manipulation of services having an impact on democratic processes and public security;
> - adverse effects on gender-based violence, and on minors and serious consequences for the physical or mental health of users.

The presentation of harmful content and disinformation is promised to suffer swift removal and financial punishment of up to 6% of the company's worldwide turnover. Although this regulation may sound less draconian than the burning and seizure of illegal books listed as punishment in the Royal Charter of 1557, it will probably make internet publishers think twice before they use dark patterns or engage in a political misinformation campaign. It remains to be seen how these new laws will be implemented and how the internet moguls, including Elon Musk's Twitter, will react to them. For now, Musk has reinstated many Twitter accounts formerly banned from the platform for abuse of rules and hate speech, which has already cost him the loss of many top advertisers that generated Twitter's income. Nesrin Malik (2022) believes that Musk will have to learn "that free speech is not simply about saying whatever you want, unchecked, but about negotiating complicated compromises." Milton's "filial freedom" was also a compromise, an inescapable one. The authority of man, according to *Paradise Lost*, lies not in total and absolute freedom, but in an informed choice that follows truth and wisdom.

NOTES

1. For a comprehensive cultural history of this dispute, see Mchangama (2022).

2. Wynkyn de Worde, Caxton's apprentice, who acquired his master's business after Caxton's death, moved the business to Shoe Lane, just off Fleet Street. The metonymic use of Fleet Street as the seat of the British press industry has much earlier roots than the modern business association.

3. For more on the continued legal interventions in the printing and publishing business in 16th- and early 17th-century England, see Clegg (1997, 2008).

4. The Court of Star Chamber was a court tribunal that emerged during the reign of Henry VII and developed into a sort of court of appeal. The Stuarts managed to seize political control of it, and Charles I used it as an instrument in his persecution of opponents and religious dissenters. The codification of the censorship of printing was one of the court's prerogatives. The Court of Star Chamber was abolished as a result of the Habeas Corpus Act of the Long Parliament. For an overview of the history and the political significance of the Star Chamber, see Cheyney (1913).

5. *The Doctrine and Discipline of Divorce* was published without license and anonymously in August 1643. It bears the initials of the publishers' names, T. P. (Thomas Payne) and M. S. (Matthew Simmons). See Lewalski (2000/2003, p. 549, note 45).

6. Another Puritan poet, Anne Bradstreet, who had read Milton, wrote the moving poem "The Author to Her Book" (ca. 1666), where a conceit metaphor of a maternal link between the poet to her text organizes the entire poem. Bradstreet calls her poems "ill-form'd offspring of my feeble brain" and expresses her distress over the success of their publication. See Jehlen and Warner (1997, pp. 550–551).

7. For a comment on the relation between Milton's divorce campaign and his marital life, see McDowell (2020, p. 412ff).

8. For a discussion of Milton's influence on *Mercurius Politicus*, see Anthony (1996, pp. 593–596, 598–609).

REFERENCES

Anthony, H. S. (1966). *Mercurius Politicus* under Milton. *Journal of the History of Ideas, 27*(4), 593–596, 598–609.

Bently, L., & Kretschmer, M. (Eds.). Stationers' Charter, London (1557). In *Primary Sources on Copyright (1450–1900).* www.copyrighthistory.org

Blake, N. F. (1991). *William Caxton and English literary culture.* Bloomsbury Academic Publishing.

Cheyney, E. P. (1913). The Court of Star Chamber. *The American Historical Review, 18*(4), 727–750.

Clegg, C. (1997). *Press censorship in Elizabethan England.* Cambridge University Press.

Clegg, C. (2008). *Press censorship in Caroline England.* Cambridge University Press.

Dittmar, J., & Seabold, S. (2019) *New media and competition: Printing and Europe's transformation after Gutenberg.* Centre for Economic Performance; London School of Economics and Political Science. https://cep.lse.ac.uk/pubs /download/dp1600.pdf

European Parliament. (2022). *Digital Services Act: Agreement for a transparent and safe online environment.* https://www.europarl.europa.eu/news/en/press -room/20220412IPR27111/digital-services-act-agreement-for-a-transparent -and-safe-online-environment

Febvre, L., & Martin, H.-J. (1976). *The coming of the book: The impact of printing 1450–1800.* New Left Books.

Gilmore, M. P. (1952). *The world of humanism, 1453–1517.* Harper.

Hughes, M. Y. (Ed.). (1957). *John Milton: Complete poems and major prose.* Odyssey Press.

Isaac, M., & Hirsch, L. (2022, April 25). Elon Musk agrees to buy Twitter. *The New York Times.* https://www.nytimes.com/live/2022/04/25/business/economy -news-stocks-inflation

Jehlen, M., & Warner, M. (Eds.). (1997). *The English literatures of America: 1500– 1800.* Routledge.

Kang, J. K. (2022, December 6). What Elon Musk doesn't know about free speech. *The New Yorker.* https://www.newyorker.com/news/our-columnists/what -elon-musk-doesnt-know-about-free-speech

Lewalski, B. K. (2000/2003). *The life of John Milton. A critical biography.* Blackwell Publishing.

Loades, D. M. (1964). The press under the early Tudors: A study in censorship and sedition. *Transactions of the Cambridge Bibliographical Society, 4*(1), 29–50.

Malik, N. (2022, November 28). Elon Musk's Twitter is fast proving that free speech at all costs is a dangerous fantasy. *The Guardian.* https://www.theguardian.com /commentisfree/2022/nov/28/elon-musk-twitter-free-speech-donald-trump -kanye-west

McDowell, N. (2020). *Poet of revolution: The making of John Milton.* Princeton University Press.

Mchangama, J. (2022). *Free speech: A history from Socrates to social media.* Basic Books.

Milton, J. (1644/1932). *Areopagitica* (J. W. Hales, Ed.). Oxford University Press.

Milton, J. (1654/1957). *Defensio secunda.* In M. Y. Hughes (Ed.), *John Milton: Complete poems and major prose.* Odyssey Press.

Milton, J. (1654/1957). *Paradise lost.* In M. Y. Hughes (Ed.), *John Milton: Complete poems and major prose.* Odyssey Press.

Milton, J. (1643/2010). *The doctrine and discipline of divorce.* In S. J. van den Berg and W. S. Howard (Eds.), *The divorce tracts of John Milton: Texts and contexts.* Duquesne University Press.

Myers, B. (2006). *Milton's theology of freedom.* De Gruyter.

Natanson, M. (1952). Jean-Paul Sartre's philosophy of freedom. *Social Research, 19*(3), 364–380.

Rahe, P. A. (2004). The classical republicanism of John Milton. *History of Political Thought, 25*(2), 243–275.

Reich, R. (2022, April 22). Elon Musk wants to own Twitter to protect his "freedom," not everyone else's. *The Guardian.*

van den Berg, S. J., & Howard, W. S. (Eds.). (2010). *The divorce tracts of John Milton: Texts and contexts.* Duquesne University Press.

What's happening regarding the Digital Services Act? (2022, April 29). *European Law Monitor.* https://www.europeanlawmonitor.org/latest-eu-news/what-s -happening-regarding-the-digital-services-act.html

KENNETH REEDS | Salem State University

Arizona as Testing Ground for School Censorship

Abstract

As censorship in the United States focuses on critical race theory and arguments about the ways history is taught in our schools, this essay examines Arizona's 2010 law HB 2281. Passed in a politically charged context, HB 2281 was widely seen to target for elimination a Mexican American studies program in Tucson's public schools. This essay locates this legislation as a precursor to today's bills, laws, and guidelines being proposed and passed by local and state governments, as well as school districts across the country. The essay argues that Arizona's law was more a reflection of the noisy political discourse from the time and disregarded both the need for and success of the Mexican American studies program in Tucson Unified School District. Indeed, research has more than demonstrated that the culturally relevant pedagogy used in Tucson produced academic success by multiple measurements. Despite this, the political discourse of the moment ruled the day, the law was passed, and the Mexican American studies program ceased to exist in the form that it was conceived. Lastly, this essay couches this discussion in political terminology from the past and argues for the need of a new definition that will help us look to the future.

Keywords: Culturally relevant pedagogy, Arizona, HB 2281, Mexican American studies, censorship, critical race theory, politics

This essay will tell a story. It is a story from Arizona in 2010, but it will sound familiar. This familiarity is because the current debates about critical race theory are echoes of the story that I am about to tell. This is not a coincidence. The past events that I will relate, it could be argued, were practice, a test run, and a proving ground for the things that are happening now. To be able to talk about and understand this story from the recent past, it is necessary to use terminology from a bit further in the past. The notion of "fascism" is well known. However, it is so familiar that it has grown to be charged with emotion and connotations that do not necessarily help us delineate and relate the story that needs to be told.

For this story to make sense, I am going to have to distance the term from its historical context and point to a more up-to-date definition. To do that I am not going to just make up a definition, but I am going to rely on recent writing. In recent months the Yale philosopher Jason Stanley employed the term "fascism" to talk about a movement, a transnational political current that he sees making inroads and making its presence felt in political discourse in places like the United States, in Mexico, in the United Kingdom, in France, in Hungary, and in Russia.

In fascism's historical formulation, the world witnessed a people develop a cult of personality around a man who promised that a socially constructed idea like a race would grow, thanks to its perfection, to dominate the world. However, Stanley argues, in the modern version it is not the domination of a supreme race that is sought, but instead the rallying cry focuses on the defense of traditional values such as family, masculine strength, the rule of the powerful, and religion's central place in society. In the Unites States' political discourse, the people who argue for these values are often said to be conservative. However, to argue that conservatism's aim is to *conserve* is a bit of a misnomer. The goal, it could be argued, is not to keep things how they are, but instead push a vision of the United States that would be different from the one where we currently live. In that sense, they are not conservatives, but instead hope to be revolutionaries. The revolution that they seek to lead, Stanley argues, is a modern form of fascism.

This modern fascism is different from the image of Germans marching across Europe. Instead of a place where a particular race or ethnicity dominates, this is fascism where like-minded leaders from various countries and cultures find common ground in conventional views of how a society should function. Stanley describes it as being "about traditionalist, ethnic nationalists dominating each of their countries with a strong, powerful, masculine leader. It's about protecting supposedly traditional values against democracy, decadence, etc." (Stanley, 2022). In simple terms, for Stanley, "[t]he global far-right fascist movement presents itself as the defender of traditional values" (2022). This vision of political platforms around the world uniting in the name of old-fashioned views about women, minorities, and religion should give us pause and should invite us to think deeply about what is at stake as well as Arizona's legislation as an early example of its influence on classroom pedagogy.

Book 8 of *Plato's Republic* contains a conversation between Socrates and Plato that both celebrates democracy's advantages while also warning us about the path to its downfall. Democracy is posited as an attractive option in that it presents the best chance for diversity and cohabitation of people from different backgrounds and varying hopes. The text describes this city in metaphorical terms: "this is the most beautiful of polities as a garment of many colors, embroidered with all kinds of hues, so this, decked and diversified with every type of character, would appear the most beautiful" (Plato, n.d.).

This desirable result is the product of freedom, or in the words of the text, a city "chock-full of liberty and freedom of speech" (Plato, n.d.). However, this freedom suffers from a risk like alternative forms of government where overindulgence in advantage was argued to force demise. Socrates contends that too much freedom is democracy's danger. Specifically, he warns that in a democracy it is "inevitable that in such a state the spirit of liberty should go to all lengths" (Plato, n.d.). This unbridled spirit of liberty takes the form of public and private accusations where one points to another and claims that they are an enemy to freedom. The other then answers that no, their accuser is the enemy because he follows the laws and therefore is a slave and not a lover of freedom. These crossed accusations are possible because freedom of speech is the rule and therefore truth is relegated to a secondary role.

With the loss of truth, then, the door is opened to the one who speaks loudest or who most vigorously exercises his freedom of speech in such a way that it silences others. This, the text warns us, is the weakness of freedom and the path to tyranny: "And so the probable outcome of too much freedom is only too much slavery in the individual and the state" (Plato, n.d.). In other words, freedom of speech brings us to a point where the importance of facts wanes because they are drowned by the person who speaks loudest. This ancient description of both democracy's beautiful potential and the simultaneous warning about how its greatest danger hides within one of its sacred ideas bring me—finally—to the story that I intend to tell.

The terminology of "institutional" or "systemic" racism dates to Stokely Carmichael and Charles V. Hamilton's 1967 book *Black Power: The Politics of Liberation*. As of June 2021, US Republican lawmakers in five states had passed bills and in another 17 states had introduced legislation aimed to prohibit the teaching of concepts like racial equity, White privilege, and arguments that contend that "racism remains central to much of American life and its legal system" (Adams et al., 2021).

These pervasive efforts to make illegal the teaching that discrimination is systemic did not appear suddenly. Over the 54 years between Carmichael and Hamilton's book and today, US lawmakers have challenged multiple times how sexuality, gender, and racism are taught. While it could be argued that today's version is especially focused on African Americans and their place in US society, an earlier test ground for today's censored teaching took place in the early 2010s in Arizona, where lawmakers focused on Hispanic people and the teaching of Hispanic culture in public schools.

Hispanic culture and the Spanish language have long suffered oppression in the United States, but the law passed in Arizona took a new form that was not the "Mexicans not welcome" or "English spoken here" of the past, and instead, HB 2281 was expressly created to eliminate a "Mexican American studies" program in Tucson public schools. In many senses, it can be argued that the language in today's laws resonates with that which was used in Arizona. Indeed, as one author put it when comparing Arizona's experience with today's debate, "the language and the politics have clear echoes" (Stephenson, 2021). As the United States enters a newly energized period of censorship, one that repeats and amplifies the techniques and language used in Arizona, it is important to look to this earlier experience to ask what lessons can be learned to prepare for today.

The Mexican American studies program in the Tucson Unified School District was created to address a problem: the high dropout rate among Latino public school students in Arizona. A 2001 study showed that the state had a generalized challenge in regard to students not reaching graduation: "Arizona has a significant dropout problem with an estimated overall attrition rate of 33 percent" (Cortez et al., 2002). In analyzing the data from a demographic perspective, the same study found that "Arizona's minority pupils dropped out at higher rates than White pupils" (Cortez et al., 2002). Focusing on Hispanic students, they showed that nearly half left school: "Attrition for Hispanic students ranged from 44 percent in the class of 1999 to 42.7 percent in the class of 2000" (Cortez et al., 2002). Considering the loss of nearly one in two Latino students, it should be unsurprising that educators were willing to try something different. Among these difficult statistics, the Mexican American studies program began in 1998.

In simple terms, the curriculum that was created centered around the Mexican American experience in the literature and history that was taught. In the dry and rather ambiguous language of the state's official audit, strong teaching of varied viewpoints and intercultural exchange were emphasized: "Tucson Unified School District's Mexican American Studies Department programs are designed to improve student achievement based on ... valuable unit and lesson design, engaging instructional practices, and collective inquiry strategies through values of diversity and intercultural proficiency" (Cappellucci et al., 2011). More specifically, the faculty in Tucson focused on what some academics have called culturally relevant pedagogy.

This approach to teaching aims to center students' cultural realities, thus teaching differently to different groups of students. Curtis Acosta, one of the professors who created the literature portion of Tucson's curriculum, has emphasized the student-centered teaching philosophy: "The mission for our Mexican American/Raza Studies Department has been to empower students by addressing the educational and academic needs of [the] Chicana/o community throughout Tucson" (Acosta, 2013). To create this empowerment, the program created materials and even physical spaces that echoed this student-centered approach: "[W]e eventually developed academic spaces, specific classrooms and classes centered on the Chicana/o experience" (Acosta, 2013). Indeed, Acosta described an educational environment that eschewed the typical classroom where his students felt marginalized and replaced it with one where they were comfortable and even felt at home by "transforming a school space, which may resemble a primarily negative place for our students, into an academic space that resembles their home, their culture, and their identity" (Acosta, 2013). This centering of the students' cultural realities described by Acosta aligned with the practices of culturally relevant pedagogy. This pedagogy, when studied in San Francisco, was shown to be effective, or in the words of researchers who analyzed the results, "Taken at face value, these findings provide a compelling confirmation of an extensive literature that has emphasized the capacity of [culturally relevant pedagogy] to unlock the education potential of historically marginalize students" (Dee & Penner, 2016). So, did this pedagogy that had worked in San Francisco produce successful results in Arizona?

Created in an environment of challenging numbers, the program sought to make a change. Or, put differently, it "was founded with the aim of reversing some disturbing academic trends for Chicano students in Tucson" (Fong, 2014). The answer to the question of whether this curriculum was successful is that yes, it did indeed appear to work well. Regarding standardized tests, students participating in the program were "64 percent more likely to pass" in 2010 and, "in the 2008 cohort were 118 percent more likely to pass" (Cabrera et al., 2012, p. 5). Another metric often employed to gauge student success is graduation rates. These were also shown to improve with students in the program "51 percent more likely to graduate from high school" in 2009 and "108 percent more likely" in 2008 (Cabrera et al., 2012, p. 6). In other words, this study showed significant improvement in standardized test scores and graduation rates for students participating in the Mexican American studies program. A National Education Association report that collectively analyzed several studies on the subject in 2020 confirmed these successes, summarizing the numbers by stating that

> [t]hey found that although students in [Mexican American studies] courses entered, on the average, with lower 9th- and 10th-grade GPA and achievement test scores than control students, by 12th grade they attained "significantly higher [standardized test] passing and graduation rates than their non-[Mexican American studies] peers." (Sleeter & Zavala, 2020, p. 8)

It can be argued that these numbers show clear and large improvement by two important metrics. Indeed, as the National Education Association emphasized in their 2020 report, the Mexican American studies program "improved the achievement of mainly Mexican American students significantly more than the traditional curriculum and the more courses students took, the stronger the impact on their achievement" (Sleeter & Zavala, 2020, p. 8). Stated succinctly, a program created in 1998 to confront a situation where close to half of Hispanic students were not finishing school, was, in a decade, showing enormous gains in measurements of student success, particularly among Hispanic students. Yes, Tucson's Mexican American studies program was a success.

The program's successes were known, but nevertheless HB 2281 was passed in 2010 targeting it and embroiling Tucson's Mexican American studies in years of court cases. How did this happen? Most versions of the history of HB 2281 point to the legislation being born with a speech given by Dolores Huerta in April 2006. Huerta was speaking to students at one of the district's schools. She stated that "Republicans hate Latinos" and encouraged students to support the reelection of Congressman Raúl Grijalva (Fischer, 2006). Republican Jonathan Paton objected particularly to a recording of the speech being stored on the district's website, calling it "blatant electioneering" and possibly illegal use of school resources (Fischer, 2006).

It did not take long for editorial columnist Doug MacEachern to intensify the rhetoric with statements that described what the program's curriculum and teaching were doing to students in provocative words: "They [the teachers in the program] were turning them into Marxist foot soldiers" (Stephenson, 2021). State Senator Russell Pearce echoed the editorial language on the Senate floor, criticizing the program's teaching by characterizing it as treason: "History is one thing. Misinformation, hateful speech, sedition is not appropriate with my tax dollars" (Zirin, 2010).

Instead of specifying aspects of the curriculum considered Marxist indoctrination or disloyal to the United States, this inflated language was aimed at the entire Mexican American studies program. This is reflected in the law's final language and bullet points that

Prohibits a school district or charter school from including in its program of instruction any courses or classes that:

- Promote the overthrow of the United States government.
- Promote resentment toward a race or class of people.
- Are designed primarily for pupils of a particular ethnic group.
- Advocate ethnic solidarity instead of the treatment of pupils as individuals. (HB 2281—492R—House Bill Summary, 2010).

This language from the legislation did not point to what specific content from the Mexican American studies program was seen as objectionable. Its more general language of prohibition also included language that stipulated that a single person, the superintendent of public instruction, is the one who determines whether a particular district complies. In other words, the law empowered a single individual with the ability to judge a curriculum's content and to determine if a program should be closed. Ignoring the fact that the Mexican American studies program had measurable positive outcomes regarding standardized test scores and graduation rates, HB 2281's language was written without pointing to specific content and reflected the inflated political rhetoric being aimed at the program.

HB 2281 was a bill focused on education. However, instead of being aimed at measurable student success outcomes, it reflected the political climate in which it was created. One of the authors of a study that demonstrated the Mexican American studies program's academic successes recognized that empirical data might not have sway in the face of such a charged political environment: "The work may not 'matter' to policy actors who are influenced by ideological commitments, political agendas, or special interest group membership" (Cabrera et al., 2014, p. 1110). He was correct and despite the fact that HB 2281 does not explicitly name Tucson's Mexican American studies or address the political climate, the legislation was written with the goal of closing the program: "The Arizona legislature passed HB 2281, which eliminated Tucson Unified School District's Mexican American Studies program, arguing the curriculum was too political" (Cabrera et al., 2014, p. 1084). Teachers, parents, administrators, and students defended the program's curriculum and pointed to its successes. Furthermore, they also argued that it was not in violation of the newly approved legislation: "School district officials and teachers in the program vigorously denied being in violation of any of the language of the law" (Acosta, 2013). Nevertheless, the law went forward, and the program ceased to exist in the form that it had been created. In 2017, a judge declared not only that the law banning the program was unconstitutional, but that it had been motivated by racism. Even with this decision, the modern-day version of Mexican American studies in Tucson avoids some of the curriculum's more controversial aspects.

So, that was the story that I wanted to tell. What I would like to emphasize is that this was not a place where discourse was based in logic and reason, where participants used dialog and disagreement to move closer to truth. The simple truth was that the Mexican American studies program worked. Culturally relevant pedagogy produced students who were far more academically successful than those who were educated in the traditional curriculum. This was the truth. However, instead of centering this truth and perhaps debating ways to improve the program, the creation of HB 2281 was a discourse about power. Just as Plato had predicted, it was a space where the winner was determined by whoever exercised their speech loudest and most politically advantageously.

It was a debate about how people in Arizona talk about the past and how that conversation about history influences both their discussion of political power and—serving as a model—today's similar and wider discourse about how we teach US history across the country. This is true throughout the United States, including the five states where laws have been passed and the 17 where legislation has been introduced that prohibits the teaching of concepts like racial equity and White privilege. Among those states is the one that hosted the conference where this essay was originally given, North Carolina. Although eventually vetoed by the governor, House Bill 324 was passed by the legislature, limiting how teachers can discuss race in the classroom. For the Yale philosopher whose ideas I described at the start, laws like these are some of the many steps that he sees where one of democracy's fundamental aspects —freedom of speech—is used against democracy and in favor of a modern version of fascism.

REFERENCES

Acosta, C. (2013, October 15). Raza studies and the battle over educational reform. *Utne Reader.* https://www.utne.com/community/raza-studies-zm0z13ndzlin/

Adams, C., Smith, A., & Tambe, A. (2021, June 17). Map: See which states have passed critical race theory bills. *NBC News.* https://www.nbcnews.com/news/nbcblk/map-see-which-states-have-passed-critical-race-theory-bills-n1271215

Cabrera, N. L., Milem, J. F., Jaquette, O., & Marx, R. W. (2014). Missing the (student achievement) forest for all the (political) trees: Empiricism and the Mexican American studies controversy in Tucson. *American Educational Research Journal, 51*(6), 1084–1118.

Cabrera, N., Milem, J., & Marx, R. (2012). *An empirical analysis of the effects of Mexican American studies participation on student achievement within Tucson Unified School District.* University of Arizona College of Education. https://old.coe.arizona.edu/sites/default/files/MAS_report_2012_0.pdf

Cappellucci, D., Williams, C., Hernandez, J., Nelson, L., Casteel, T., Gilzean, G., & Faulkner, G. (2011). *Curriculum audit of the Mexican American studies department Tucson Unified School District.* Cambium Learning, Inc.; National Academic Educational Partnership. https://www.tucsonweekly.com/images/blogimages/2011/06/16/1308282079-az_masd_audit_final_1_.pdf

Cortez, A., Danini Cortez, J., & Robledo, M. (2002, September). *Dropping out of school in Arizona: IDRA conducts new study.* IDRA. https://www.idra.org/resource-center/dropping-out-of-school-in-arizona/

Dee, T., & Penner, E. (2006, January). "The Causal Effects of Cultural Relevance: Evidence from an Ethnic Studies Curriculum." Cambridge, MA: National Bureau of Economic Research. https://doi.org/10.3386/w21865.

Fischer, H. (2006, May 20). Legislator asks official ruling on Huerta talk. *Arizona Daily Star.* https://tucson.com/news/local/education/precollegiate/legislator-asks-official-ruling-on-huerta-talk/article_af0d5329-c12e-5da9-9ee3-e4fc1cb42567.html

Fong, J. (2014, April 26). When this teacher's ethnic studies classes were banned, his students took the district to court—and won. *YES! Magazine.* https://www.yesmagazine.org/issue/education-uprising/2014/04/26/interview-with-curtis-acosta

HB2281—492R—House Bill Summary. (2010). Arizona Legislature. https://www.azleg.gov/legtext/49leg/2r/summary/h.hb2281_05-03-10_astransmittedtogovernor.doc.htm

Plato. (n.d.). *Plato, Republic, Book 8.* http://www.perseus.tufts.edu/hopper/text?doc=Perseus%3Atext%3A1999.01.0168%3Abook%3D8

Sleeter, C. E., & Zavala, M. (2020). *Transformative ethnic studies in schools: Curriculum, pedagogy, and research* (chapter 3). Teachers College Press.

Stanley, J. (2022, April 7). *Putin thinks U.S. democracy is weak and hypocritical* [Video]. YouTube. https://www.youtube.com/watch?v=_9aKODtay6c

Stephenson, H. (2021, July 11). What Arizona's 2010 ban on ethnic studies could mean for the fight over critical race theory. *POLITICO.* https://www.politico.com/news/magazine/2021/07/11/tucson-unified-school-districts-mexican-american-studies-program-498926

Zirin, D. (2010, May 12). New reason to protest the Arizona D-backs: House Bill 2281. *The Nation.* https://www.thenation.com/article/archive/new-reason-protest-arizona-d-backs-house-bill-2281/

WŁADYSŁAW CHŁOPICKI | Jagiellonian University

Humor in the European Public Sphere as an Expression of Freedom of Speech

Abstract

The increasing polarization in European nations and in European politics as well as debates on the limits of freedom of expression have been the stimuli to develop a project titled "Humor in the European Public Sphere: Fostering Societal Debate About Contested Expression in a Globalizing World," which was funded in 2021 by the consortium of major European universities, including Catholic University of Leuven, University of Bologna, and the Jagiellonian University of Kraków. As part of the project, the international team of researchers from across the European Union have presented how humor (largely visual) has been used in public by politicians, journalists, and other members of the public in different European countries, frequently causing or responding to what has been called humorous controversies or scandals. On the website humorinpublic.eu, 24 short contributions are presented in an attempt to explain the humor across the borders of language and culture in a way that will be understandable and interesting not just for scholars but also for the general public. Specifically, each contribution is divided into three sections: (1) what do we see? (the content that perhaps would not all be noticed by readers from outside the culture), (2) what public issue is addressed?, and (3) what does humor do? Each contribution is also tagged with three kinds of keywords: (1) humor form/genre, (2) humor mechanisms, and (3) themes. The website also comprises a glossary with the key terms in humor studies, including humor mechanisms, explained to the interested readers in relatively simple terms. The website is set to develop and turn into a major vehicle of commenting on the growing number of humor scandals across Europe, although due to increasing globalization, it does not avoid references to global controversies either. Its general aim is to foster an understanding of the multifarious nature of humor.

Keywords: humor controversy, public sphere, humor mechanisms, free speech

Introduction: Humor in the Public Sphere

The sociopolitical conflicts that shattered Europe and North America in recent decades, with all their differences, have a great deal in common—they result from variously defined "culture wars" between conservatives and progressives (Nagle, 2017). The increasing polarization of political scenes has run deeper than before and with the parallel process of growing digitization of political debates (Shifman, 2014), it has gone online. The recent debates on the use of humor in the public sphere (especially in social media, very much in line with Habermas's (1991, p. 176) definition of public sphere as "virtual or imaginary community which does not necessarily exist in any identifiable space"[1]) have resulted from the fact that online humor and memes have become tools in these wars (see Galeotti, 2019, for the discussion of hybrid war). The debates by Western scholars highlight the centrality of freedom of speech, echoing various humor controversies, such as when the Turkish government demanded a criminal prosecution of German satirist Jan Böhmermann over a poem ridiculing president Erdoğan (Calamur, 2016), when Chinese government officials objected to European cartoons about COVID-19 (Galle, 2020), not to mention the frequent persecutions of stand-up comedians in India (Mogul, 2022). Researchers such as Kuipers (2011) and Herkman and Harjuniemi (2015) stress the necessity to express open criticism of those in power and for such disagreement to be accepted even though the temperature of public debate runs high.

Kuipers (2011) discusses the famous "Danish cartoons controversy" in 2006: As a result of the publication by the Danish newspaper *Jyllands-Posten* of 12 cartoons, some featuring the prophet Mohammed, particularly one where he was portrayed as having a bomb in his turban, protests erupted across the Islamic world, including the countries where Muslims are a minority, with protesters burning Danish flags, Danish ambassadors being recalled, and the cartoonists receiving death threats. She calls this the first "transnational humour controversy" (Kuipers, 2011, p. 63, see also Fraser, 2007), since the repercussions reached the government level in countries like Iran. She explains why the controversy was sparked specifically by cartoons and points out that this is a special genre understood cross-culturally as belonging "to a non-serious domain that is linked with fun and freedom, but also with ridicule and disparagement. Even if the cartoons were not necessarily funny (Lewis, 2008), the genre signals frivolity and irreverence" (Kuipers, 2011, p. 68). And this irreverence is found incompatible with religion generally, and with Islam in particular.

Following the publication of the cartoons, the public debate started where the left and right used their own arguments, which boiled down respectively to "trivializing religion," on the one hand, and "Muslims lacking a sense of humor" on the other. Crucially for the analyses in the present article, Kuipers identified two sides of the debate, which have remained the same ever since, even though many events and instances of culture wars have occurred since then (suffice it to mention the attack of Islamic militants on the editorial office of the French satirical newspaper *Charlie Hebdo* in 2015, in retaliation for their publication of cartoons depicting the prophet Mohammad). Both sides of the argument play the "modernity" card. Conservatives emphasize the essential nature of free speech for Western democracies, while progressives point out the need to accept and respect cultural differences. Interestingly, these differences extend further—conservatives stress respect for tradition and are opposed to non-European migration, while progressives condemn violence and oppression and appeal to the public to adopt a cosmopolitan approach that stresses the values shared by all humanity and to move beyond the national, provincial, parochial, and narrow-minded stance of conservatives in the name of progress (cf. Kuipers, 2011, p. 67).

With regard to the cartoons themselves, what Kuipers (2011) rightly emphasizes is the essentially ambiguous nature of humor, which cannot be directly turned into argument and statement (see also Mulkay, 1988); even cartoonists themselves may not know what the "right" interpretation of their cartoons is. "When we take a closer look at the *Jyllands-Posten* cartoons, it is not evident who is being ridiculed—the prophet Muhammad, militant Muslims, or the Western media" (Göktürk, 2008, p. 1707). Taking the most controversial bomb cartoon as an example, Muslims took offense as in their minds it portrayed the prophet Mohammad as a terrorist and was thus an impermissible attack on their religion; in contrast, the cartoonists as well as a large proportion of the Western audience read the cartoon as expressing criticism of Islamic fundamentalists: "Some individuals have taken the religion of Islam hostage by committing terrorist acts in the name of the Prophet. They are the ones who have given the religion a bad name" (Rose, 2006).

Kuipers points out one aspect of the Danish cartoon controversy that is rarely mentioned. There actually was a Muslim response to the controversy that was not a public protest, but rather an international Islamic cartoon competition organized by an Iranian satirical newspaper, although—significantly—there was no response on the part of Danish Muslims. Apart from its direct purpose, the international competition also aimed at disproving the long-lasting stereotypical conviction held by Westerners that Muslims have no sense of humor. The winning entries played on European taboos that are nonreligious in nature; namely, they referred to the Holocaust or its denial: one "shows a bulldozer with a Star of David building a wall in front of a mosque. On the wall, in black and white, is a picture of the Auschwitz railway station" (Kuipers, 2011, p. 73). Another portrayed Anne Frank sleeping with Hitler.

This calls forth a discussion of the ethical nature of humor. Humor has a corrective function as emphasized already by Henri Bergson (1911); it can build rapport and heal divisions (cf. Zelizer, 2010), but it can also hurt its audience's sensibilities. The principles advanced by Morreall (2009, p. 79) may be helpful in this regard: "Do not promote a lack of concern for something about which people should be concerned"; "Do not laugh at sb's problem when compassion is called for" (2009, p. 73). He seconds Kuipers, however, on the "non-committal nature of humor," which becomes problematic from the ethical point of view when seriously getting involved is required. He makes a distinction between humor by politicians, which tends to promote stereotypes and trivialize issues, and that about politicians, which tends to promote critical thinking. The former is a strategy and is essentially targeted (a notorious example are the Nazi cartoons targeted at Jews, which proliferated their stereotypes of greed and dirtiness). Such humor is not considered honest and does not aim at amusement, but is a means of achieving a persuasive effect (cf. Gérin, 2018, on the instrumental use of satire by Soviet authorities). It may block a political issue by blocking critical thinking about it. Morreall provides an example of the election debate in 1984 between the incumbent Ronald Raegan and the younger candidate Walter Mondale, where the ageism issue was blocked that way. During the debate, when the question of candidate age was raised, as Reagan expected it would be (he was 73 at the time), he said to Mondale: "I will not make age an issue in this election. I will not exploit for political gain my opponent's youth and inexperience" (Morreall, 2009, p. 77).

Morreall, somewhat idealistically, concludes that "ideal political humor" should be playful and honest—like in conversation among friends. In fact, for humor to have an impact, it does need to be critical or "edgy," which does amuse some people—and not only those in agreement with the viewpoints expressed.[2] Others, often those with different opinions, however, are sometimes offended, indignant, hurt; in short, they are not amused. When they make their objections public, we have a humor controversy: a moment of public contestation of a humorous expression, leading to a dramatization of social and political divides and oppositions.

Case Studies of Humor in the Public Sphere

The problem of humor in the public sphere, briefly presented above, has been severely understudied. This essay serves the purpose of outlining the issues concerned, which is made possible thanks to a cooperation of a team of European scholars who attempted to fill this research gap. They received a grant from UNA Europa—a consortium of Europe's oldest and leading universities, including five participant universities—the universities of Bologna, Madrid, Leuven, Kraków, and Helsinki, whose researchers participated in the project titled "Humor in the European Public Sphere" in 2021.

This first phase of the project (to be continued in the following research projects in the years 2022–2024) aimed to showcase examples of how humor works in the public sphere. Researchers from across Europe have chosen particularly telling instances of public, often controversial, uses of humor from their country, ranging from cartoons and memes to performances, artwork, and street happenings. The website humorinpublic.eu (UNA Europa, n.d.) has been designed and was edited by the team of three researchers: Giselinde Kuipers (University of Leuven), Delia Chiaro (University of Bologna), and Władysław Chłopicki (Jagiellonian University of Kraków), with two other research team members being Carmen Maíz-Arévalo (University of Madrid) and Juha Herkman (University of Helsinki). Twenty-two scholars who have so far contributed 24 examples to the website came from 19 countries of Europe, including the United Kingdom and Russia.

At the outset of the project, in order to ensure a degree of uniformity of examples, which represent a huge variety of humor used in the European public sphere, it was assumed that each example should contain a visual element, which could be a photograph, artwork, another kind of image, or video. The genres that the examples were classified as thus represented artworks, cartoons (most popular category with 10 examples), (photographs of) events (3 examples), memes and other images (7 examples), news articles (1 example), posters (2 examples), and videos (3 examples).[3] Apart from the variety of genres, each of the examples was attributed a theme, the most popular of which represented gender (7 examples), international politics (5 examples), or artistic freedom (4 examples).

In order to bring the humor examples closer to the general public across the barriers of culture and language, we have formulated three basic questions that each contributor was asked:

1. What do we see here?
2. Which public issue is addressed here?
3. What does humor do?

The first two questions stem from the realization that virtually nothing can be taken for granted when presenting cases of humor use across culture and language barriers. Thus, as per the first question, international readers must be told what they need to pay attention to when examining the visual(s) in each case. Second, the sociopolitical circumstances need to be brought to bear on the case, so that foreign readers can place the visual and its accompanying commentary in the appropriate context, assumed by the original target receivers of the humorous example. Third, and most importantly, it cannot be taken for granted that international readers will recognize the humorous nature of the visual, even when the first two questions have been answered. Thus, a range of humorous mechanisms (18 in total, but the list is not complete) have been assigned to the humorous examples, sometimes more than one per example. The most frequent mechanisms included exaggeration (12 examples), satire (10), parody (8), transgression (7), or irony (4). In order to facilitate the understanding of the mechanisms to readers, their simple, nontechnical definitions were offered in the glossary developed for the website, each with a typical example. Here is a sample of glossary entries:

- **Exaggeration** "consists in overemphasizing an element of a scene or image for humorous effect; the mechanism can be understood as a schematic opposition within one script, e.g. fatness: 'Yo mamma so fat the elephant at the zoo thought they were related'";
- **Satire** is "a humorous way of highlighting faults and weaknesses of politicians, their policies and their ideas. It is often considered a social practice rather than a specific genre and it can involve parody, irony, sarcasm, wordplay as well as other humor mechanisms" (the example is the *Charlie Hebdo* case[4] described also at the website);
- **Parody** is "a humorous imitation of a piece of art, a book, a film or even of a famous person or an event, usually not targeted at anyone" (clowns are given as an example);

- **Transgression** is "the mechanism which evokes humor by directly or indirectly referring to topics which are socially sensitive or taboo, such as sex, homosexuality, bodily functions, religion or violence. Humor makes it possible to refer to them, although the topics still remain sensitive, like a reference to rape";
- **Irony** "(verbal irony, often referred to as sarcasm in American English) is a rhetorical technique which involves opposed or contextually inappropriate meanings, with the negative meaning usually being intended (e.g., 'I like your shirt' in reference to a worn out and partially torn shirt). Irony tends to be humorous because it usually involves an opposition, but it does not have to be, given a serious context."

In the following part of the essay, I will attempt to bring closer four examples of a public use of humor in three countries (Poland, Portugal, and the United Kingdom), using three genres (a cartoon, a poster, and a news article), different themes (gender, social movements, national politics, corruption), and different mechanisms (including exaggeration, parody, satire, irony, and transgression).

Case 1: Online Controversy Over a Cartoon

The first case (described on the website by Agata Hołobut from the Jagiellonian University) illustrates very well what can be called an online humor controversy. The visual stimulus of the controversy was the cartoon by the well-known Polish artist Janek Koza. The cartoon (see Figure 1) was first published in the Polish *Polityka* weekly in 2017 and then republished on Facebook, coinciding with the first wave of "women's strike" in Poland against the planned restrictions on abortion. The specific public issue involved was that striking women particularly strongly protested against potential restrictions on terminating pregnancies resulting from rape. What we see in the black-and-white cartoon, drawn in a naïve style, is a number of women standing in various poses and wearing different outfits, more or less revealing their bodies. The caption (translated from the original Polish) says: "Indicate women who ask for rape (color them in)," thus presenting the viewers with a nontask (ethically and logically provocative) and at the same time parodying a children's coloring exercise. As to humor, there is an incongruity here between the stated message (complete the task) and the intended message (it is not women's way of dressing that is responsible for rape, as claimed by some), which should

Figure 1. "Indicate women who ask for rape (color them in)". Cartoon by Janek Koza (by permission of the artist) https://humorinpublic.eu/project/hopelessly-awkward/

evoke the sense of irony, but, due to the ambiguous and noncommittal nature of humor discussed above, often does not (as shown by comments below). The incongruity is accompanied by a comic tension, which results from the sense of transgression the viewer experiences when looking at the cartoon.

This elaborate cartoon evoked a number of responses on Facebook, some supportive of the cartoonist's message and others nonsupportive. The supportive comments frequently mirrored the original irony, by offering contextually inappropriate, and thus ironic comments (cited here in translation), such as "So much coloring," "What address do I send the crayons to?" (both drawing on the nontask at hand), as well as metalinguistic, nonhumorous explanations offered to other commenters: "This is good irony—I think I got it," "Only potential rapists can indicate." Nonsupportive comments were most revealing as they demonstrated how easy it is to misinterpret an ironic message; they included sexist and racist comments, and some of the commenters indeed failed to recognize the irony, blaming the author for promoting rape: "Shame on you," "Disgusting." When put right by others, they emphasized the fact that certain themes were taboo and should not be taken as subject of cartoons, and defended their perspective—"There are matters on which no sarcastic images can be made, but you won't get it" (thus claiming their own superiority)—or questioned the suitability of the use of irony in this context, expressing a "concern" about the likelihood of others to misinterpret the cartoon—"Consider how a simple man may react to this image: as an encouragement or permission."

Case 2: Provocative Poster Profanity

The second example (described by Dorota Brzozowska from Opole University) is also Polish, but represents a different genre and illustrates an interesting interplay of intertextual references. What we see is a poster with an elegant lady (who happens to be the well-known British actress Maggie Smith), well dressed in an old-fashioned way, smiling lightly and confidently (see Figure 2). She is attributed the words (in translation): "Would you be so kind and fu...[ck off]" ("wyp"... are first letters of the word: *wypierdalać*—get the fuck out, considered obscene in Polish), placed above her head in an elegant script. The phrase "to jest wojna" (this is a war) incorporates the letter "j" in the shape of a lightning bolt (the recognized emblem of the protesters), the symbol being repeated on the left-hand side of the poster against the female silhouette that features the words "strajk kobiet" (women's strike).

In 2021, *wypierdalać* became a slogan of angry Polish women who took to the streets to protest against the conservative establishment, after the abortion law had finally been declared unconstitutional by the government-controlled Constitutional Tribunal, and the Polish conservative government adopted a new law banning most cases of abortion (including that of serious, moribund pregnancies). The public protests erupted, with young people being the majority participants, and adopted *wypierdalać* as their main slogan as well as a range of equally slang references to the taboo sphere of sexual intercourse and body gases (see Chłopicki, 2019, for a longer explanation of the origin of Polish obscenities).

What humor does in Figure 2 is evoke the elegant versus vulgar/obscene opposition (known in humor studies in more general terms as high–low stature opposition; cf. Raskin, 1985), with the poster designer attributing the request, which is partly polite and partly rude, to the dignified lady impersonated by Maggie Smith; the poster uses the mechanism of exaggeration by comically inflating the lady's request.

There are several twists here, some of them being intertextual. The poster itself draws on earlier posters, including the 2020 poster in support of a women's strike, which uses the figure of Sarah Connor as terminator (see Figure 3). On the poster, the woman with muscular arms carries a huge machine gun, and in the background we can see the *wypierdalać* word again, this time in a recognizable script, known in Poland as the Solidarity script, which goes back to the 1980s and the rise of Solidarity movement in Poland. The lightning bolt—the symbol of the women's strike—is placed at the bottom of the poster.

Figure 2. "Would you be so kind and fu … [ck off]? This is war. You need abortion? You are not alone. Women's strike." Poster by Jarosław Kubicki (https://humorinpublic.eu /project/maggie-smith-gets-politely-vulgar/)

Figure 3. Sarah Connor (Terminator) in support of women's strike (2020). Poster by
Jarosław Kubicki. https://humorinpublic.eu/project/maggie-smith-gets-politely-vulgar/

Figure 4. Tomasz Sarnecki "High noon 4 June 1989", Solidarity poster. https://
humorinpublic.eu/project/maggie-smith-gets-politely-vulgar/

This time the polite–rude humorous opposition is not there, and instead the man–woman incongruity is evoked, not only because of the presence of the gun as a stereotypically male prop, but also due to the reference to the famous Solidarity election poster from 1989 with Gary Cooper, which had successfully encouraged voters in Poland to support Solidarity candidates in the crucial parliamentary elections that ended the communist system in Poland (see Figure 4).

Case 3: Artistic Cartoon on International Politics

The next example is an artistic cartoon by a British artist Dave Brown (see Figure 5), described on the website by Delia Chiaro from the University of Bologna. What we see there is the former UK Prime Minister Boris Johnson, sitting at a table, in a Union Jack chair, across from Ursula von der Leyen, EU president, who is sitting in an EU-flag chair. On the table, there is a golden tray in the shape of Ireland. Over the tray, Ursula von der Leyen, with a vicious look on her face, is holding a fork with part of a "sausage" stuck onto it. It is visually implied that the "sausage" has just been cut off from Johnson's crotch with the sword she is holding in her other hand; she is clearly planning to cut the sausage in half, thus implying evil intent. As if to corroborate the implication, Boris Johnson seems to be holding his crotch, obviously in pain and all sweaty.

Figure 5. The war of Johnson's sausage. Cartoon by Dave Brown. https://humorinpublic .eu/project/the-war-of-johnsons-sausage/ (by permission of the artist)

Figure 6. "The Plumb Pudding in Danger" by James Gillray. https://humorinpublic.eu/project/the-war-of-johnsons-sausage/

The intertextual reference is present here too, the cartoon being a parody of the well-known editorial cartoon from 1805 called "The Plumb Pudding in Danger" by James Gillray (see Figure 6). We can see William Pitt the Younger (on the left) and the newly crowned Emperor Napoleon (on the right), sitting in the chairs with their national emblems, at a table with golden plates on it. They are carving up the world with their swords, as if it was a Christmas pudding (hence the title). Pitt is holding a trident, symbolizing British naval supremacy, and cuts off the ocean, while Napoleon, a fork in hand, cuts off Europe, with high anxiety (possibly madness) in his eye.

What humor does in Figure 5 (with the cartoon from Figure 6 being alluded to) is evoke many incongruities: English versus French interests, French versus European interests, successful versus unsuccessful politician, 19th-century versus 21st-century European politics, as well as plays on the "allusive semiotics of sausages," to use Delia Chiaro's words. There is also a specific reference to the difficulties in importing sausages from Britain into Northern Ireland in 2021, due to Brexit (cf. de Gruyter, 2021).

Case 4: Spoof News Article Condemning Corruption

This last case, that of a mock article from the Portuguese spoof newspaper *O Inimigo Público* (The Public Enemy), was described on the website by Isabel

Figure. 7. Arrested teddy bear. Mock article from *O Inimigo Público*. http://inimigo
.publico.pt/2021/12/12/joao-rendeiro-detido-de-pijama-juntamente-com-urso
-de-peluche-cumplice/, discussed in English at: https://humorinpublic
.eu/project/teddy-bear-guilty-of-portuguese-bank-corruption/.

Ermida from the University of Minho in Portugal. The text of the article in translation is as follows:

> João Rendeiro was arrested by the South African authorities in his pajamas and taken to the police station along with the teddy bear he was with at the time. The Portuguese Police believes the teddy bear to be the real culprit of all the embezzlement and swindles of BPP [Banco Privado Português],[5] while poor João Rendeiro is nothing more than a front man. João Rendeiro should be released and go back to bed, while the teddy bear will stay in the same cell in Évora prison where José Sócrates[6] stayed the night. (https://humorinpublic .eu/project/teddy-bear-guilty-of-portuguese-bank-corruption/)

What we see in the visual in Figure 7 are two shots of the teddy bear (the banker's apparent companion at the time of the arrest, although this might be the spoof news item), which are like typical shots of a convicted criminal before he starts his prison sentence. The public issue that the article alludes to is that of rampant corruption among Portuguese bankers, who—from the perspective of the public—even when convicted remained completely unpunished and were able to continue their lavish lifestyle. Even against this background and no doubt populist argument, the case of João Rendeiro is unique and blatantly extreme: the bank manager was sentenced to a prison term for financial crimes leading to his bank's collapse, but he escaped to South Africa, where several months later, in December 2021, he was arrested in a five-star hotel one early morning while he was still in his pajamas. Upon his arrest he defiantly claimed he had "no intention" of presenting himself "to the Portuguese authorities or the Portuguese courts."[7]

What humor does in this case is evoke the oppositions of human versus animal, adult versus child (a teddy bear is a cute animal toy used by children to calm them down before going to sleep), sex versus no sex (a teddy bear is not a usual sleeping companion of a sexually active adult), guilt versus innocence (the teddy bear is not a real culprit as claimed by the article and in the spoof picture), thus contributing to a range of comic interpretations when the reader thinks of João Rendeiro as the real protagonist of the story. With regard to the form of the spoof article, the additional opposition of news article versus its parody is evoked, since the article assumes the standard news article form with the catchy title ("João Rendeiro arrested in pajamas together with accomplice teddy bear") and the typical information structure from the general to the specific (known as the inverted pyramid), including formal vocabulary. The ironic clash between the serious form and the nonsensical content is intended to amuse the readers.

Conclusions

To conclude, humor controversies differ across cultural boundaries, due to humor's inherent ambiguity as well as different cultural priorities, but certain public issues, when explained in considerable detail, can be conveyed to international audiences. All of the four examples illustrate the use of humor about politicians (as per Morreall's distinction), other public figures, and governments. Thus, they "punch up," support the public's right to freedom of speech, and contribute to the public control of the government. This raises the issue of possible limits of freedom of speech as raised by the left-wing part of the public opinion, who cite the respect for the sensibilities of minorities and quote, like Morreall, the following principle: "Do not laugh at sb's problem when compassion is called for." The humor controversies evoked by the examples comprised: the reference to rape and the irrational view, held by some and inflaming others, that the way women dress encourages rapists; the public use of profanity, considered culturally inappropriate, particularly in the Polish public sphere, which values and protects social hierarchy; making a sophisticated political point by a mocking portrayal of a prominent politician and alluding to mutilation of his genitals; and portraying a corrupt banker as a teddy bear and ironically attributing to the bear all the guilt for the banker's crimes.

It can be argued that the degree of likelihood that a humor controversy will be sparked depends on the ability of the audience to interpret the satirist's intention as humorous. Among the four examples, the Facebook cartoon caused the greatest controversy with its open rape reference and the ensuing misunderstanding of its irony, and the blatant public profanity used in the street of Warsaw (and broadcast on public television) met with a wave of indignant comments as well. In contrast, the sophisticated intertextual references in the Maggie Smith poster and Dave Brown's cartoon published in the *Independent* as well as the Portuguese spoof article published in a satirical newspaper all seem to have been more clearly understood as artistic and thus escaped public outrage; still, the associations of public figures with genital mutilation, the use of profanity, or alluding to strange sexual practices potentially called for such outrage. The humorous mechanisms of parody (the Portuguese example) seem to be the least prone to evoking controversy, while irony, exaggeration, and transgression are more likely to do so.

Overall, it should be emphasized again that the study of humor as it is used in the public sphere and that of its limitations, functions, and potential controversies is only beginning, and thus the present article sheds only some light on the issues concerned. The problem of the relation between free speech, so essential in the Western democratic tradition, and potential vulnerability and sensibilities of humor targets opens the true Pandora's box of cultural values and assumptions that, if taken too seriously, may lead to stifling democratic freedoms, not to mention humorous expression. The culture wars that have been unleashed in recent decades do not serve the purpose of unconstrained expression well, all the more so because many governments drift toward greater and greater control over the media. Still, as the example of humor thriving behind the Iron Curtain demonstrates (cf. Davies, 1998), while political humor may not bring down governments directly, it can potentially contribute to their downfall by rallying public opinion behind the (anonymous) figure of the "wise jester."

NOTES

1. There is an ongoing debate on the notion of public sphere, and some scholars tend to prefer the less straightforward approach to it, stressing its ambiguity and adopting the Bakhtinian perspective on it (see e.g. Gardiner, 2004).

2. There is no room to explore this issue further here, but humor researchers (such as Zillmann & Bryant, (1980) with their misattribution and disposition theories) assume that people tend to laugh more at the jokes that target those they do not like; on the other hand, well-structured jokes can be appreciated across social and political divides (cf. Davies, 1998).

3. Some of the examples included items belonging to multiple genres, e.g. both photographs of events and posters.

4. The famous caricature of a kissing Muslim, published on November 8, 2011, a week after after a bomb attack in Paris organized by radical Muslims.

5. One of the major banks in Portugal; João Rendeiro was its founder and CEO.

6. José Sócrates is a "former Portuguese prime minister, himself a suspect of major economic crimes which are currently in court and which caused him to spend a year in pre-trial detention" (https://humorinpublic.eu/project/teddy-bear-guilty -of-portuguese-bank-corruption/)

7. In May 2022, just before his extradition trial in Durban, South Africa, Rendeiro died in police custody (see https://www.thesouthafrican.com/news/portuguese -banker-joao-rendeiro-dies-in-sa-custody-following-arrest-last-year/).

REFERENCES

Ambroziak, A., Sitnicka, D., Szukalska, H., & Kocejko, B. (2020, October 22). Protest w Warszawie po zakazaniu aborcji. Tłum idzie pod dom Kaczynskiego [Protest in Warsaw after the abortion ban. The crowd moves towards Kaczyński's house]. *OK Press*. https://oko.press/protest-w-warszawie-po-zakazaniu-aborcji -tlum-idzie-pod-dom-kaczynskiego/

Bergson, H. (1911). *Laughter: An essay on the meaning of the comic*. MacMillan.

Calamur, K. (2016). Jokes about Erdogan aren't funny in Germany. *The Atlantic*. https://www.theatlantic.com/international/archive/2016/04/german -erdogan-insult-case/478437/

Chetty, R. C. (2022, May 13). Fugitive Portuguese banker Joao Rendeiro dies in SA custody. *The South African*. https://www.thesouthafrican.com/news/portuguese -banker-joao-rendeiro-dies-in-sa-custody-following-arrest-last-year/

Chłopicki, W. (2019). Conventional expletives as indicators of emotion, impoliteness and amusement in Polish spoken discourse. *MediAzioni, 24*, 1–27. http://mediazioni.sitlec.unibo.it

Davies, C. (1998). *Jokes and their relations to society*. Walter de Gruyter.

de Gruyter, C. (2021, June 23). Boris Johnson's "sausage war" was deadly serious. *Foreign Policy*. https://foreignpolicy.com/2021/06/23/boris-johnsons -sausage-war-was-deadly-serious/

Fraser, N. (2007). Transnationalizing the public sphere. In S. Benhabib, I. Shapiro, & D. Petranovich (Eds.), *Identities, affiliations, and allegiances* (pp. 45–66). Cambridge University Press.

Galeotti, M. (2019). *Russian political war: Moving beyond the hybrid.* Routledge.

Galle, C. (2020). Chinese ambassadeur in België: "Die corona-cartoons kwetsen 1,4 miljard Chinezen." [The Chinese ambassador in Belgium: Those corona cartoons hurt 1.4 billion Chinese] *De Morgen.* https://www.demorgen.be/nieuws/chinese-ambassadeur-in-belgie-die-corona-cartoons-kwetsen-1-4-miljard-chinezen~/

Gardiner, M. E. (2004). Wild publics and grotesque symposiums: Habermas and Bakhtin on dialogue, everyday life and the public sphere. *The Sociological Review, 52*(1_suppl), 28–48.

Gérin, A. (2018). *Devastation and laughter: Satire, power, and culture in the early Soviet state (1920s–1930s).* University of Toronto Press

Göktürk, D. (2008). Jokes and butts: Can we imagine humor in a global public sphere?. *PMLA, 123*(5), 1707–1711.

Habermas, J. (1991). *The structural transformation of the public sphere: An inquiry into a category of bourgeois society.* MIT Press.

Herkman, J., & Harjuniemi, T. (2015). Unity or heterogeneity: The promise of European public sphere? In R. G. Picard (Ed.), *The Euro crisis in the media: Journalistic coverage of economic crisis and European institutions* (pp. 221–235). I. B. Tauris.

Kuipers, G. (2011). The politics of humour in the public sphere: Cartoons, power and modernity in the first transnational humour scandal. *European Journal of Cultural Studies, 14*(1), 63–80.

Lewis, P. (Ed.). (2008). The Muhammad cartoons and humour research: A collection of essays. *Humor. International Journal of Humor Research, 21*(1), 1–46.

Mogul, Rhea. (2022, February 12). In India, comedians can face arrest for making the wrong kind of jokes. *CNN.* https://edition.cnn.com/2022/02/12/india/india-comedians-crackdown-intl-hnk-dst/index.html

Morreall, J. (2009). Humor and the conduct of politics. In S. Locker & M. Pickering (Eds.), *Beyond a joke: The limits of humour* (pp. 65-80). Palgrave MacMillan.

Mulkay, M. (1988). *On humour: Its nature and place in modern society.* Polity Press.

Nagle, A. (2017). *Kill all normies: Online culture wars from 4chan and Tumblr to Trump and the alt-right.* John Hunt Publishing.

Raskin, V. (1985). *Semantic mechanisms of humor.* Reidel.

Rose, F. (2006, February 19). Why I published those cartoons. *The Washington Post.* www.washingtonpost.com/wp-dyn/content/article/2006/02/17/AR2006021702499.html

Shifman, L. (2014). *Memes in digital culture*. MIT Press.

UNA Europa. (n.d.). *Humour in the European public sphere*. http://humourinpublic.eu

Zelizer, C. (2010). Laughing our way to peace or war: Humour and peacebuilding. *Journal of Conflictology, 1*(2), 1–9.

Zillmann, D., & Bryant, J. (1980). Misattribution theory of tendentious humor. *Journal of Experimental Social Psychology, 16*(2), 146–160.

ALICJA WITALISZ | Pedagogical University of Kraków

Weaponized Words

LGBTQ+ Anglicisms at the Service of
Polish Sociopolitical Discourse

Political language is designed to make lies
sound truthful and murder respectable.
—George Orwell (1946)

Abstract

The essay investigates the pragmatic functions of English-sourced LGBTQ+-related terms used in Polish sociopolitical discourse. Over the last century, English, as a *lingua franca*, has exerted a growing lexical impact on world languages. Affected are not only national standard varieties but also professional jargons and sociolects. The Polish language is no exception. English words, catch phrases, and idioms have been willingly adopted by Poles, either to fill in lexical gaps (in cases where Polish lacks equivalents) or for reasons of linguistic snobbery (in cases where Polish equivalents are available), or both. In the two recent decades, English has also become a handy reservoir of LGBTQ+-related terms that have been adopted not only by the Polish LGBTQ+ communities for the liberating self-definition and for constructing identity, but also by their allies willing to refer to LGBTQ+-related issues in a neutral and friendly manner. While we recognize the ways in which the English LGBTQ+-related lexis is used in Polish as a means of neutral designation of concepts that either have not been lexicalized or possess offensive names, the essay focuses on how LGBTQ+-related words are used in Polish as an effective means of ideological propaganda and antagonization, achieved through a conscious manipulation and semantic distortion of English words by far-right politicians and Church representatives. As for the research method, the author adopts a functionally oriented, usage-based approach to the analysis of the phenomena, illustrated with a sizeable body of authentic language data retrieved from the two largest corpora of contemporary Polish.

Keywords: LGBTQ+, political discourse, Anglicism, semantic distortion, language functions

Introduction

In the last century, English has grown to achieve the status of an international medium of communication; it is the language of scientific conferences, air traffic control, multinational events and organizations, and the internet. This unique position of English has allowed it to exert an unprecedented and continually growing lexical impact on European and world languages (see, e.g., Görlach, 2002; Furiassi et al., 2012; Imamura, 2018; Choi, 2021). English words are used in worldwide communication in all spheres of life to name objects, tools, inventions, people, cultural phenomena and abstract concepts, including sociopolitical phenomena. For instance, the name of one of the symbols of the American Wild West has found its way to Czech *džíny/džínsy*, French *jeans*, Spanish *jeans/bluyín*, German *jeans*, Polish *jeansy/dżinsy*, Russian *джинсы*, Swedish *jeans*, Italian *jeans*, Norwegian *jeans* (Görlach, 2001, p. 168), and even Chinese 牛仔裤 (literally "cowboy pants"). *Political correctness*, a US-born ideal of promoting tolerance and avoiding offense, has been rendered into Czech *politická korektnost*, French *rectitude politique*, German *politische Korrektheit*, Hungarian *politikai korrektség*, Italian *correttezza politica*, Polish *poprawność polityczna*, Russian *полити́ческая корре́ктность*, Spanish *corrección política*, Swedish *politisk korrekthet*, and Chinese 政治正确 (literally "political correctness") (Witalisz, 2015, p. 273). English words find their way not only into national standard varieties but also, and perhaps predominantly, into professional jargons and sociolects. The Polish language is no exception. English-sourced vocabulary was welcomed by Polish speakers before World War II (Koneczna, 1936/1937) and then in pre-1989 communist Poland (Fisiak, 1970). Since the historic political overturn of 1989, which guaranteed an opening to Western culture, values, and technologies, the number of anglicisms (i.e., words borrowed from English) has quadrupled.[1] This is also facilitated by the current foreign language teaching policy and the growing Polish–English bilingualism of Polish citizens.

English words, including catch phrases, idioms, and proverbs, are used in standard Polish in all spheres of life such as sports, technological advancements, fashion, popular culture, occupations, and many more (Mańczak-Wohlfeld, 1995; Witalisz, 2015). English-sourced terms also appear in professional languages and sociolects (e.g., in the language of information technology specialists, international corporation employees, medical doctors, as well as in the slang used by the youth and various subcultures, such as hip-hop and skateboarding) (e.g., Zabawa, 2017; Cierpich, 2019). In the two recent decades, English has also become a source of LGBTQ+-related terms that have been chiefly used by the Polish LGBTQ+ communities for the liberating self-definition and for constructing identity, and also by their allies for neutral and nonoffensive reference to LGBTQ+-related issues.

While English LGBTQ+-related lexis used in Polish usually serves as a means of neutral designation of concepts that either have not been lexicalized or whose native names are offensive, LGBTQ+-related vocabulary happens to be used purposefully in a politically motivated propaganda. Referring to authentic corpora-excerpted language data, I focus on how LGBTQ+-related anglicisms are distorted semantically in Polish ideological–political discourse and how they are used for conscious manipulation of the public.

This essay is organized as follows. First I address current Polish political discourse, whose main features do not deviate from other-language political discourses but which is marked by a distinctive Poland-specific attribute. Second, I discuss the notion of anglicism and its overt and covert faces, as well as the theoretical background behind the study of foreign linguistic influences. Next, I briefly refer to the research methodology and corpora used for the excerption of language data, to finally present and discuss the ways in which Polish public opinion is manipulated by the use of semantically distorted LGBTQ+-related anglicisms in far-right political discourse.

Features of Polish Sociopolitical Discourse at Present

Current Polish political discourse, especially the one associated with the conservative faction that is currently in power, does not differ much from the kind of political language heard elsewhere. It uses the same rhetoric and the same strategies used to effectively persuade and influence the way of thinking of the public. One of the major components of political discourse are political ideologies, defined as "basic belief systems that underlie and organize the shared social representations of groups and their members" (van Dijk, 1998, p. 17). To disseminate those beliefs, political figures and people in (some sort of) power undertake discursive actions, such as public speeches, interviews, and advertisements, directed at voters. Political discourse often exploits catchy and attention-attracting keywords and slogans, which, if used at the right time and in the right place, serve as keys to ideas that must be inculcated in the public's mind. The content of political talk proves effective if it is designed according to the laws of rhetoric and text pragmatics (Ożóg, 2004), which include the art of argumentation and the ability to find lexical means that will persuade the addressee.

Therefore, political talk is often associated with social engineering (Podgórecki, 1996), performed by the media, governments, politicians, or other parties, to influence society, its attitudes, and behaviors on a large scale. The aim of social engineering is to instill a certain way of thinking in those individuals who respond positively to a calculated appeal and whose perception of reality is often governed by prejudice (van Dijk, 2006, 2008). This is achieved by a frequent repetition of populist slogans and oversimplified concepts about particular issues, individuals, or social groups, which are based on stereotypes that are mostly negative and evoke axiological tension (Ożóg, 2004). Thus, slogans are not only meant to persuade and influence somebody's attitudes/behavior, but also to unite against the political or other opponent. Slogans are an effective linguistic weapon that is used in political discourse to attack individuals or groups by evoking negative associations and emotions (Reboul, 1980).

The major goal of Polish far-right political discourse is the shaping and regulating of social reality and an uncritical acceptance of doctrines and attitudes. This is often achieved by presenting black-and-white scenarios that evoke negative connotations and by constructing artificial contrasts or polarization between us and them (Czechowski, 2019). The key features of political discourse that aims at manipulation of the public opinion are ethically doubtful communicative acts, characterized by one-sidedness of argumentation and by the use of language mechanisms such as repeatability of the main thesis. Unethical verbal activities in Polish political discourse often involve the use of negatively connoted words (Benenowska, 2019), whose function is to distort the meaning of other words that appear in their context, especially such words that may not be comprehensible to an average voter.

Polish Sociopolitical Discourse and the Polish Catholic Church

The feature of Polish political discourse that may not be found in other (European) states is the active involvement in political disputes of the Polish Catholic Church representatives, including members of higher orders of clergy. It is not uncommon that during a pre-election period parishioners are instructed more or less directly on who (which political party) will "guarantee safe, stable, and Catholic Poland," which is a popular slogan heard in Polish churches. In return, conservative and far-right politicians openly support the

Church, also financially, using state budget funds to contribute to the building of new churches and (Catholic) Church-related infrastructure. This happens despite the formal separation of the state and the church, guaranteed in the Polish Constitution, and despite many Poles' objections to this active presence of the Church in Polish political life. Church representatives are invited to open and bless new bridges, motorways, schools, and other secular objects.

The Church–government relationship (or "marriage," as some put it) has been particularly intense since 2015, when the very conservative Law and Justice political party came to power. Despite the objections of the growing numbers of agnostics and atheists in Poland, it is not uncommon to see the symbol of a cross hanging on the wall in classrooms or in the Polish parliament, but no other symbols of any other minor denominations, despite their active presence in Poland (Orthodox, Protestant, Greek Catholic, Muslim, Jewish).[2] The ultraconservative representatives of the Polish Catholic Church get actively involved in Polish political discourse, as will be illustrated in the empirical section of this essay.

It is must be added that this continuous presence of the Church in the lives of many Poles and its strong position in Poland have been built throughout Poland's complex history and the hardships suffered by Poles in various periods of time, especially during the communist era and the 1981 Martial Law, when it was the Church that united Poles and offered consolation. This explains the sentiment and respect many Poles have felt toward it. At present, despite the rapid pace of the secularization of Poles (Sikora, 2021; Flis, 2021), the Church, perhaps encouraged by the currently ruling political party, still exerts its historical influence and gets involved in Polish politics.

Language Functions

The features of Polish political discourse well correspond to some of the functions of language. Although the major functions of language are communication and denomination (naming the reality), generally language may also be used for various other purposes, such as persuasion, positive or negative, for self-expression, as well as for the creation of literary and other works. Human language also has an aesthetic function when it is used to evoke positive or negative connotations, and a cognitive function used for the categorization and interpretation of the world. While maintaining social contacts we apply the phatic function of language, and when we use language in a humorous and playful way, we realize the ludic function (Markowski, 2005, pp. 9–11).

The analysis of English LGBTQ+-related words used in Polish allows for the delineation of the functions they perform. English-sourced LGBTQ+-related vocabulary has been found to realize the nominative, communicative, and group-bonding functions; it is also used for self-identification and self-expression (Witalisz, 2022). In this essay, I focus on the persuasive function of LGBTQ+-related words as used in Polish sociopolitical discourse. I will show that the same word may be used for positive or negative persuasion, depending on the linguistic context and the participants of a communicative act.

Anglicisms: English Words Abroad

The language data used in this essay are unusual in the sense that while analyzing Polish sociopolitical discourse, I will focus on English words. As has been noted in the Introduction, Polish speakers, just like speakers of many other languages, have been borrowing English vocabulary to refer to Anglo-American concepts, not only where native words were missing, but also to replace native words with English ones for various pragmatic reasons (e.g., to attract attention, to make an impression on others, or just to play on words).

Words and expressions borrowed from English are known as anglicisms (or Anglicisms) in language contact literature (e.g., Pulcini et al., 2012). They may be borrowed directly, as the word *jeans* quoted above, in which case the word, at least at its entrance in a foreign language, is perceived as of foreign origin due to English-like spelling, phonetics, and morphology. At a later stage, due to the assimilation processes, it may become adapted to the recipient language phonetic, spelling, and morphological rules, as in Polish *dżinsy/jeansy* and Czech *džíny/džínsy*. It is estimated that European languages each have several thousands of English words (Görlach, 2001) and the numbers are continually growing (GLAD, n.d.). Words such as *e-mail, Halloween, businessman, fast food, surfing, OK, know-how, fair play*, and *rock'n'roll*, to mention just a handful of examples, are recognized worldwide and associated with American culture.

English words and idioms may also be borrowed indirectly through word-for-word translation, as in the case of *political correctness*, quoted in the Introduction. For instance, the expressions *First Lady, e(lectronic) mail, skyscraper, fast food, rat race, greenhouse effect, headhunter, popular culture, soap opera, white collar workers*, and *glass ceiling*, have all been loan translated (i.e., translated directly) into, among others, Chinese, Czech, French, German, Hungarian, Italian, Polish, Russian, Spanish, and Swedish (for details on the respective forms, see Witalisz, 2015, pp. 273–275). Loan translated expressions are composed of native words and usually remain unrecognized by nonexperts as English-induced; see, for example, these renderings of the expression *dream factory*, as Hollywood is often referred to, into Chinese 梦工厂 (literally "dream factory"), Czech *továrna na sny*, French *usine à rêves*, German *Traumfabrik*, Hungarian *álomgyár*, Italian *fabbrica di sogni*, Polish *fabryka snów*, Russian *фабрика грёз*, Spanish *fábrica de sueños*, and Swedish *drömfabriken*.

Anglicisms vary in form and type, representing various "loanword nativization techniques" (Bańko et al., 2022), which are the different ways in which foreign words are rendered in the recipient language. Borrowed phenomena range from overtly foreign loanwords, such as *selfie*, *wellness*, and *drag queen*, to maximally nativized loan creations, such as Polish *zaplecze intelektualne* (literally "intellectual backup") (< English *think tank*) and Polish *sygnalista* (literallly "signal maker") (< English *whistleblower*). In the latter case, it is only the concept that is foreign and the English word serves only as a stimulus for the creation of a native equivalent. An English expression may be half-translated as in Polish *Krwawa Mary* (< English *Bloody Mary*) and Polish *długi drink* (< English *long drink*) (for other types of borrowed phenomena, see, e.g., Pulcini et al., 2012). The extent to which English is penetrating other languages is best illustrated by the so-called pseudo-anglicisms (i.e., English-looking and sounding words that do not exist in English, such as *before party*, formed in Polish by analogy to *after party*, *Handy* "a mobile phone" created in German, and *mobbing*, used in most European languages to mean "bullying at a workplace") (for more examples, see, e.g., Furiassi and Gottlieb, 2015).

The reasons why speakers of other languages borrow English words are various. I illustrate those reasons with LGBTQ+-related anglicisms, showing at the same time the variety of borrowing techniques available. The most important motive for borrowing foreign words is the need to fill lexical gaps (i.e., to name new (to the recipient language speakers) foreign concepts in cases where their languages lack native equivalents, for example, Polish *darkroom*, *gender mainstreaming*, *queer*). Language speakers also resort to borrowing foreign lexis in situations when a concept exists in the recipient language culture but it has not been lexicalized (i.e., it has no name, for example, Polish *gejdar* (< English *gaydar*), Polish *płynny płciowo* (< English *gender fluid*), *LGBT*, *cishet*, *cisseksizm* (< English *cissexism*)). Foreign words are also borrowed as alternative names for native words that are either offensive, negatively connoted, obsolete, or simply avoided for some reason by the recipient language speakers (e.g., the English word *gay* has been used as a neutral and nonoffensive alternative to Polish *pedał, ciota, pederasta, homoseksualista,* all offensive and referring to "a male homosexual person"). In this case, the borrowed foreign word performs specific pragmatic functions in the speech of the borrowers. There are also situations in which a new concept (foreign meaning) is attached to a native word that is a partial semantic counterpart of the foreign word (e.g., Polish *ciemnia* (< English *darkroom*), *duma* (< English *pride*), *tęcza* (< English *rainbow*), all in their LGBTQ+-related senses). Foreign words are also borrowed due to the prestige of the foreign language, its status of an international language, cultural dominance of the donor language speakers, the appearance of new semantic fields (e.g., information technology), word play and linguistic creativity, speakers' bilingualism, low frequency of native words, translator's incompetence/idleness, and linguistic snobbery (see, e.g., Rohde et al., 2000; Mańczak-Wohlfeld, 1995; Grzega, 2003; Haspelmath, 2009).

The theoretical background adopted for the study of anglicisms is a cognitive-onomasiological approach (Blank, 2003; Grzega, 2003; Zenner et al., 2012, 2014), which recognizes the active role of the recipient language speakers in the act of borrowing foreign words. Borrowing of foreign vocabulary is seen as a conscious word-finding and name-giving process, governed by the recipient language speakers' communicative and expressive needs. This approach is mind- and concept-oriented (rather than word-oriented) (i.e., it emphasizes the semantic component of language and the importance of the extralinguistic reality in the borrowing process) (Fernández-Domínguez, 2019). Borrowed words are studied as they are used in authentic communicative acts (in real-life texts) rather than as isolated words. Analyzing a whole context guarantees or at least brings us nearer a proper understanding of the intentions of the speaker/writer and tells us what pragmatic needs are fulfilled by a specific lexical choice, especially when that choice involves foreign words whose meaning may not be entirely clear for the recipient language audience. As will be illustrated below, a single word can be used to mean different things and evoke different connotations and reactions.

LGBTQ+-Related Anglicisms in Polish Far-Right Sociopolitical Discourse

LGBTQ+ Anglicisms in Polish

Research into Polish anglicisms in the area of LGBTQ+-related vocabulary has not been extensive. The few articles that can be found (see bibliography in Witalisz, 2021) mention single instances of English-sourced words used chiefly in the sociolect of Polish homosexual people. The most comprehensive, corpus-based collection that has been gathered so far is presented in Witalisz (2021), who lists over 230 LGBTQ+-related borrowings of various types, including direct loanwords (e.g., Polish *drag queen*), half-translations (e.g., Polish *studia genderowe* < English *gender studies*), loan translations (e.g., Polish *językoznawstwo lawendowe* < English *lavender linguistics*), and semantic loans (e.g., Polish *sojusznik* < English *ally*).

A corpus-based study shows that the sociolect(s) of Polish LGBTQ+ community(-ies) abound(s) in English-sourced words, which are borrowed to name: (1) people and groups (e.g., Polish *ally, buczka* (< English *butch*), *daddy, drag king, fag hag, friend of Dorothy, gay, LGBT, skate* (< English *skater*), *twink*); (2) places and events (e.g., Polish *darkroom, cruising bar, drag show, underwear party, naked party, klub misiów* (< English *bear club*)); (3) sexual practices, activities, and behaviors (e.g., Polish *bareback, bug chasing, chemsex, (sex)czat* (< English *sex chat*), *cyberseks/cyberek* (< Engilsh *cybersex*), *spanking, wyautowany* (< English *outed*)); (4) types of sexuality and sexual orientation (e.g., Polish *cisgender, gender, transgender, queer, tożsamość gejowska* (< English *gay identity*)); (5) symbols (e.g., Polish *flaga tęczowa* (< English *rainbow flag*), *jednorożec* (< English *unicorn*), *fiołki* (< English *violet*)); (6) organs and sexually stimulating agents (e.g., Polish *boner, cock ring, soksy* (< English *socks*); (7) medical conditions (e.g., Polish *AIDS, FFS, GRS, HIV, terapia konwersyjna* (< English *conversion therapy*)); and (8) scientific and legal concepts (e.g., Polish *gender studies, queer studies, płeć prawna* (< English *legal gender*) (Witalisz, 2021). The specific sociolectal vocabulary shared by a particular social group provides communal awareness and has a group-forming and group-bonding function. It is a social group that creates their own language, but it is also the language that creates a social group (Grabias, 2019). A sociolect unifies the members of a social group by evoking sameness and a sense of belonging. It also lets them separate from other social groups by evoking otherness.

While most LGBTQ+-related Polish anglicisms are semantically equal to their English etymons, some others, which are the focus of this essay, are distorted semantically to achieve specific goals. Authentic language data presented below point to the different understanding and use of some of the key terms and concepts related to the LGBTQ+ community (e.g., *gender, LGBT*) by particular individuals and groups.

Corpora and Method

The language data presented and analyzed in this section come from two web-based corpora of contemporary Polish. The 7-billion-word Monco Monitoring Corpus (http://monco.frazeo.pl) registers post-2008 texts and is daily supplemented with authentic language data from over a thousand websites and portals of the Polish internet. The 60-billion-word plTenTen Corpus is part of Sketch Engine, a large internet-based database that includes corpora of 90 languages (https://auth.sketchengine.eu). Both corpora guarantee sociolinguistic and genre variation of texts.

For the analysis, I use usage-based research methodology (see, e.g., Zenner et al., 2012; Backus, 2014; Winter-Froemel, 2014), which advocates the study of language, including contact-induced phenomena, in authentic communicative acts. This allows for the recognition of speakers' individual communicative needs and their intentions revealed through the conscious choice of specific linguistic means. Though the study focuses on the use of individual LGBTQ+-related expressions, I analyze them as they are used in the company of other words, which may, as will be illustrated here, significantly change their meaning. Separating words from the context would deprive them of the pragmatic functions they perform in authentic communication and blur or conceal the speakers' intentions.

Sociopolitical Background in Poland

The exemplary language data presented in this essay constitute only a small sample of a larger corpus of authentic texts that have been collected. Their content requires putting in context those readers who are unfamiliar with and do not experience Polish political discourse on a daily basis. The sociopolitical background for the linguistic phenomena described in this essay is a nation that is polarized and divided, generally speaking, into two groups that present totally different mindsets. On the one side, there are European Union-supporting cosmopolitans, open-minded, well-travelled, tolerant, environmentally aware, often well-educated, many of them Catholics, and on the other, there are conservative and ultraconservative Catholics who seem to confuse patriotism with nationalism, and who are intolerant of whatever is considered by them "against the norm." In respect to gender-related issues, the representatives of the latter group demonstrate socially negative attitudes toward members and ideals of the LGBTQ+ community by setting up "LGBT-free zones" in their hometowns and resorting to homophobic rhetoric, supported by the Polish president, Andrzej Duda's pre-election slogan "LGBT is not people, it's an ideology" and his comparison of the so called "LGBT ideology" to "neoBolshevism" (see, e.g., BBC, 2020; Picheta & Kottasová, 2020). Perhaps this worldview dichotomy described above is an unjust overgeneralization, but one that helps understand the sociopolitical background in Poland.

Language Data and Discussion

In modern politics, one of the most effective tools used to manipulate people's minds, activated chiefly during parliamentary and presidential campaigns, is the strategy of imposing threat and pointing at an enemy, whether real or imagined. This strategy is also useful as a replacement topic to hush up inconvenient scandals, such as, for instance, the recently publicized pedophilia acts in the Polish Catholic Church (see, e.g., Stawiany, 2019; EuroNews, 2021).

Using foreign words whose meaning is unclear or unknown seems the most effective strategy of manipulation and diverting the public attention from real problems. The first set of data is a sample of *gender*-related statements expressed by Polish far-right media, far-right politicians, and representatives of the Polish Catholic Church (English translation in square brackets):

(1) "Diabeł, gender i feminizm: w Sejmie o szkodliwych treściach w e-podręcznikach" [Devil, **gender** and feminism: Parliamentary debates about the harmful contents in e-textbooks] – title of a feature article (https://www.prawo .pl/oswiata/diabel-gender-i-feminizm-w-sejmie-o-szkodli-wych-tresciach -w-e-podrecznikach,131625.html);

(2) "Gender ideologią szatana? To zniszczy polskie rodziny" [Is **gender** Satan's ideology? This will ruin Polish families] – title of a radio report (https://www.polskieradio.pl/7/3040/Artykul/1026484,Gender-ideologia -szatana-To-zniszczy-polskie-rodziny);

(3) "Słusznie mówi się o gendertotalitaryzmie, bo genderyści rzeczywiście chcą władzy totalnej" [**Gender**-totalitarianism is the right name, as genderists want, in fact, total power] – fragment of a Catholic priest's comment (http:// niedlagender.info/gender-ideologia-totalitarna/);

(4) "Gender to ideologiczna zaraza" [**Gender** is an ideological plague] – fragment of a far-right politician's comment (https://www.rp.pl/artykul /1110496-Gender-to-ideologiczna-zaraza.html);

(5) "Szkodliwość tzw. ideologii gender" [Harmfulness of the so-called **gender** ideology] – title of a newspaper article (https://www.eostroleka.pl /szkodliwosc-tzw-ideologii-gender,art39182.html);

(6) "[...] o współczesnych zagrożeniach kulturowych. [...] To gender, erotyka i smartfon" [on contemporary cultural threats [...] These are **gender**, erotica and smartphone] – fragment of a lecture by a Catholic bishop (https://bydgoszcz.wyborcza.pl/bydgoszcz/7,48722,25728470,wyklad-o -szkodliwym-gender-w-urzedzie wojewodzkim-biskup-zacheca.html).

In these examples, the otherwise widely used neutral sense of English *gender*, understood commonly in Polish as "a sociocultural role," is deliberately semantically distorted to mean "threat, evil" and evoke negative connotations.[3] This is achieved through the use of negatively connoted words, such as "threat," "plague," and "harmfulness" (cf. examples 4–6).

The second set of authentic data illustrates how the English acronym *LGBT*, as well as the noun *tęcza* "rainbow" and adjective *tęczowy* "rainbow," both referring to the LGBTQ+ community, are used by far-right politicians, media, and the representatives of the Polish Catholic Church, to function as tools of imposing threat by actually naming the alleged enemy. Consider the following examples:

(7) "LGBT jest ideologią będącą rodzajem umysłowej zarazy [...] czymś, co nas atakuje oraz nam zagraża" [**LGBT** is an ideology that is a kind of a mental plague [...] something that attacks us and threatens us] – a Catholic bishop's comment (https://www.fronda.pl/a/lisicki-amerykanska-ambasada -splunela-w-twarz-katolikom,162417.html);

(8) "LGBT. Zagrożenie dla państwa, narodu i człowieka" [**LGBT**. A threat for the state, nation and man] – a Catholic bishop's comment (https:// wiadomosci.wp.pl/biskup-wieslaw-alojzy-mering-o-lgbt-zagrozenie -dla-panstwa-narodu-i-czlowieka-6544525776956032a);

(9) "LGBT to nie są ludzie, to jest ideologia" [**LGBT** are not people. It is an ideology] – a comment by a Polish MP J. Żalek; later repeated by the Polish president, Andrzej Duda (https://www.rp.pl/polityka /art672461-lgbt-to-nie-ludzie-to-ideologia-posel-zalek-wyproszony-z-tvn24);

(10) "trzeba bronić dzieci przed ideologią LGBT" [we must defend our children against the **LGBT** ideology] – comment by a prominent far-right MP (https://wiadomosci.gazeta.pl/wiadomosci/7,114884,26239433,morawiecki -komentuje-slowa-terleckiego-o-lgbt-nie-ma-u-nas.html);

(11) "[Flaga tęczowa] symbol neomarksistowskiej cywilizacyjnej destrukcji" [The **rainbow flag** is a symbol of neo-Marxist destruction of civilization] – comment by a far-right journalist (https://dorzeczy.pl/kraj/149646/znana

-aktorka-broni-teczowych-flag-ziemkiewicz-nie-wytrzymal-juz-mnie-mdli
-od-ich-plenia.html);

(12) "[...] tęczowa zaraza zastąpiła czerwoną zarazę" [the **rainbow** plague
has replaced the red [communist] plague] – fragment of a Catholic bishop's
sermon (https://dorzeczy.pl/tygodnik/116270/lgbt-to-zaraza.html);

(13) "samochodzik obsmarowany satanistyczną tęczą" [a car painted in a sa-
tanic **rainbow**] – comment by a prominent far-right politician (https://www
.wprost.pl/kraj/10467838/final-euro-2020-krystyna-pawlowicz-pisze-o
-satanistycznej-teczy.html).

The language data presented above, published between 2019 and 2022, show
that some politicians, media, and spiritual leaders realize the persuasive
function of language through very conscious choices of lexical means. They
influence others by transmitting and imposing a specific way of thinking by
pointing at antivalues (i.e., undesirable and negatively connoted qualities).
Yet, LGBTQ+-related anglicisms, as a tool for transmitting a specific worldview, may perform the persuasive function in two different ways.

First of all, anglicisms, which are foreign words and not comprehensible
to every Pole, may be used as a tool to manipulate and consciously mislead
others, to achieve desired goals through intellectual violence. This is done
through the intentional, or perhaps only ignorant, distortion of the meaning
of words. Lack of linguistic competence of the addressees does not allow for
the recognition of this semantic distortion. For instance, the meaning of the
word *gender* in Polish seems to be dependent on the political views and worldview of the speaker. Anglicisms, especially those whose meaning is not entirely
clear to many Poles, can be used to negatively influence the public opinion
and their behavior. This is done through combining the innocent word *gender*
with Polish negatively connoted words such as *devil, Satan, plague, totalitarian,
harmful,* and *threat* (Polish *diabeł, szatan, zaraza, totalitarny, szkodliwy,* and
zagrożenie, respectively). This results in the change of the meaning of the word
gender, which now becomes a *condemnandum* (i.e., a term that evokes negative
associations and emotions (Pisarek, 2000)) and represents antivalues that deserve to be condemned by the public opinion. Frequently repeated, it serves
to diminish the range of possible thought. Using negatively connoted words
as collocators is a frequent rhetorical mechanism used to manipulate through
semantic distortion.

In the case of the word *gender* as used in the language data quoted above, its
expressive layer dominates its meaning, and it is not important what *gender,*

in fact, means, but what kind of emotions and reactions it will evoke in the voters. Examples 1–6 illustrate how the word *gender* is semantically degraded to stigmatize a whole social group (Rejter, 2013, p. 130).

It is interesting to note that far-right politicians and media, and some Church officials, hardly ever refer to the representatives of the LGBTQ+ community with native derogatory terms. Instead, they surround words such as *LGBT* and *gender* with negatively associated vocabulary. When they use the English-sourced *gay* or the acronym *LGBT*, their lack of understanding and respect may be signaled either by the context of other words that are derogatory, such as *zaraza* "plague" and *diabeł* "devil," as in these Polish-specific collocations: Polish *tęczowa zaraza* ("rainbow plague"), *diabeł gender* ("gender the devil"),[4] or by the use of specific prosodic features (a scornful tone of voice). Publicly performed verbal abuse of certain social groups by people in power (i.e., showing contempt through the use of specific words) may evoke violent reactions in the anti-LGBTQ+ public.[5]

A similar persuasive effect can be achieved through the creation and use of new words or phraseological units derived from anglicisms, such as *genderyzm* ("genderism") and *ideologia gender* ("gender ideology"). The Polish word *genderyzm* was coined by analogy to *racism, sexism, ageism*, in which the suffix –*ism* is used to express negative concepts. Negatively connoted in Polish is also the noun *ideologia* ("ideology") through its connotation with some negatively perceived ideologies of the past, so collocating *ideologia* with the word *gender* automatically affects the meaning of the latter. *Gender*, and the related expressions (*genderyzm* and *ideologia gender*), have become, for some Poles, a way to express negative content, which violates both the original English meaning of *gender* and its scientific sociological understanding.

To end on a more optimistic note, it is necessary to mention the other way in which anglicisms are used as persuasive means of expression. One of the main reasons for borrowing foreign words is naming new concepts. In the case of many LGBTQ+-related anglicisms, the concepts have been there but their native names either did not exist or were derogatory. Borrowing English expressions allows for nonoffensive, neutral reference to what has previously been taboo and unspoken of. "Socially, to have a name is to be" (Peyron, 2018). English words do not replace native offensive words but coexist with them, fulfilling different pragmatic functions. This has also been attested for other languages, Spanish for instance (Rodríguez-González, 2008; see also Leap & Boellstorff, 2004). Adopting foreign words to be able to refer to taboo or negatively associated concepts has been labeled *therapeutic borrowing* (Haspelmath, 2009, p. 50).

Authentic language data also show that much more often LGBTQ+-related anglicisms are used to disseminate positive values and shape attitudes based on respect for other people. Many anglicisms, especially those that are semantically more generic and used also outside of the sociolect or slang of the LGBTQ+ community, such as *gay, LGBT, sexual minorities, gender fluid, rainbow flag, gay rights, rainbow march,* and *pride parade* (in Polish *equality parade*), are used neutrally by the opposite side of the political scene and in discourse that is not related to political propaganda.

Conclusion

The analysis shows that the way LGBTQ+-related anglicisms are used in Polish socio-political discourse automatically reveals the (positive or negative) attitudes of the speaker and reflects their interpretation of reality. Words borrowed from English may be seen as those that facilitate nonoffensive, neutral, and friendly discourse, but also as those that are used as a means of political manipulation and indoctrination of the public mind. This social engineering and influencing the society on a large scale may be either positively or negatively oriented, which depends not only on the represented worldview but, most importantly, on the desired political goals. The analyzed language data show that LGBTQ+-related anglicisms are (positively or negatively) evaluative expressions and function as the lexical exponents of the intentions of the speaker, who intends either to please and appreciate or threaten and mislead. In the latter case, LGBTQ+-related anglicisms are notoriously used to discredit the other, often the unknown, to humiliate and dehumanize a whole social group. The very choice of derogatory words as collocators for LGBTQ+-related vocabulary reflects negative evaluation. The dynamics of heated political disputes and the creation of negative connotations evoke various, often negative, emotions, which may lead to discrimination and violence against LGBTQ+ individuals.

NOTES

1. The year 1989 marked the final abolition of communism and the end of the 44-year-long Soviet dominance over Poland. The events that led to this include the Martial Law, introduced in Poland in 1981 to crush political opposition, the formation of the "Solidarność" [Solidarity] trade union movement under the leadership of Lech Wałęsa, and a series of factory strikes throughout the 1980s. The political changes initiated in Poland resulted ultimately in the fall of the entire Eastern and Central European communist bloc, whose symbol was the opening of the Berlin

Wall in 1989. Ultimately those events brought the end of the Cold War in 1991 and resulted in lifting the Iron Curtain that divided Europe throughout the major part of the second half of the 20th century.

2. See Religious denominations in Poland, 2019–2021, at https://stat.gov.pl /obszary-tematyczne/inne-opracowania/wyznania-religijne/wyznania-religijne -w-polsce-2019-2021,5,3.html.

3. Polish uses a native word *rodzaj* "type, gender" to refer to a grammatical category. The English word *gender* was borrowed by Polish speakers to refer to a new concept of a sociocultural role or "a set of behaviours and values ascribed to a particular sex by society and culture" (SJP, n.d.).

4. "Diabeł mieszka w Polsce i nazywa się Gender" [The Devil lives in Poland and his name is gender] – title of a feature article published in a liberal weekly, used as a comment on the words of Archbishop Michalik about "gender ideology" (from *Polityka*, September 6, 2019).

5. See reports on attacks on LGBTQ+ people and their allies in the Polish press (e.g., https://trojmiasto.wyborcza.pl/trojmiasto/7,35612,26892940,napad-na -trenujace-osoby-lgbt-dwie-osoby-w-szpitalu.html; https://www.fakt.pl /wydarzenia/polska/slask/chlopak-pobity-w-autobusie-bo-stanal-w-obronie -osoby-lgbt/xgobsy).

REFERENCES

Backus, A. (2014). A usage-based approach to borrowability. In E. Zenner & G. Kristiansen (Eds.), *New perspectives on lexical borrowing: Onomasiological, methodological and phraseological innovations* (pp. 19–39). De Gruyter Mouton.

Bańko, M., Witalisz, A., & Hansen, K. (2022). Linguistic purism and loanword adaptation techniques (the case of Polish). *Language Awareness, 31*(1), 95–116. https://doi.org/10.1080/09658416.2021.1990306

BBC. (2020, June 14). Polish election: Andrzej Duda says LGBT "ideology" worse than communism. *BBC*. https://www.bbc.com/news/world-europe-53039864

Benenowska, I. (2019). Normy etycznej komunikacji, ich łamanie i sankcje (na wybranych przykładach) (Norms of ethical communication (illustrated with selected examples)). In I. Benenowska, E. Laskowska, & B. Morzyńska-Wrzosek (Eds.), *Aksjologiczne aspekty komunikacji* (Axiological aspects of communication) (pp. 23–39). Wydawnictwo Uniwersytetu Kazimierza Wielkiego.

Blank, A. (2003). Words and concepts in time: Towards diachronic cognitive onomasiology. In R. Eckardt, K. von Heusinger, & C. Schwarze (Eds.), *Words in time: Diachronic semantics from different points of view* (pp. 37–65). De Gruyter Mouton.

Choi, H. (2021). Anglicisms in Korean: A diachronic corpus-based study with special reference to translation as a mode of language contact. *Journal of Language and Linguistic Studies, 17*(1), 115–138.

Cierpich, A. (2019). *Zapożyczenia angielskie w polszczyźnie korporacyjnej* [English loanwords in Polish corporate language]. Wydawnictwo Naukowe Akademii Ignatianum.

Czechowski, W. (2019). "Totalna opozycja" i "poprzedni rząd" w polityce infor-macyjnej programu telewizyjnego *Wiadomości TVP* ["Total opposition" and "the former government" in the information policy of the television program *Wiadomości TVP*]. In I. Benenowska, E. Laskowska, & B. Morzyńska-Wrzosek (Eds.), *Aksjologiczne aspekty komunikacji* (Axiological aspects of communication) (pp. 43–70). Wydawnictwo Uniwersytetu Kazimierza Wielkiego.

EuroNews. (2021, June 28). Polish Catholic Church reveals hundreds of new sexual abuse claims. *EuroNews.* https://www.euronews.com/2021/06/28/polish -catholic-church-reveals-hundreds-of-new-sexual-abuse-claims

Fernández-Domínguez, J. (2019). The onomasiological approach. In M. Aronoff (Ed.), *Oxford research encyclopedia of linguistics* (pp. 1–26). Oxford University Press.

Fisiak, J. (1970). The semantics of English loanwords in Polish. *Studia Anglica Posnaniensia, 2*, 41–49.

Flis, D. (2021, September 6). Socjolog: Obowiązkowa religia tylko wkurzy młodych. Kościół ich nie zatrzyma (Sociologist: Compulsory religion will only make the youth angry. The Church will not stop them from leaving). *OKO.press.* https://oko.press/sekularyzacja-religia-mlodzi-kosciol/

Furiassi, C., & Gottlieb, H. (Eds.). (2015). *Pseudo-English. Studies on false anglicisms in Europe.* De Gruyter Mouton.

Furiassi, C., Pulcini, V., & Rodríguez-González, F. (Eds.). (2012). *The Anglicization of European lexis.* John Benjamins.

Görlach, M. (Ed.). (2001). *A dictionary of English anglicisms.* Oxford University Press.

Görlach, M. (Ed.). (2002). *English in Europe.* Oxford University Press.

Grabias, S. (2019). *Język w zachowaniach społecznych. Podstawy socjolingwistyki i logopedii* [Language in social behaviour. The rudiments of sociolinguistics and logopedia). (4th Ed.). Wydawnictwo Uniwersytetu Marii Curie-Skłodowskiej.

Grzega, J. (2003). Borrowing as a word-finding process in cognitive historical ono-masiology. *Onomasiology Online, 34*, 22–42.

Haspelmath, M. (2009). Lexical borrowing: Concepts and issues. In M. Haspel-math & U. Tadmor (Eds.), *Loanwords in the world's languages. A comparative hand-book* (pp. 35–54). De Gruyter Mouton.

Imamura, K. (2018). The lexical influence of English on Japanese language: Toward future comparative studies of Anglicisms. *Global Studies, 2*, 101–116.

Koneczna, H. (1936/37). Wyrazy angielskie w języku polskim (English words in Polish). *Poradnik Językowy, 9*, 161–170.

Leap, W. L., & Boellstorff, T. (Eds.). (2004). *Speaking in queer tongues. Globalization and gay language.* University of Illinois Press.

Mańczak-Wohlfeld, E. (1995). *Tendencje rozwojowe współczesnych zapożyczeń angielskich w języku polskim* (Development trends of present-day English loanwords in Polish). Universitas.

Markowski, A. (2005). *Kultura języka polskiego. Teoria. zagadnienia leksykalne* (The culture of the Polish language. Theory, lexical issues). Wydawnictwo Naukowe PWN.

Orwell, G. (1946). *Politics and the English language*. Broadview Press.

Ożóg, K. (2004). *Język w służbie polityki* (Language at the service of politics). Wydawnictwo Uniwersytetu Rzeszowskiego.

Peyron, D. (2018). Fandom names and collective identities in contemporary popular culture. *Transformative Works and Cultures, 28*. http://dx.doi.org/10.3983/twc.2018.1468

Picheta, R., & Kottasová, I. (2020). "You don't belong here": In Poland's "LGBT-free zones," existing is an act of defiance. *CNN*. https://edition.cnn.com/interactive/2020/10/world/lgbt-free-poland-intl-scli-cnnphotos/

Pisarek, W. (2000). Polskie słowa sztandarowe i ich publiczność: lata dziewięćdziesiąte (Polish flagship words and their audience: the 1990s). *Zeszyty Prasoznawcze, XLIII*(3–4), 19–41.

Podgórecki, A. (1996). Sociotechnics: Basic problems and issues. In A. Podgórecki, J. Alexander, & R. Shields (Eds.), *Social engineering* (pp. 23–58). Carleton University Press.

Pulcini, V., Furiassi, C., & Rodríguez-González, F. (2012). The lexical influence of English on European languages: From words to Phraseology. In C. Furiassi, V. Pulcini, & F. Rodríguez-González (Eds.), *The anglicization of European lexis* (pp. 1–24). John Benjamins.

Reboul, O. (1980). Kiedy słowo jest bronią (When a word is a weapon). In M. Głowiński (Ed.), *Język i społeczeństwo* (Language and society) (pp. 299–337). Czytelnik.

Rejter, A. (2013). *Płeć – język – kultura* (Gender – language – culture). Wydawnictwo Uniwersytetu Śląskiego.

Rodríguez-González, F. (2008). Anglicisms in Spanish male homosexual terminology. In R. Fischer & H. Pułaczewska (Eds.), *Anglicisms in Europe. Linguistic diversity in a global context* (pp. 247–270). Cambridge Scholars Publishing.

Rohde, A., Stefanowitsch, A., & Kemmer, S. (2000). Loanwords in a usage-based model, *Series B: Applied and Interdisciplinary Papers*, Paper No. 296, 1–14, Essen: LAUD. file:///C:/Users/Komputer/AppData/Local/Temp/B296.pdf

Sikora, P. (2021, November 21). Jednak sekularyzacja (After all, secularization). *Tygodnik Powszechny*. https://www.tygodnikpowszechny.pl/jednak-sekularyzacja-169832

Stawiany, J. (2019, May 10). Film Sekielskiego ujawnia nowe fakty o pedofilii w Kosciele (The movie by Sekielski reveals new facts about pedophilia in the Church). *Press.* https://www.press.pl/tresc/57246,film-sekielskiego -ujawnia-nowe-fakty-o-pedofilii-w-kosciele

van Dijk, T. A. (2006). Discourse and manipulation. *Discourse & Society, 17*(3), 359–383.

van Dijk, T., A. (2008). *Discourse and power.* Palgrave Macmillan.

van Dijk, T. A. (1998). What is political discourse analysis? In J. Blommaert & C. Bulcaen (Eds.), *Political linguistics* (pp. 11–52). John Benjamins.

Winter-Froemel, E. (2014). Formal variance and semantic changes in borrowing: Integrating semasiology and onomasiology. In E. Zenner & G. Kristiansen (Eds.), *New perspectives on lexical borrowing: Onomasiological, methodological, and phraseological innovations* (pp. 65–100). De Gruyter Mouton.

Witalisz, A. (2015). *English loan translations in Polish: Word-formation patterns, lexicalization, idiomaticity and institutionalization.* Peter Lang.

Witalisz, A. (2022). Mieć nazwę to istnieć: funkcje anglicyzmów w dyskursie związanym ze społecznością LGBTQ+ [To have a name is to be: the functions of anglicisms in the LGBTQ+ community-related discourse]. *Socjolingwistyka, 36,* 247–262.

Witalisz, A. (2021). Polish LGBTQ+-related anglicisms in a language contact perspective. *Studia Anglica Posnaniensia, 56,* 631–653. https://doi.org/10.2478 /stap-2021-0013

Zabawa, M. (2017). *English semantic loans, loan translations and loan renditions in informal Polish of computer users.* Wydawnictwo Uniwersytetu Śląskiego.

Zenner, E., Speelman, D., & Geeraerts, D. (2012). Cognitive sociolinguistics meets loanword research: Measuring variation in the success of anglicisms in Dutch. *Cognitive Linguistics, 23*(4), 749–792. https://doi.org/10.1515/cog-2012-0023

Zenner, E., Speelman, D., & Geeraerts, D. (2014). Core vocabulary, borrowability, and entrenchment: A usage-based onomasiological approach. *Diachronica, 31*(1), 74–105. https://doi.org/10.1075/dia.31.1.03zen

Corpora and dictionaries

GLAD – Global Anglicisms Database, https://www.nhh.no/en/research-centres /global-anglicism-database-network/resources/

Monco – Monco Monitoring Corpus, http://monco.frazeo.pl/

plTenTen – Corpus of Polish in Sketch Engine, https://www.sketchengine.eu /pltenten-polish-corpus/

SJP – Słownik języka polskiego [A Dictionary of Polish], https://sjp.pwn.pl/sjp/

**BRITTANY M. W. THOMPSON,
ERIKA K. JOHNSON | East Carolina University**

Amplifying Black Voices

#SOCBlackVoices Social Media Campaign
Discourse Analysis Using Critical Race Theory

Abstract

This research analyzes photos and text content of a Black Voices social media-based campaign, a publicly available university-based campaign that started in the summer of 2020 on Instagram and Facebook with a weekly post of school alumni featuring a photo and text about their experiences with being Black in America. This campaign draws from the Photovoice as an intervention trend and applies critical race theory as a framework. Researchers employed critical discourse analysis and cycled open coding. Themes were professionalism, gender differences, safe spaces and belonging, and empowerment.

Keywords: critical race theory, critical discourse analysis, Black voices, social media

Introduction

Since events leading to social reckoning in 2020 (e.g., George Floyd killing), corresponding social media discourse emerged to spotlight underserved communities on social media (e.g., Black voices takeovers, listening campaigns, etc.). In this study, research team members analyzed photos and text content of a Black Voices social media-based campaign. This is a publicly available university-based campaign that started in the summer of 2020 on Instagram and Facebook with a weekly post of school alumni and students featuring a photo and text about their experiences with being Black in America. The Black Voices social media campaign initiated from a "share the mic" movement for people from minority populations whose voices are often underrepresented in media. This campaign draws from the Photovoice as an intervention trend (e.g., using photos to illustrate issues in underserved communities), which is often applied in public health and other disciplines (Wang & Burris, 1997).

Literature Review

Black Voices emerged as a social media trend to spotlight communities and individuals of color with the premise that usually the public and most audiences primarily hear and see the experiences of White people (Literat & Brough, 2019; DeBiasse et al., 2021). The idea of Black Voices is that there is a need for underrepresented voices to be heard and for experiences of Black people to be seen on social media and via other social media vehicles (Literat & Brough, 2019; DeBiasse et al., 2021).

Photovoice, initially called Photo Novella, is a participatory methodology/technique developed to assess the needs/issues, such as injustice, inequality, or health issues, that certain communities face and for educating the public about those needs/issues (Wang & Burris, 1997). Photovoice emerged as a tool to learn the needs of a community by placing cameras in the hands of community members and letting their documentary images tell the stories of daily life (Wang & Burris, 1994, 1997). Photovoice is often applied in public health and other disciplines, to spotlight underserved communities. Photovoice recognizes the role of the participant in the education-empowerment process, so the technique fully embraces the participatory component of highlighting the participant voice and experience (Wang & Burris, 1997).

The foundation of Wang & Burris's (1994) Photovoice is Paulo Freire's (1970) concept on problem-posing education, deriving from community dialogue and empowerment through shared experiences of community members. The premise of Freire's (1970) concept is when conversations occur within a community, issues that impact that community come to the surface. If there are common trends in those issues, then the community can collectively identify it as a need and move to educate on the issues and create change through policy (Freire, 1970; Wang & Burris, 1994).

Photovoice also has roots in feminist theory by focusing on empowerment through sharing one's voice. Feminist theory is "meant to empower vulnerable populations" from within (Wang & Burris, 1997; Budig et al., 2018, p. 2). With a combination of community participation and empowerment, the goals of Photovoice are (1) to provide an opportunity for members of a community to document their lived experiences and reflect on what is documented, (2) to initiate critical conversations about issues that are uncovered through the documentary process, and (3) to inform policy makers of the issues within the community (Budig et al., 2018, Wang & Burris, 1997; Capous-Desyllas & Bromfield, 2018).

Since its conception, Photovoice has become popular as a method across many disciplines from the health sciences to visual arts. There are many ways to adapt Photovoice into participatory research. Traditionally, the Photovoice method steps include: (1) selecting a target community, (2) recruiting participants from the community, (3) introducing and training the participants on the concept of Photovoice and obtaining their consent, (4) distributing cameras and other needed equipment to participants for them to start their documentary, (5) engaging in conversations through focus groups with the participants about their images and the descriptions for those images to tease out common themes and how they relate to community needs, and (6) using collected visual and verbal information to inform policy makers of community needs (Wang & Burris, 1994, 1997; Kile, 2021).

It is important to remember that the Photovoice method focuses on both captured images and the voice of the participants (Sarrica & Brondi, 2018). The voice can be captured during focus group discussions or through reflections. Themes in both the voice and the images help give a platform to suppressed voices in marginalized communities (Borron, 2013). This type of multimethod participatory approach helps community members isolate key issues within communities. The Photovoice method has been used in diverse fields of study and used in a variety of adaptions from the original process developed by Wang and Burris (1994, 1997).

Photovoice is not used in the traditional sense for this research project, but rather as an intervention to analyze a university-based Black Voices social media campaign following the murder of George Floyd and other social injustice events that occurred in the summer of 2020. The social media campaign was initiated under the "share the mic" premise with Black students within a communication program at the university (current students and alumni). The students were provided a prompt to simply reflect on communication and race and to provide an accompanying image of themselves. The research team members recognized the potential to learn about Black student needs by retroactively applying Photovoice principles to uncover themes from the public social media campaign.

Theoretical Framework: Critical Race Theory

Critical race theory (CRT) is an academic framework centering racism as a systemic issue in our institutions and influencing mainstream culture that originated within the legal tradition by a group of scholars at Harvard Law School (Delgado & Stefancic, 2017). The ideas and work of Derrick Bell, and later Alan Freeman, in the 1970s laid the groundwork for CRT. Bell was a key figure in the civil rights movement and desegregation law during the 1950s and 1960s (Steinberg, 2012; Cobb, 2021). By the late 1960s and early 1970s, Bell shifted his thought on the progress of the civil rights movement. He started writing and discussing how antidiscrimination laws of the civil rights movement did not have the full impact of their intent (Crenshaw, 2017; Steinberg, 2012; Cobb, 2021). Bell believed that racism was so fundamental to our society that it could not be eradicated and, in fact, even after successful movements that push forward reforms, racism is easily able to reinsert itself into our society (Steinberg, 2012; Cobb, 2021; Delgado & Stefancic, 2017). In the beginning of his 1978 article, Alan Freeman wrote:

> The law has outlawed racial discrimination, it has affirmed that Black Americans can be without jobs, have their children in all-black, poorly funded schools, have no opportunities for decent housing, and have very little political power, without any violation of antidiscrimination law. (p. 1050).

Freeman also adjacently examined the relationship between antidiscrimination laws and our social structure (Freeman, 1978).

Though the foundation of CRT was codified in law, many different veins of study branched out from the original idea, endeavoring to explore other institutional or societal structures that perpetuate racism by just existing and to bring to light the role racism has in our society. Scholars from education, political science, ethnic studies, feminist studies, theology, and health care, to name a few, use the lens of CRT to examine concepts around race and racism in their fields. To date, there are many contributing voices to the collection of ideas in CRT. However, it has been misunderstood and many individuals as well as larger systems (i.e., local and state governments, schools, parents, etc.) have expressed disapproval of the theory being taught in schools or being mentioned in public discourse (Kim, 2021).

CRT asserts that race is constructed, and that racism is a phenomenon experienced in everyday life (Delgado & Stefancic, 2017, Goessling, 2018). CRT assumes that there is systemic racism, where racism and inequality are reinforced and structured by legal systems and government, policies within government and institutions, other systems, and cultural norms (Delgado & Stefancic, 2017). CRT and systemic racism assert that racism does not fall (in terms of responsibility or source) within an individual necessarily, but rather within the constructs of a society (Delgado & Stefancic, 2017, Goessling, 2018).

This research employed CRT and critical discourse analysis (CDA). CDA emphasizes how "social power abuse, dominance, and inequality are enacted, reproduced, and resisted by text and talk in the social and political context" (Van Dijk, 2001, p. 352). CRT will be applied to examine how race is constructed in posts as a reflection of societal systemic racism (e.g., exploring personal experiences/voices in regard to larger legal systems/government, policies, culture, and other societal systems) and racism experienced in everyday life (Delgado & Stefancic, 2017).

The following questions will be addressed:

Research Question 1: What are the (a) rhetorical and (b) visual strategies used to present Black voices?

Research Question 2: How do elements of CRT emerge in the posts (visual and writings)?

Method

The method used to analyze the posts was textual analysis, specifically CDA. CDA is able to allow researchers to understand how "social power abuse, dominance, and inequality are enacted, reproduced, and resisted by text and talk in the social and political context" (Van Dijk, 2001, p. 352). The researchers used open coding initially and thematic analysis.

Specifically, authors openly coded the content from these voices and images in a three-stage process. The two researchers conducted primary-cycle coding to put the data into manageable pieces (Tracy, 2013). The authors used the research questions as guidelines to consider themes at this stage. After primary-cycle coding, they employed secondary-cycle coding, which involves "classifying, prioritizing, integrating, synthesizing, abstracting, conceptualizing, and theory-building" (Saldaña, 2009, p. 45). Authors grouped initial codes into themes and patterns in this second focused cycle of coding

(Tracy, 2013). After that stage, authors created descriptions and emphasized key examples for each of the themes (i.e., ideas that appeared consistently and became prominent within and among the posts). The focus of this research leans more heavily on the voice part of the sample.

Sample

There were 16 total posts as part of the #SOCBlackVoices Instagram campaign with 10 posts created by women and 6 posts created by men. July 2, 2020, was the first post and June 10, 2021, was the last one. The campaign ended after a stall in recruitment efforts of participants. The campaign solicited posts from current School of Communication (SOC) students and alumni on LinkedIn and the SOC's social media on Instagram and Facebook starting after the Floyd tragedy in late May 2020. Each post featured a photo of the person and a blurb for Instagram consisting of several paragraphs. Each post was also re-posted on SOC's Facebook. Participants that were interested in creating content for the campaign were given the following prompt to reply to:

> I hope you are doing well during these unique and transformative times! The School of Communication is focused on making lasting changes within our walls to ensure the unraveling of systemic racism.
>
> We are embarking on a social media campaign that uplifts the voices of our Black alumni and current students. We would love for you to be a part of this meaningful campaign.
>
> Every week we will showcase #SOCBlackVoices. We are simply asking for one-post content that includes an image and a caption that focuses on any (positive or negative) experience that you have had that looks at racism through a communication lens. We know this is broad, but we want authentic and organic content from you if you are willing to participate in this campaign. (B. Wright Thompson, personal communication, July – October, B2020)

Participant posts were not edited other than correcting egregious grammatical or spelling errors in order to not censor the creators' voices.

Results

Following the rhetorical (written) coding process, four preliminary themes emerged from the analysis of the 16 #SOCBlackVoices posts. The themes included professionalism, gender differences, safe spaces and belonging, and empowerment. These themes are also interconnected and do not to stand alone (i.e., multiple themes emerged within individual posts). In addition to the text, the images were also evaluated.

The theme of professionalism appeared in multiple posts. The focus of this theme was more on being Black in the field of communication and drew on the pressure of Black communication professionals to prove they belong in the professional space. These voices were empowering as well in that they clearly stated Black communicators belonged in these professional spaces and possessed the skill and knowledge.

Two posts by Black men commented on the rarity of Black male communicators. In an excerpt from a post, the writer even went on to emphasize the importance of "intentional excellence" when it comes to producing work: "Black male communicators are rare. Every presentation, interaction, and project must be executed with intentional excellence.... We indeed do speak and write well" (SOC Instagram, 2020). At the end of the quote, there is almost a mocking of stereotypes by adding in that Black men do "indeed speak and write well." One post stated, "One must know that men of color, specifically Black males, exist and belong in the communication space.... Our presence and work matters" (SOC Instagram, 2020). This illuminates pressures that Black communicators feel to be the best representation of their community by working hard and delivering exemplary work in the field of communication.

Another post focused on professionalism states that Black men "have a unique presence within the field of communication, and it's important that we demonstrate that, not only through our work, but also through the way we communicate as professionals" (SOC Instagram, 2020). We felt this specific post highlighted a call for Black communicators to recognize their rarity and the pressure of delivering strong work and being the consummate professional. In one post that intersected with professionalism, the creator voiced concerns that Black students may limit their range of interest in communication to sports broadcasting and journalism out of fear of failing in other areas of communication, such as public relations (SOC Instagram, 2020).

In the context of professionalism, many of the posts touched on a lack of representation in communication fields. This theme connects professionalism with the second theme of safe spaces and belonging. Many touched on the thread of not seeing people that looked like them in their classes or experiences and encounters that made them feel like outsiders and uncomfortable.

There has been extensive research on the impact of belonging in higher education (Allen et al., 2021). Ranging from academic success to feelings of isolation felt by students, researchers have examined a variety of associations with a sense of belonging (Allen et al., 2021). The content we reviewed had a more negative connotation where students felt isolated and in one case a student felt as if their culture was openly attacked in the educational setting.

One post stated, "My first years at ECU were uncomfortable, due to the lack of black faces and black voices," and another stated, "I didn't know if I was going to see anyone I knew or if there were going to be people that look like me" (SOC Instagram, 2020). There is almost a sense of resignation that goes with feelings of not belonging with statements like, "turned out what I thought was right; there were not that many black students in the room but I did have a friend in the class" (SOC Instagram, 2020). As educators with a focus on creating a positive learning environment, these are revelations with implications that counteract our goals in higher education.

It is important to note that the content focusing on a lack of belonging and not having a safe space was created by Black women. Within these posts about lack of belonging and safe spaces, there are threads of gender difference that start to unravel. Many posts that we reviewed discussed starkly the burden of being a Black woman and the lack of representation in the professional space.

For instance, one student noted, "When I was growing up, ... I did not see many Black women on my screen doing travel journalism. I want to be one of them, exploring the world and sharing my perspective while learning from others" (SOC Instagram, 2020). A similar sentiment echoes that lack of representation in the professional world: "Growing up, I didn't see many black women journalists on television. So, seeing women like Robin Roberts inspired me to take on the journalism profession and be a voice for the unheard" (SOC Instagram, 2020). These sentiments tie into the third theme to arise, gender differences, along with intersectionality. Intersectionality, a concept pioneered by CRT critical scholar Kimberlé Crenshaw, can be defined as a thorough "examination of race, sex, class, national origin, and sexual orientation and how their combination plays out in various settings" (Delgado & Stefancic, 2017, p. 58).

From our analysis of the content, there are differences in experiences among the male and female posts. Messages created by Black men conveyed the need to showcase their excellence mostly in a professional setting. One post states, "Black male communicators are rare. Every presentation, interaction, and project must be executed with intentional excellence" (SOC Instagram, 2020). Messaging created by the Black women revealed the need to (1) acknowledge gender differences, (2) show self-pride in having agency, and (3) demonstrate sociopolitical activism while enacting and holding professional roles.

There was a focus on the gender differences throughout the content posted by the Black women. That focus touched on the intersectionality concept that layers of inequality exist and that identity complexity must be considered when addressing marginalized and oppressed populations (Gillborn, 2015). The gender difference content directly noted the importance of being a woman and being Black.

Another impression from the content is that creators take pride in being Black women and successful professionals, while engaging in sociopolitical activism. Some of the posts mentioned being able to use professional platforms as a tool for empowerment and movement forward (e.g., "Being a black woman and having the opportunity to highlight such powerful and meaningful protests meant the world to me" and "seeing women like Robin Roberts inspired me to take on the journalism profession and be voice for the unheard" (SOC Instagram, 2020)). The connection to empowerment is noted throughout CRT literature. Goessling (2018) posited that the "goal of CRT scholarship is not to make accessible or convey experiences or arguments of discrimination to the majority, but to resist and deconstruct dominant racial narratives through the powerful telling of counter narratives" (p. 654). Solórzano and Yosso (2001) write about majoritarian stories creating a normative in our society that is a misrepresentation of the population. The majoritarian stories are mostly privileged, middle-class, heterosexual White experiences that project a systemic racism into our societal and institutional structures (Solórzano & Yosso, 2001; Goessling, 2018). Counter-narratives are the stories of minorities that "serve to dismantle" the reality that majoritarian creates (Goessling, 2018, p. 655). These counter-narratives serve as a tool of empowerment. It is fitting that a final theme of empowerment arises from the #SOCBlackVoices narrative.

Empowerment as a move to creating awareness and change through open dialogue is a goal of Photovoice methodology. Many of the 16 posts were threaded with empowering messages from the creators about sharing their voices or using their platforms for awareness. Some messages were focused on being a part of change, which highlighted the importance of community and a collective voice to be forces for change. A specific post states it is key to foster and grow positive change, and that "all depends on our ability to organize" (SOC Instagram, 2020). Other messages contain positive messages about personal growth and empowerment. For example, one post shared an inspirational message of "I encourage other black youth to not hide your light and stand firm in your blackness" (SOC Instagram, 2020).

We felt it important to note that though this essay is using Photovoice as a retroactive lens for discovery instead of in its original intent of participant participatory methodology, content images were also analyzed. Some posted images depicted positive emotion and hope, while others showed serious or pensive emotional states. Many photos showed professional or profession-specific dress. One content creator showcased their poems and a stoic photo of themselves and depictions of Black men in self-embrace and mixed emotions.

The posted images depicting positive emotion and hope included smiles and relaxed postures. All images with a positive emotion were captured outside in natural sunlight. These positive emotion and hope themes connected with a variety of the written analysis themes including professionalism, empowerment, and gender differences. When considering the posted images that were interpreted as professional, the clothing was business dress including suits, dress pants, and dress shirts. The participants' bodies were either directly facing the camera and looked like professional images or candid images that seem to capture energy with movement in the images. The professionally themed images were posted with similarly themed content.

A smaller number of the posted images (4) were perceived as pensive or emotionally serious. In images perceived as serious or pensive, the subjects were not showing recognizable smiles and all were making direct eye contact with the camera lens. Body posture in those images varied from directly facing the camera while sitting and standing to leaning against walls.

When combined with the written text that accompanied these serious and pensive images, the images seem to support the messages of empowerment and sense of belonging. Combined with the words, these images helped create a strong message to send out to audiences. The serious and pensive images felt authentic and connected to the accompanying written content. A few images were very artistic and had been altered with design elements and were accompanied by poetry.

During our analysis, we recognize that the 16 voices shared during the 2020 #SOCBlackVoices campaign are unique and individual. Four themes were identified from the written content and four distinct visual connections can be identified in the images. Finally, CRT was used as a lens to guide our review of the #SOCBlackVoices content. CRT brings critical awareness to the systemic racism present in societies with an eye toward change. The reviewed content touched on systems of inequality that the creators experienced and aligned with CRT concepts of intersectionality and empowerment.

Discussion

There are limitations to consider with this project and for future continuations. This essay is an analysis of publicly published content from Instagram related to a specific hashtag, #SOCBlackVoices. Photovoice was used as a retroactive intervention, where the research examined the content post hoc through the lens of Photovoice methodology. This is a limitation in the use of the data and, more importantly, a loss of rich insight that the Photovoice, in its pure form, could provide as a participant narrative on lived experiences. Used to its full potential, Photovoice could provide valuable clues to charting communities' needs and developing meaningful strategies to achieve change. The image analysis from the participants' viewpoint is a valuable component of Photovoice, and it is missing from this project due to the retrospective nature of the analysis of publicly posted social media content. Informed interpretations of the images were provided in this analysis but do not capture the subject's "why" for selecting that specific image. In future diversity, equity, and inclusion research, using the Photovoice method in a more traditional process according to Wang and Burris (1994, 1997) could yield more meaningful data on the individual's unique experience. Being able to capture participants' intent from their submitted images could provide more insight on the meaning attached to the images.

There were certainly recruitment and implementation limitations of the #SOCBlackVoices social media campaign. In regard to recruitment, it proved to be difficult to engage people to create content to share during the campaign. If the authors move forward to a larger, true Photovoice project, it would be pertinent to develop diverse recruitment strategies (e.g., on multiple communication channels with more frequent outreach). After a galvanizing event fades from the spotlight in many media platforms, people may forget about the importance of Black (or Black, Indigenous, people of color) voices and perhaps people do not want to volunteer if there is not an agitating event or crisis; this presents another barrier to future recruitment. CRT, race, and social injustice issues are very controversial currently and can add potential challenges (e.g., students and alumni may be shy to speak out and may not want to make potential connections or employers on social media upset).

This is important work to keep an open dialogue about the needs of all our students in our universities and colleges. In terms of feasibility and the exploratory nature of this research, the focus was very narrow in this essay. In a future project, expanding the focus to more marginalized populations in the community would give more insight into community inequalities and needs.

REFERENCES

Allen K. A., Gray, D. L., Baumeister, R. F., & Leary, M. R. (2022). The need to belong: A deep dive into the origins, implications, and future of a foundational construct. *Educational Psychology Review, 34*(2), 1133–1156. https://doi .org/10.1007/s10648-021-09633-6

Borron, A. S. (2013). Picturing the underserved audience: Photovoice as method in applied communication research. *Journal of Applied Communications, 97*(4), https://doi.org/10.4148/1051-0834.1124

Budig, K., Diez, J., Conde, P., Sastra, M., Hernán, M., & Franco, M. (2018). Photovoice and empowerment: Evaluating the transformative potential of a participatory action research project. *BMC Public Health, 18*(432). https://doi.org/10.1186/s12889-018-5335-7

Capous-Desyllas, M., & Bromfield, N. F. (2018). Using an arts-informed eclectic Approach to Photovoice data analysis. *International Journal of Qualitative Methods, 17*(1). https://doi.org/10.1177/1609406917752189

Cobb, J. (2021, September 13). The man behind critical race theory. *The New Yorker*.

Crenshaw, K. (1989). Demarginalizing the intersection of race and sex: A Black feminist critique of antidiscrimination doctrine, feminist theory, and antiracist politics. *The University of Chicago Legal Forum, 1989*(1), 139–167.

Crenshaw, K. W. (2017). Race liberalism and the deradicalization of racial reform. *Harvard Law Review, 130*(9), 2298–2319. http://www.jstor.org /stable/44867674

DeBiasse, M. A. S., Qamar, Z., & Burt, K. G. (2021). A social media intervention for dietetics professionals to increase awareness about racial/ethnic diversity and inclusion in dietetics: Black voices centered. *Critical Dietetics, 6*(1), 40–48.

Delgado, R., & Stehancic, J. (2017). *Critical race theory: An introduction.* 3rd ed. New York University Press.

ECU School of Communication Instagram [@ECU_SOC]. (July 2, 2020 – June 10, 2021). Series of posts - Today we amplify #SOCBlackVoices by sharing the experiences of. https://www.instagram.com/ecu_soc/

Freeman, Alan David. (1978). Legitimizing racial discrimination through antidiscrimination law: A critical review of Supreme Court doctrine. *Minnesota Law Review, 804.* https://scholarship.law.umn.edu/mlr/804

Freire, P. (1970). *Pedagogy of the oppressed.* Seabury.

Gillborn, D. (2015). Intersectionality, critical race theory, and the primacy of racism: Race, class, gender, and disability in education. *Qualitative Inquiry, 21*(3), 277–287.

Goessling, K. P. (2018). Increasing the depth of field: Critical race theory and Photovoice as counter storytelling praxis. *Urban Review, 50,* 648–674. https://doi.org/10.1007/s11256-018-0460-2

Kile, M. (2021). Uncovering social issues through Photovoice: A comprehensive methodology. *Health Environments Research and Design Journal, 15*(1), 29–35.

Kim, R. (2021). Under the law: "Anti-critical race theory" laws and the assault on pedagogy. *Phi Delta Kappan, 103*(1), 64–65.

Literat, I., & Brough, M. (2019). From ethical to equitable social media technologies: Amplifying underrepresented youth voices in digital technology design. *Journal of Media Ethics, 34*(3), 132–145.

Saldaña, J. (2009). *The coding manual for qualitative researchers.* Sage Publications Ltd.

Sarrica, M., & Brondi, S.(2020). Photovoice as a visual-verbal strategy for studying contents and processes of social representations: A participatory project on sustainable energy. *Qualitative Research in Psychology, 17*(4), 565–586. https://doi.org/10.1080/14780887.2018.1456587

Solórzano, D. G., & Yosso, T. Y. (2001). Critical race and LatCrit theory and method: Counter-storytelling. *Qualitative Studies in Education, 14*(4), 471–495.

Steinberg, S. (2012). Derrick Bell: Fighting Losing Battles. *New Politics, XIII*(4).

Tracy, S.J. (2013). *Qualitative Research Methods.* Wiley-Black Well, West Sussex.

Van Dijk, T. A. (2001). Critical discourse analysis. In D. Tannen, D. Schiffrin, & H. Hamilton (Eds.). *Handbook of discourse analysis* (pp. 352-371). Oxford: Blackwell.

Wang, C., & Burris, M. A. (1994). Empowerment through Photo Novella: Portraits of participation. *Health Education Quarterly, 21*(2), 171–186.

Wang, C., & Burris, M. A. (1997). Photovoice: Concept, methodology, and use for participatory needs assessment. *Health education & Behavior, 24*(3), 369–387.

DOROTA RYGIEL | State University of Applied Sciences in Krosno

Far From Home

The Portrayal of Polish Migrant Groups in
Britain in 21st-Century Polish Fiction

Abstract

The aim of this essay is to show the way Polish migrants in Britain are portrayed in the selected Polish novels written after Poland's accession to the European Union in 2004. The two novels are: *Polska szkoła boksu. Powieść emigracyjna* (The Polish Boxing School. An Emigration Novel) (2009) by Adam Miklasz, and *Emigrantka z wyboru. Opowieść londyńska* (The Emigrant by Choice. A Story from London) (2008) by Dana Parys-White. The essay discusses the most important determining factors of Polish migration and focuses on the daily life of Polish migrants in Britain. It shows how they cope with the new reality, cultural differences, and limitations that sometimes result from their own inferiority complex or personal weaknesses. Being displaced from an ethnically and culturally homogenous society, Polish migrants must adapt to living in a multicultural society, among people of different origins, who practice different religions. At times it is difficult for conservative migrants, who grew up in the society where Catholics make up the largest religious group. The essay also aims to show how much migration changes people's identity and how adherence to traditional values and conservative upbringing affects the process of their assimilation into the host society. The essay intends to answer the question of whether Polish migration to Britain is an exciting adventure and release from personal dependencies, unemployment, and imposed limitations, or rather a curse that causes intense mental suffering and evokes the feeling of alienation.

Keywords: Polish migrants, Polish prose after 2005, identity, assimilation, stereotypes, inferiority complex

Introduction

The aim of this essay is to show the realistic portrayal of Polish migrants in Britain on the basis of two contemporary novels written after Poland's accession to the European Union: *Polska szkoła boksu. Powieść emigracyjna* (The Polish Boxing School. An Emigration Novel) (2009) by Adam Miklasz, and *Emigrantka z wyboru. Opowieść londyńska* (The Emigrant by Choice. A Story from London) (2008) by Dana Parys-White.

Polska szkoła boksu is a debut novel, which, as the writer's biographical note states, "was inspired by [Miklasz's] two work stays in the British Isles" (2009). (All quotations from Polish authors are my translations unless otherwise noted.) It draws heavily on his personal turbulent experience of migration and close observation of British society and Polish migrants in Britain. It is a vibrant portrait of the Polish community in London told through the story of four friends who leave for England to improve their living conditions right after Poland's accession to the European Union. They eventually end up in the imaginary town of Buckby, a typical provincial English town, whose monotonous routine is interrupted by new waves of migrants from different parts of Eastern Europe.

Dana Parys-White was born in Ostrów Mazowiecka, Poland, and moved to Britain to study English. She has been living there ever since. She used to work as a journalist for *Jazzwise*, the most popular English-language music magazine in Europe, and with radio HeyNow, where she hosted her popular show. She has turned her personal experience of cultural differences, identity dilemmas, and communication problems into *Emigrantka z wyboru*, which was shortlisted for the Literary Award of the Union of Polish Writers Abroad in 2009. The novel revolves around Ewa, a 26-year-old woman with a university degree in Polish philology, who moves to London.

Both novels were written after Poland became a member state of the European Union. According to Dariusz Nowacki's typology of Polish migrant fiction, *Polska szkoła boksu* falls into the category of *proza inicjacyjno-formacyjna*, which is similar to a typical bildungsroman. Parys-White's novel belongs to the category of *proza "przebojowych Polek,"* which uses themes common for women's writing. This kind of the migrant narrative text revolves around female characters who are able to rise to a higher social or economic position and do not conform to the stereotype of poor and helpless migrant women (Nowacki, 2016, p. 225).

Determinants of Migration to Britain

During World War II and in the postwar period, forced migration prevailed. A number of refugees who escaped the Nazi invasion of Poland left for Western Europe or the United States, later to be joined by those oppressed by the communist regime. In 1968, nearly 13,000 Polish Jews left Poland as a result of the anti-Zionist campaign triggered by the communists (Hurrle, 2019). In the early 1980s the imposition of martial law encouraged a new wave of migration. In 1982 the communist government eased the way for the interned and those who posed danger for the communists' one-party rule to leave Poland. As a result, over 4,000 people fled the country (Stola, 2002, p. 63). Furthermore, a significant number of emigrants left Poland illegally due to the repressive migration policy of the communist authorities. After the fall of the Iron Curtain, the key determinants of migration were better labor market conditions and economic factors, which played a vital role in motivating Poles to emigrate. Migration to the United Kingdom was no exception to that pattern.

Most people who left Poland for Britain right before the EU accession were motivated by those economic pull factors (see Lee, 1966, for the push–pull theory). They came to Britain with the aim of increasing income and improving their and their families' economic status in Poland. International mobility of Poles expanded due to the visa-free entry to Britain and the lifting of the unfavorable passport policy. However, these were not the only drivers of migration. In the early 1990s an estimated 20,000 Polish Roma settled down in Britain because they were disadvantaged by the post-1989 economic transition and experienced widespread anti-Roma discrimination in Poland (Düvell & Garapich, 2011, p. 3). While political emigrants mostly left their country to live abroad permanently, for post-1989 economic migrants it was not a rule. Mullan and Frejka (1995) point out at two factors that affected that trend: greater political stability ensured by the new authorities and fewer opportunities for permanent settlement (p. 228).

When Poland became a member state of the EU, Britain decided not to impose migration restrictions on Poles, which facilitated the mass migration of the young. The UK government took only one control measure: migrants were obliged to register in the Workers Registration Scheme. The rising unemployment rate in Poland and no prospects of improvement in the economic situation led people to emigrate to Britain. The main characters of *Polska szkoła boksu* are economic migrants who intend to stay temporarily in Britain.

They are young men in their 20s or early 30s who flee poverty and want to increase their household's income. One of them is getting married and needs money to cover the cost of his wedding. Some have to pay off their debts and others plan to set up their own companies in Poland. The prospect of higher earning motivates them to work hard and endure hardship. The protagonist of the novel dreams of saving £1,000, whereas his friend's intention is to earn enough to buy an A8 Audi to show off when he returns home and meets his old friends again. He says he wants to return to his hometown "and fulfil his lifelong dream—drive up to the concrete batching plant, where he used to work for PLN500 per month, in his brand new Audi A8 ... and do dough-nuts to make everyone jealous" (Miklasz, 2009, p. 94). All of the characters of Miklasz's novel view money and material possessions as a symbol of a suc-cessful life.

People migrate for a range of different reasons, including political and eco-nomic factors. In late 20th century, it became possible to identify yet another type of international migration: existential migration, where the main motiva-tion is beyond political relations and material improvements (Czapliński, 2013, p. 15). An existential migrant flees stagnation and routine, moving across an international border in search of greater independence or the mere experience of something unfamiliar and foreign. As Natasza Goerke puts it, existential migration is not escape from something but rather leaving for the unknown or unidentified (2006, p. 173). An individual leaves the place of his or her habitual residence to have new and exciting experiences different from what the home-land can offer. In his thorough study, Greg Madison (2006) gives compelling reasons for existential migration. He confirms the significance of moving into the unfamiliar and also points at the importance of identity formation, per-sonal preferences and desires, wider life perspectives, and last but not least, family relations and housing conditions (p. 246).

The protagonist of *Emigrantka z wyboru* is definitely neither a political nor economic migrant. The title of the novel translated as *The Emigrant by Choice* reflects Ewa's free will and no economic or political pressure to leave Poland. She is fed up with her dead-end job in the underfunded local community cen-ter, which is likely to close down. She sees no prospects of things improving in Poland. The sight of her friend, a physicist dreaming of a career in scientific research, who sells fish to make ends meet, is the last straw. As she puts it, "I didn't want to waste my potential and youth energy passively waiting for better times to come" (Parys-White, 2008, p. 17). Ewa feels that the development of her self-potential is obstructed not by the parental pressure but by her surroundings and environment, which offer nothing but a monotonous and predictable routine. She believes that migration will let her develop herself according to what Madison calls "an inner call" (Madison, 2006, p. 246). Before moving to London, Ewa has a rather vague vision of her future in a foreign country and no specific expectations of what her life should be like. She perceives London as a perfect place not in an economic sense but as the one that offers freedom of choice and equal opportunities. Her desire to move to an unfamiliar country and begin a new life is greater than the fear of alienation by the host society.

The Promised Isle

The characters of both novels have an idealized vision of life in Britain. The host country is referred to as the promised land for immigrants that offers an opportunity to make a fresh start and is synonymous with equality and freedom. It attracts people who believe that it will make them successful both in an economic and existential sense. The protagonists leave behind their homes in Poland, prepared to struggle with the many challenges of a long journey, culture shock, or home sickness because they feel England will alleviate their problems.

Both Ewa and the protagonist of *Polska szkoła boksu* cannot afford the airfare; therefore they board an overcrowded ramshackle bus that will take them to the better world, where their living conditions will radically improve. Their uncomfortable journey and the bus "congested with passengers, bags and emotions" are not viewed as a problem. The prospect of material improvements in the "land of well-being and tolerance" is very comforting and takes their minds off their arduous journey (Parys-White, 2008, pp. 21–22). In *Polska szkoła boksu*, the passengers are overwrought with the thought of a customs procedure. Most of them do not speak a foreign language, so the idea they will have to talk to an immigration officer is very stressful. Some of them are terribly afraid of the border control because they are smuggling cigarettes. The only way to ease the stress is alcohol, which makes the migrants loud, quarrelsome, and disturbing. They are exhausted with their long journey and much more worried about their future life in Britain than the protagonist of

Parys-White's novel. During infrequent stops, the migrants in *Polska szkoła boksu* either smoke or articulate their worries, of which the most nagging are their poor command of English and searching for a job or a place to live. However common these concerns are for each migrant, they greatly affect the characters' mood and self-esteem. Those who were self-confident and ready to fulfil their rags-to-riches dream, now have lost their courage and pride.

Economic migrants travel with heavy luggage because they do not intend to change the place of residence. They are planning to stay in one place, earn a living, and help their relatives financially. Even if economic or social conditions become unfavorable and force them to change their location, they avoid moving to distant places, unlike existential migrants, who consider their frequent move natural and welcome. They are like contemporary nomads who feel no need to settle in one place. They own only things they truly need and can carry all their possessions in a small backpack, which becomes a symbol of the change and, as Pasterska (2019) puts it, of the freedom of choice (p. 76). In *Emigrantka z wyboru*, Ewa seems to live according to a classical dictum *Omnia mea mecum porto* [All that is mine I carry with me] and puts all her belongings into her small backpack. She says, "My friend had two heavy backpacks—and I actually little to pack" (Parys-White, 2008, p. 19). She can easily move from one place to another without developing a sense of belonging to any of them.

The idealized vision of Britain is an incitement to many migrants, but the reality proves much bleaker. The ideal land the migrants arrive in turns out to be the place full of injustice, social inequalities, and exploitation. In Miklasz's novel, the protagonist does not feel at home in England. He calls England "an obligatory labor camp, a prison in which [he is] going to stay for a few months and do the simplest task to scrape together as much as possible" (2009, p. 61). He shares a tiny room in a crowded flat in central Buckby rented from Turkish migrants, which does not meet his expectations of an easy and comfortable life in England. He says, "On the first floor there was a shared kitchen and bathroom that was a horrible combination of a shower and the crapper" (Miklasz, 2009, p. 41). Ewa has a more optimistic outlook on London. She also shares a room with her Polish friend in King's Cross. This part of London offers relatively cheap rents and the regular sight of homeless people, prostitutes, and people involved in some shady business. However, all this does not mar her vision of London. In the beginning, she adores the city, especially London's beautiful Victorian architecture and well-kept parks full of various birds and squirrels patiently waiting for some food. She is also impressed with friendly and polite Londoners whose "short 'I'm sorry' … improved [her] mood and made [her] relaxed" (Parys-White, 2008, p. 37).

Paradise With Equal Opportunities

After a few months of living in London, Ewa feels bitterly disappointed because London is not the "[p]aradise with equal opportunities" she expected (Parys-White, 2008, p. 19). Remembering the times of social inequality, oppression, and tyranny of the communist regime, she leaves Poland for the promised land in the hope of settling down in the country, where all people regardless of their ethnicity, social status, or religion are treated fairly. However, she experiences exploitation, and the hard reality does not meet her expectations. In the beginning, she works as a maid at a three-star hotel, whose grumpy owner breaks "most of human rights of the 20th century" (Parys-White, 2008:, p. 30) and has never defined her workload, weekly wage, and duties. Migrants, especially those with a poor command of English, work hard for the "cash in hand" and have little or no time off work. It is not rare for employers to bully migrant workers who cannot even complain officially because they are undocumented workers with no rights.

The narrator of *Polska szkoła boksu* also realizes that most migrants are assigned to menial jobs, which require little schooling and hardly any formal qualifications, which the British are reluctant to do. Migrants make a living as refuse collectors or by doing gardening jobs, which offer bleak job prospects and very low wages. He says, "Low-paying manual jobs, which an average British disdained, provided the migrant with a steady income and a sense of stability" (Miklasz, 2009, p. 30). The migrants dream of working in a factory or warehouse, where they can earn more, but with their poor command of English, they will never get their dream job. Polish migrants depicted in both novels are desperate to get a job. Some of them spent the last penny to buy a ticket to England and unless they find a job, they will have difficulty in surviving in the host country. As the protagonist of *Polska szkoła boksu* states, "I needed this job just like a little child needs a toy" (Miklasz, 2009, p. 25). That is why the migrants often abandon their ambitions and downgrade their skills in order to get any job. In *Emigrantka z wyboru*, Ewa admits that it was common for migrants to lie about their qualifications. The protagonist of Miklasz's novel does not reveal he has no experience in gardening because he hopes he will be able to acquire some practical know-how quickly. The main character of *Emigrantka z wyboru* in turn has a university degree in Polish studies but is never picky in her job search. She has decided to blank out her master's degree not to influence her choice and admits that in London her job requirements "disappeared like the first snow—rapidly" (Parys-White, 2008, pp. 21, 29). Therefore, she does not reveal her academic qualifications but can do any job that is offered in a job center or she can find on her own.

Migrants are vulnerable to exploitation: they work long hours and have very little time on their hands. In Miklasz's novel most characters have to get up at the crack of dawn to catch the train in order to get to work on time. Because the migrants have low-paying jobs, they work hard or have more than one job to make ends meet. In *Polska szkoła boksu*, some characters start their work early in the day in order to be able to have another job in the evening. Others go around exclusive Buckby housing estates and search for items the owners no longer need. They want to sell the things they find and make some extra money. The protagonist of the novel gets into trouble with rival Albanian migrants who forbid the Poles to "work" in their area. In *Emigrantka z wyboru*, some characters are willing to have another job to earn more despite the fact they are exhausted. No wonder they look forward to the weekend when they can wind down and forget their worries for a while.

In their novels, both writers depict the real life of the migrants with all their concerns and worries because, as Nowacki states, they may want to convey an important message. The nasty work experiences the migrants have may serve as a warning for future Polish migrants who are considering leaving for England (Nowacki, 2016, p. 223). Nowacki may be right because only a few times in both novels, the narrators cast some positive light on their working lives. In one of her jobs, Ewa develops a close working relationship with her friendly and helpful employer, whereas Miklasz's narrator meets some friendly workmates when he gets a job in a factory.

Inferiority Complex

Migrants' inferior position at work and social degradation contribute to their inferiority complex, which according to Dariusz Skórczewski (2013), is "a natural mental and cultural consequence of foreign domination," in this case the Soviet control (p. 398). The oppressor perpetuated negative stereotypes of Polish people to make them feel submissive and helpless. This led to what Skórczewski calls *hypernegative self-stereotyping*, which directly results from internalization and is typical of the oppressed, for example, migrants from postcommunist countries of Eastern Europe. What is more, such negative self-stereotyping inhibits assimilation into the dominant society.

Scholars who deal with Polish national character uncover other reasons for inferiority complex, which sometimes result from underestimating one's own heritage (e.g., Legutko, 2008; Szyszkowska, 1998). Szyszkowska (1998) admits that Poles show too much humility toward the West and praise what is foreign. She attributes it to the lack of rudimentary knowledge of their own history of philosophy (p. 283). Ryszard Legutko (2008) puts forward a more convincing reason for the inferiority complex of Poles. According to him, it is caused by the ignorance of the history of Poland. Legutko explains that a strong dislike for history was initiated by the communist regime, which encouraged disrespect for the prewar Polish culture and history and broke the cultural continuity. On the one hand, Poles have unlearned to appreciate their own history and ignored the need to remember the past times, for example, time of the communist oppression. On the other hand, they feel the need to follow foreign trends and modern fashions, one of which is ignorance of history. Legutko (2008) states:

> [D]etachment from the past is obviously noticed. It is supposed to show we are gradually becoming part of the global world, where the spatial distance is smaller than the temporal distance: an individual living in contemporary Poland is in closer proximity to a New Yorker than to a countryman living 50 or 100 years ago. (p. 103)

This is exemplified by the migrants in *Polska szkoła boksu*, whose inferiority complex may stem from their being unable to recognize Polish heritage values. They are impressed with anything foreign and regard it as better and more valuable than anything Polish. However, the bitter reality of being a migrant breaks the spell. When the narrator of the novel arrives in England, he is disappointed by the way Poles are treated there. He is shocked by the very entry application process, which classifies Slavic migrants as Eastern Europeans instead of Europeans. He is angry with the authors of the application form, who

> created a new race called "Eastern European"! That means that according to English bureaucrats, psychopathic Adolf was right saying that Poles, Czechs, Slovaks ... differ mentally and racially from the rest of civilized Europe and they do not deserve to be called ordinary, true Europeans. (Miklasz, 2009, p. 25)

This surely intensifies his inferiority complex that even the recognition at work cannot diminish. For a moment he does not feel inferior because he has established intimate relations with Sonia, an English girl who lives nearby, whom he regards as "an English princess, a representative of the dominant caste" (Miklasz, 2009, p. 231). That she is attracted to a poor Polish migrant boy increases his self-confidence. However, when Sonia's father, who is a police investigator, asks if he knows a dangerous Albanian criminal who may be living among the migrants, his feelings of inferiority overwhelm him again. He realizes he will never be able to raise his marginal status and in England will always be treated as an inferior Polish migrant. He says,

> We lived in two parallel but very distant worlds that knew nothing about each other and had nothing in common. I was only one of those faceless types, with no history, past and future, meaningless creatures flashing silently and unnoticed from work to work and living in the cheapest basement flats.... (Miklasz, 2009, p. 231)

The protagonist of *Emigrantka z wyboru* also suffers from inferiority complex. Ewa is aware that Polish migrants are abused by their English employers, like her close friend, Jagoda, who works at a hairdresser's. She is overwhelmed by a heavy workload and her employer keeps imposing new duties on her:

> She told me recently to wash her car but only after the hair salon has been closed. I had been waiting for an hour till she did her shopping, so I finished polishing her wheels at 9 p.m. And what did she do? ... She cut my wage rate because I forgot about the bumpers, and some smudges left on the rear window. But it was already dark. How could I do it properly under the streetlight? (Parys-White, 2008, p. 52–53)

Despite having a university degree, Ewa knows that being a migrant she cannot expect to get a well-paid job. For this reason, she willingly accepts an offer to clean hotel rooms. In the beginning, she puts up with the unfair treatment from her boss because she desperately needs money to support herself, but later she proves to be strong enough to resign from her menial job and criticize him in public. Ewa is aware that fluency in English can raise her social status. She realizes that "a good command of English will boost [her] career prospects and ensure a better future" (Parys-White, 2008, pp. 52–53). That is why she buys the cheapest food and scrimps and saves to pay for her English course at London College.

What helps the male migrants in Miklasz's novel to overcome their feeling of inferiority and boost their confidence is verbal overcompensation. In *Polska szkoła boksu*, the narrator states that normally there were

> [f]ive or six "fucks" in the compound sentence, whereas a simple sentence had to contain at least two "fucks," always at the beginning of the sentence to emphasize something, and always at the end to show the emotional attitude of the speaker to what he has just said. (Miklasz, 2009, p. 78).

The reason for using so many obscenities is to cover the helplessness of the protagonists and increase their self-confidence. The narrator states that "[he] understood the most appropriate synonym for 'fuck' is 'helplessness'" (Miklasz, 2009, p. 314).

The migrants also bolster their ego by humiliating others and labeling them. Many of them have never been abroad before, so meeting a foreigner can be a nerve-racking experience. What is more, some of Miklasz's main characters are unskilled people with rather poor knowledge and little cultural awareness, therefore they label other migrants using very basic connotations. In *Polska szkoła boksu*, Miklasz shows a wide variety of derogatory words the characters use with reference to foreigners. For example, Turks are called Kebabs, Czechs are called Czech Dumplings, Italians are called Eyeties, the French are called Frogs, whereas Pakistanis and Indians are called Chapattis. The protagonist provides more examples of how Asians are referred to. He points out that disrespectful terms like Chink or Nip have become old-fashioned and have been replaced by more modern ones, like Pokémon or Ping-Pong. The labels used by Miklasz's characters with reference to other migrants are also based on religion and physical appearance. Thus, Muslims are labelled as Mahomets, whereas Arabs, who, according to Polish migrants, tend to forget about the importance of personal hygiene, are called slobs (Miklasz, 2009, pp. 45–46, 177, 185).

The offensive tone seems to be a way to boost self-confidence of insecure and exploited Polish migrants. It can help diminish the feeling of inferiority a bit and endure the hardships of everyday life. As Jarosław Wach (2010) argues, the only way to separate and defend oneself from the unpleasant and unfriendly world is through "laughter, mockery, irony and loutishness."

Migrant Identity

The weekends spent together playing cards and drinking are not only a way of relaxing but they also give the migrants a strong sense of unity. The characters become a close-knit community of the same ethnic descent, who have the common aim to improve their economic conditions and protect their families from poverty. The appalling conditions they live in, common aims, and shared everyday experience increase their sense of belonging. Ewa admits that "being part of the group gave a sense of security and suppressed the feeling of loneliness. It was the best way to survive, the best source of relaxation after work and after everyday stresses in a foreign country" (Parys-White, 2008, p. 69). On the other hand, the idea of ethnic solidarity can be violated by economic competition for a better-paying job or personal savings. However jealous the migrants might be of their flatmates' successes, they support each other. Their loved ones were left behind in Poland, so it is the flatmates who have become family. As there are hardly any elderly and experienced characters in the novels who could advise the young, they have to rely on their own or their friends' experience, or search for constructive advice in books, like Ewa, who seeks useful hints about how to be happy in a self-help book.

The protagonists depicted in both novels appreciate their national identity very much. They are living in England, but it is their Polishness that maintains the bond between them. Despite having different social backgrounds, skills, and even the level of fitness, they can join forces to train together to take part in the migrant football tournament. What strengthens the bond between them is the national spirit during the match against another migrant team or while watching sports competitions where they support Polish athletes. Cultural and religious traditions are also significant because they give the migrants a sense of unity with other Poles in England and help preserve their Polish national identity. Culture plays a vital role in the process of identity formation and gives the migrants the feelings of security and belonging. According to Homi Bhabha (2004), culture is crucial to survival as it provides safe refuge for migrants and prevents them from feeling alienated (p. 247).

Leaving their homes behind, the migrants remain conservative and celebrate all the major religious festivals in the same way as they did in Poland. During Christmas they follow the custom of putting some hay under the table cloth, eating Polish bread and traditional dishes, singing Christmas carols, and participating in the midnight service to make Christmas a unique time and preserve tradition. Ewa describes the family atmosphere of Christmas spent in London and calls her flatmates "the foster family but best we could have here" (Parys-White, 2008, p. 89). The migrants care about the tiniest details while preparing celebrations of Easter, birthday, or wedding parties. Every single Polish custom makes them feel spiritually close to their homeland. The importance of preserving tradition is revealed by Ewa, who states that "it maintained the sense of belonging and quite well deceived the heart that was missing the homeland. With the pursuit of the Western lifestyle, traditions in Poland declined. Ironically, here they were carefully preserved because they were familiar" (Parys-White, 2008, p. 90).

Polish migrants' traditional upbringing sometimes prevents the full assimilation into British society. With their conservative views on gender roles, the male migrants seem to be the victims of the patriarchal order. They regard themselves as breadwinners, earning money to support their families. The woman is expected to be like mythological Penelope who remains faithful to her husband when he is away and cares for the household. One of the migrants in *Polska szkoła boksu* states,

> "When I get back to Poland, my Grażynka will make me Polish hunter's stew, make the bed, brew the tea.... She is better than a thousand English women!" We agreed with him, made a toast to our homeland, to all decent Grażynkas, Bożenkas, and Helenkas ..., to all these true reflections of the mythical woman of Sienkiewicz's prose who, like Penelope, is waiting faithfully for us to return home.... We praised Slavic delicate beauty, honesty, loyalty, attachment to Poland and tradition.... [W]e shouted each other down with the ideas of Polish women's wisdom, honor, honesty and loyalty (i.e., cardinal virtues that the islanders missed). (Miklasz, 2009, pp. 96–97)

The male migrants idealize their girlfriends, who were left behind in Poland. However, this idealized picture of their fiancées is superseded by the real life at times, arousing the feelings of frustration and disappointment. On the one hand, the men miss their girlfriends, but if they had an opportunity to establish an intimate relation with English women, they would take advantage of it. Miklasz's narrator says that "[t]hose more persistent were watching in solitude the main streets of the city ... dreaming of buxom English women" (Miklasz, 2009, p. 87). When they see a nice-looking girl passing by, they shout excitedly, "Look! Look at this bit of fluff!" (Miklasz, 2009, p. 97). On the other hand, they are aware that their female compatriots do not fit the image of submissive women and deal much better with their new life in England than the men. Miklasz's protagonist admits that Polish women "with the speed of chameleons adopted the rules that governed this new, better world, its trends and the manner of existence in the society of Übermenschen" (Miklasz, 2009, p. 87).

The male migrants prove to be socially marginalized losers who can achieve success neither at work nor in love, which is illustrated by the way Miklasz's narrator describes other male migrants:

> [Poles] tired of working the whole week, meticulously counting their pounds, frequently not very attractive physically and intellectually, burdened by their complexes and huge language barrier, completely unadjusted, forgotten by history, the media and God, with no friends, despised even by their female compatriots, were drinking vodka and chewing hot dog sausages. (Miklasz, 2009, p. 87)

In *Emigrantka z wyboru*, women are stereotypically portrayed as typical housewives confined to the domestic sphere, who have no other aspirations than a clean house, a delicious dinner, and a satisfied husband. Parys-White depicts Polish female migrants through the oppressive paradigm of Matka-Polka (Mother-Pole), which forms Polish identity and has been deeply rooted in Polish culture. It places women in the role of patriots, submissive wives, and exemplary mothers who are responsible for preserving Polishness and will sacrifice themselves for the sake of their homeland and families. Ewa says that Polish women are very popular with English men, who

> were looking for practical, solicitous, caring, and loving [women] with a motherly and tender heart. … That is why Eastern European women arouse great interest [of men]. Their modesty and no excessive demands for men were endearing. They didn't have to be taken to an expensive restaurant every week. A meager takeaway was definitely enough. They didn't hold out against housework duties. They didn't make constant demands for gifts and flowers. It was enough to have a man who gave them a hello kiss and kissed them goodbye, and occasionally took them to a pub for beer. (Parys-White, 2008, p. 68)

Traditional upbringing and Catholic teaching bear responsibility for this oppressive patriarchal structure that imposes limitations and causes family conflicts. Parys-White's novel illustrates this point clearly. One of the characters, Julia, has an argument with her father who objects to her interethnic marriage with an Egyptian. However, the new reality provides opportunities for the change of traditional stereotypes and redefinition of the identity. Ewa notices that "[i]n our country it was not allowed to change the natural order of things, make mistakes, provoke fate, fall out of the established framework"

(Parys-White, 2008, p. 69), whereas the host country enables spontaneity and provides migrants with freedom and independence. Ewa states that in England "[e]veryone had an opportunity to make a fresh start" (Parys-White, 2008, p. 69). No wonder that the deeply rooted stereotypes and traditional views can be eventually rejected.

The female protagonists depicted in *Emigrantka z wyboru* often fail to live up to the men-made image of submissive women. They eradicate prejudices and reject stereotypes. England provides them with self-confidence and the ability to challenge the established order, like Julia who is strongly opposed to her father's vision of her marital life. They become self-reliant and strong women who deal with the harsh migrant reality much better than the men. They leave for England not only to earn money but also to enable their personal development, and they adapt to the new reality much more easily and faster than the men. As Van Heuckelom argues, contemporary migrant women's prose depicts "going abroad as the upward mobility (not downward). The stories of degraded Odysseus are replaced by a modern version of the Cinderella fairy tale" (Van Heuckelom, 2013, p. 326). The women prove to be more flexible in their assimilation into the host society, which makes them feel fulfilled and satisfied. After a series of initial failures and problems, Parys-White's protagonist finds a good job, gets married to an English man, and settles down in England, whereas Miklasz's protagonist returns to Poland.

The migrants in both novels value friendship, which not only eases the pain of loneliness but also increases their sense of belonging. They tend to be sympathetic and willing to help their friends when they are in need. They are very supportive to each other. For example, when Julia, one of the characters of *Emigrantka z wyboru*, is upset when her father objects to her marriage with an Egyptian, her friends are sympathetic and try to comfort her. When Jagoda, who is abused by her employer, is complaining about her excessive workload, her flatmate offers her help to find a better-paying job: "When a vacancy has arisen in our pizza restaurant, I'll immediately pull strings to get you a job" (Parys-White, 2008, p. 53). When Ewa gives up her job in the hotel, she feels it is necessary to help her workmates who are also Polish migrants. She makes them realize they are abused by the boss and encourages them to search for a better-paying job, where they will be treated humanely. She persuades them: "Give up this job! You sweat blood from dawn to dusk and you get paid peanuts! You already have some experience in hotel industry. You will easily find something better" (Parys-White, 2008, p. 32).

In his useful study, Marek Butrym (2010) states that the shared space, common experiences and bonds drawn on common ethnic origin make the migrants become a close-knit community, which provides them with physical and emotional security. On the other hand, a shared bathroom or kitchen can provoke conflicts and disputes. It is sometimes hard to put up with the flatmates' irritating habits of messing up or behaving improperly. The protagonist of Parys-White's novel (2008) complains about dirty dishes in the kitchen sink or stale food in the fridge (p. 38), whereas the narrator of *Polska szkoła boksu* (2009) objects to a dirty washbasin, muddy shoes left in the middle of the kitchen, tobacco on the kitchen table, or sweaty T-shirts lying all over the floor (p. 139). In a shared bathroom long showers have become a thing of the past and exceeding a time limit provokes anxiety and ill feelings. The main character of Miklasz's novel (2009) speaks about constant control of the time spent in the shower: "Everyone felt watched by the other, not a single move went unnoticed, which even more took away the sense of intimacy" (p. 140). No intimacy, a dull reality, and inferior positions at work make the migrants want to strengthen their position at least at home. As Ślósarska (2016) argues, no decision-making potential at work and lack of individual autonomy lead to the fight for their superiority at home and defense of their private space, for example, a kitchen shelf in the migrants' Buckby flat, "which was among the shared loo, shared washing machines, shared cabinets, shared plates, mugs, and cutlery our only inviolable private sphere. We were proud of this poor substitute for privacy…" (Miklasz, 2009, p. 140). The kitchen shelf grows into the role of the private sphere, where others are not allowed. There occurs a binary opposition of "mine" and "his/hers," which symbolizes a conflict between the need for socializing and belonging to a group on the one hand, and the struggle for personal development and strong position on the other (Ślósarska, 2016, p. 166).

Most migrants depicted in both novels feel little need to assimilate into British society. They perceive the world as a clash between "here" (England) and "there" (Poland), "our" world of dirty, congested flats and "their" world of London or Buckby. This struggle carries emotional baggage because what is "mine" mostly has positive connotations, whereas "their" is associated with inequality, exploitation, and negative stereotypes about Poles. The narrator of *Polska szkoła boksu* is part of the Polish migrant community in England, which he strongly identifies with. However, he seems to be a bit more open to the new culture and English people than his friends. For him, the world beyond his crowded flat in Buckby is tempting and has a lot to offer. This is the ordered and safe world, where he meets his girlfriend and spends quality time with her, whereas the daily life he shares with his flatmates is compared to "the brutal reality closed in Polish immigrants' kitchen" (Miklasz, 2009, p. 201). Therefore, he reckons that his move to Sonia's place will allow him to cut himself off from "the brutal world of the drunken immigrants in Buckby" (Miklasz, 2009, p. 301). He also skips regular weekend benders and slightly changes his physical look as a symbol of his breakaway from his Buckby life: "My conventional hairdo and neutral clothes including casual black shirt and cords made them believe I was not one 'of them' [migrants]" (Miklasz, 2009, p. 316). Despite the attempts to break out of his Polish lifestyle, the bond with his Polish friends proves to be stronger than the relationship with Sonia.

The small communities where the migrants live strengthen their national identity and also provide them with a sense of security in language. They speak Polish, which makes them unmotivated, as they do not have to make an effort to learn English, which most of them do not know at all. They can always find someone who will help them at a job agency or at work where speaking English is necessary. This becomes a vicious circle: many Polish migrants are frustrated because they have to do menial jobs as their command of English is poor, but they are reluctant to learn it. They attribute their poor command of the language to high costs but never to their laziness. Only the narrators of both novels realize the importance of being fluent in English. In the beginning, Ewa knows only a few basic phrases and relies entirely on her friend Zofia, who speaks much better English. However, when she has managed to save some money, she enrolls in an English course in a nearby language school. The protagonist of Miklasz's novel can speak English well enough to communicate with his English-speaking workmates and his English girlfriend. However, most of his flatmates, for example, Boruta, speak no English, which prevents any social interaction with the natives. This, in turn, hinders their assimilation and increases their frustration and inferiority complex. At times the narrator of *Polska szkoła boksu* feels appreciated and more self-confident thanks to his being fluent in English.

Poles in England frequently use a strange code consisting of Polish and English words, which does not result from their poor command of English but rather reveals their new migrant identity that combines the elements of both cultures. This may be a symptom of their conscious or unconscious assimilation into British society. In the analyzed novels the migrants mix Polish with some English words, for example: "A ty to ... *who are you?*"; "He, he, he ... ale *funny*"; ""Do diabła z tą *power of word*" (Parys-White, 2008, pp. 64, 131); " [t]y na głupim *forklifcie* zarabiasz więcej niż u was w urzędzie"; "menedżer wyzywał od *lazy bastardów*" (Miklasz, 2009, pp. 61, 201). In Miklasz's novel (2009) the migrants also tend to translate Polish sayings literally, for example: "Who wakes up in the morning, God gives him" instead of "the early bird catches the worm" or "[h]e is laughing like a stupid to cheese" for laughing for no reason (p. 262).

It is sometimes hard for the migrants to preserve their identity. They are in between the past and present, Poland and England. They must redefine their identity to adjust to the new conditions, for example, when they have to accept jobs below their qualifications or when they are regarded as inferior by the host society. It is hard at times because of their Polish upbringing. In early childhood their parents instilled disdain in them for some humiliating jobs. They emphasized the importance of education and regarded manual jobs as shameful. Therefore, Ewa is very ashamed of having to change a bed as part of her job in the hotel and avoids speaking about it when she meets her friends.

Some Polish migrants feel a sense of superiority and think they are power-ful enough to impose their own vision of England. This is what Skórczewski (2013) calls *hyperpositive self-stereotyping*, which is a way to fight against the ste-reotypes perpetuated by the Soviet authorities during their control of Poland (p. 398). Parys-White (2008) calls Polish migrants "[c]ontemporary warriors of light" (p. 10), whereas Miklasz (2009) views them as "proud conquistadors of the British Isles" (p. 6) and "cocreators of this world" (p. 30). Sadly, the characters' high expectations are crushed by a harsh reality, and instead of having impressive careers, they are often viewed as inferior and unimportant.

Conclusion

The migrants portrayed in the two novels come from different social back-grounds and have different qualifications, but share the dream of changing their life for the better and of improving their economic status. Despite the fact that capitalism replaced the communist regime in Poland several years before, the new system is still not reassuring for the young, who would like to live a better life than their parents. The better life they dream of relates either to better employment prospects and improved economic conditions (*Polska szkoła boksu*) or to simple wanderlust, the need to break a routine, fulfill indi-vidual potentials, and feel independent (*Emigrantka z wyboru*).

The work stay in England does not meet the migrants' expectations of easy money and the promised isle, where everybody regardless of race, ethnicity, religion, and gender is treated equally. What the migrants have to face on a daily basis is inequality, the feeling of displacement, and social degradation because they often "convert their intellectual competence into the broom and shovel" (Parys-White, 2008, p. 96). They have to bear prejudices stemming from their poor command of English, or negative and unfair stereotypes of Poles as drunkards and criminals. All this adds up to their deeply rooted inferiority complex, which is hard to overcome.

The protagonists feel the bond with their home country and miss the families they left behind in Poland. They feel a strong need to be part of the Polish community in England because it gives them the sense of belonging and security. For this reason they preserve Polish customs and traditions and form a lasting friendship with their compatriots who substitute for their families and support them in difficult situations. Such close-knit communities, which often hinder migrants' assimilation, are believed to be caring and protective of their members. They are very important for the migrants who frequently feel alienated by the host country. Their identity is at a crossroads: on the one hand, they still feel a strong bond with their homeland, but they are also exposed to new cultural influences, which shape processes of identity formation. The protagonists follow what Dąbrowski (2016) calls *the code of the Other* (p. 307). They neither rely on their former identity nor fully integrate into British society, but they form an entirely new identity that is in between both cultures.

Ultimately, the way Polish migrants are portrayed in the novels is influenced by gender. Most male migrants are depicted as losers, who are unable to achieve success either in their professional or love life, and are reluctant to learn English and assimilate into the host society. The protagonist of Miklasz's novel feels he will always be treated as one of the migrants and therefore returns to Poland. In his article about Polish migrant prose, Nowacki (2016) states that "men in the UK lose, women win" (p. 220), which sounds convincing especially in relation to Parys-White's novel, where most of the women are flexible and reasonable. They do not conform to culturally assigned gender stereotypes and are not victims of patriarchy. They never reject their Polishness but can rationally plan their future without viewing assimilation as risky or dangerous. For Ewa her migration is like a happy ending adventure: she achieves fluency in English, gets married to an English man, and settles down in England.

REFERENCES

Bhabha, H. (2004). *The Location of Culture*. Routledge Classics.

Butrym, M. (2010). Kapitał społeczny i stosunek do ojczyzny młodych emigrantów zarobkowych (Social Capital and Relationship to Homeland of Young Economic Migrants). In R. Bera (Ed.), *Wielka emigracja zarobkowa młodzieży. Wyzwanie dla edukacji* [Great Youth Migration. Educational Challenge] (pp. 125–132). UMCS.

Czapliński, P. (2013). Kontury mobilności (Mobility Contours). In P. Czapliński, R. Makarska, & M. Tomczok (Eds.), *Poetyka migracji. Doświadczenie granic w literaturze polskiej przełomu XX I XXI wieku* [The Poetics of Migration. The Experience of Bordering in Polish Literature at the Turn of the 21c.] (pp. 9–42). Wydawnictwo Uniwersytetu Śląskiego.

Dąbrowski, M. (2016). Proza migracyjna: źródła i znaczenie [Migrant Prose: Sources and Meaning]. *Teksty drugie, 2016*(3), 288–307. https://rcin.org.pl /dlibra/show-content/publication/edition/59162?id=59162

Düvell, F., & Garapich, M. (2011). *Polish Migration to the UK: Continuities and Discontinuities* (Working Paper No.84). Centre on Migration, Policy and Society. University of Oxford. Download WP-2011-084-Düvell-Garapich_Polish _Migration_UK (PDF)

Goerke, N. (2006). Koktajl wielowarzywny (Mixed Vegetable Cocktail). In M. Pollack (Ed.), *Sarmackie krajobrazy. Głosy z Litwy, Białorusi, Ukrainy, Niemiec i Polski* [Sarmatian Landscapes]. The Voices of Lithuania, Belarus, Ukraine, Germany and Poland) (pp. 169–194). Wydawnictwo Czarne.

Hurrle, J. (2019). The Polish-Jewish Emigration of 1968 and Their View of Poland. *Migration Online*. https://migrationonline.cz/en/the-polish-jewish-emigration -of-1968-and-their-view-of-poland

Lee, E. (1966). A Theory of Migration. *Demography, 3*(1), 47–57. https://doi.org /10.2307/2060063

Legutko, R. (2008). *Esej o duszy polskiej* [An Essay on Polish Spirit]. Ośrodek Myśli Politycznej.

Madison, G. (2006). Existential Migration. In S. du Plock & J. M. Heaton (Eds.), *Existential Analysis*, 17.2 (pp. 238–260). https://www.gregmadison.net /documents/MigrationEA.pdf

Miklasz, A. (2009). *Polska szkoła boksu. Powieść emigracyjna* (The Polish Boxing School. An Emigration Novel). Księgarnia Wydawnictwo Skrzat Stanisław Porębski.

Mullan, B., & Frejka, T. (1995). The UN/ECE International Migration Surveys in Lithuania, Poland, and Ukraine: Methodological Issues. In R. van der Erf & L. Heering (Eds.), *Causes of International Migration* (pp. 223–253). Office for Official Publications of the European Communities.

Nowacki, D. (2016). Wyspy obiecane. Rekonesans krytyczny [The Promised Isles: A Critical Reconnaissance]. *Teksty drugie, 2016*(3), 205–228. https://rcin.org
.pl/dlibra/doccontent?id=59158

Parys-White, D. (2008). *Emigrantka z wyboru. Opowieść londyńska* [The Emigrant by Choice. A Story from London]. Videograf II Sp. z o.o.

Pasterska, J. (2019). Modele polskiej prozy „unijnej." Próba klasyfikacji [Models of Polish 'Union' Prose. An Attempt at Classification]. *Tematy i konteksty, 9*(14), 70–92. https://doi.org/10.15584/tik.2019.4

Ślósarska, J. (2016). "Zmartwychwstanie śmieciarzy". Interakcjonizm symboliczny i narracyjne trajektorie biograficzne w tekstach polskich migrantów przebywają-cych w Wielkiej Brytanii i Irlandii po roku 2004 ["Resurrection of the Dustmen": Symbolic Interactionism and Narrative Biographical Trajectories in the Texts by Polish Migrants in Great Britain and Ireland after 2004]. *Przekładaniec,* 32(2016), 163–175. https://doi.org/10.4467/16891864PC.16.010.6550

Skórczewski, D. (2013). *Teoria – literatura – dyskurs. Pejzaż postkolonialny* [Theory-Literature-Discourse: a Postcolonial Landscape]. Wydawnictwo KUL.

Stola, D. (2002). Milion straconych Polaków [A Million Lost Poles]. *Biuletyn Instytutu Pamięci Narodowej, 3*(14), 62–65.

Szyszkowska, M. (1998). *Filozofia w Europie* [Philosophy in Europe]. Temida 2.

Van Heuckelom, K. (2013). Od "Polish Remover" do *Polskiej szkoły boksu.* Polskość w najnowszej literaturze migracyjnej (From "Polish Remover" to the *Polish Boxing School.* Polishness in the Recent Migrant Literature). In G. Filip, J. Pasterska, & Magdalena Patro-Kucab (Eds.), *Polonistyka w Europie. Kierunki i perspektywy rozwoju* [Polish Studies in Europe. Directions and Development Prospects] (pp. 319–329). Wydawnictwo Uniwersytetu Rzeszowskiego.

Wach, J. (2010). Sen wariata tudzież marne losy polskich emigrantów [A Lunatic's Dream and a Miserable Life of Polish Migrants]. *Akcent, 4*(2010). http://akcentpismo.pl/spis-tresci-numeru-42010/jaroslaw-wach-sen-wariata
-tudziez-marne-losy-polskich-emigrantow/

CHRA RASHEED MAHMUD | Canterbury Christ Church University

Why Do Things Matter? Kurdish Material Culture and Identity

Abstract

This essay focuses on the dynamic role of material culture in reflecting individuals' identities. It aims to highlight the importance of making and remaking material objects and examines the emotional impacts of objects. It also places on the individual's identities by drawing on the interplay of "posthumanism" and "nonessentialist" standpoints. For this study, three research participants, two male and one female, narrated their stories and explained how their identities had been influenced by the objects they used and the places they visited. The analysis in this essay is part of a larger project that looks at identity negotiation and navigation within a group of Iraqi Kurdish migrants in the United Kingdom. The findings reveal a robust association between humans, material possessions, and places. Hitherto, neither persons nor objects can withstand alone since the two function together and are intertwined in many respects. They are associated with deep emotional investment and powerfully influence an individual's identity, emotions, and well-being. To the participants, objects are material capsules that make places "sticky"; they are a connecting product that links the feeling, sites, and landscapes from the past in establishing a better future.

Keywords: material culture, identity, posthumanism, nonessentialism, narrative analysis.

Throughout history, humans have used every available means to survive by implementing their skills and abilities to build shelters out of the available resources, make weapons for hunting, fishing, and self-protection, or simply as a decorative means like clothing and artwork. These material objects are socially and culturally dependent and embody an individual's cultural reality (Prown, 1982; Lynch, 2009; Woodward & Fisher, 2014).

Countless interdisciplinary studies addressed the significance of material objects concerning identity, lifestyle, and homemaking processes (e.g., Khrenova & Burrell, 2021; Ran & Liu, 2021; Marschall, 2019; Money, 2007).

This essay highlights the importance of studying material culture and identity within the Kurdish context. It aims to (1) investigate how a group of Kurdish migrants use objects to express their sense of being, and (2) examine the role of objects in retrieving an individual's memories while living in the diaspora. To do so, three people, two male and one female, all first-generation Iraqi Kurds, told their stories about their relationship with objects and explained the emotional impacts of objects and places on their identities. Then, the participants' first-hand experiences were analyzed and discussed qualitatively using literature from "posthumanism" (Miller, 2010) and "nonessentialist" standpoints (Holliday, 2013).

The Kurds are the largest ethnic and linguistic community without an independent state (McDowall, 2021). The region inhabited by the Kurds is known as Kurdistan, or the homeland of the Kurds, a strategic area in the Middle East (Mahmud, 2018). Kurdistan comprises an integral part of Turkey, Iraq, Syria, Iran, Azerbaijan, and Armenia (Ünver, 2016). According to McDowall (2021), Kurds are estimated at around 34 million people dispersed across many regions and continents. Among this number, 18 million Kurds live in Turkey, 8 million in Iran, 7.2 million in Iraq, 1.8 million in Syria, and 2 million in the diaspora and Caucasus (McDowall, 2021). However, these numbers are not an accurate representation of the Kurds. A systematic survey is required in Kurdistan and the diaspora to reveal the actual number of the Kurdish community.

My reflection on studying material culture concerning identity began two years ago when I started exploring cultural identity within the Kurdish context. While collecting data for the Ph.D. project, I interacted with different objects inside the participants' private dwelling. Listening to the participants talk about their experiences in the United Kingdom was interesting. However, I was flabbergasted by their attention to material objects in their daily lives. After some investigation, it becomes evident that limited studies on material culture in the Kurdish context are available (Mahmud, 2023 [forthcoming]; Eagleton, 1996; Kren, 1996). Therefore, I sought to know more about those objects and examine their role in establishing research participants' identities. Indeed, delving into such a process was challenging and overwhelming, yet exciting. They required a detailed understanding of what counts as a material object/culture and its impact on people's identities.

This study uses material objects and material culture interchangeably to avoid complications because both concepts are associated with physical entities, possessions, and spaces that define people's culture (see Badwan & Hall, 2020). In this stance, it is necessary to provide a pellucid definition of what constitutes material culture/objects and clarify their meaning. Material culture refers to the personal possessions, goods, resources, and spaces one encounters, interacts with, and uses regularly. Indeed, the object choices vary depending on the person's preferences, history, and memory around them.

The essay begins by reviewing and conceptualizing personal, social, and material culture and materiality. Next, the context in which the study was undertaken will be explained. Then some empirical data will be presented and analyzed in relation to personal and social identity development, material culture, and materiality.

Conceptualizing Material Culture, Personal, and Social Identity

Material Culture and Materiality: Life Beyond the Self

Material culture is not new in human history. The term appeared for the first time in 1843 (Buchli, 2004). Material culture has become the dominant study area within the social science disciplines, and the concept is defined differently across disciplines. The term is perceived as "something of a contradiction ... since material culture is not culture but its product" (Schlereth, 1999, p. 2). Hence, material culture is "culture made material" that is unique to humans (Sheumaker & Wajda, 2008, p. xi).

Material culture is "an object or physical structures that had a particular use, meaning or set of values attached to them" (Greig et al., 2015, p. 5). These objects should have a direct influence on people and "are acted upon by people" to carry out a social function, "regulating social relations and giving symbolic meaning to human activity" (Woodward, 2007 p. 3). In other words, material culture is the physical objects or "stuff" that people make, interact with, and use to define their cultures, such as clothing, food, artwork, tools, and other household objects (Miller, 2010). In addition, the collected objects might be influenced by technological advancement, intercultural encounters, and various sociocultural and sociopsychological factors. Individuals become familiar with society's beliefs, ideas, values, and attitudes through objects. Therefore, the importance of using material objects lies in their meaning and relationship with the owner, whether they are "real" or "imagined," "lost" or "forgotten" (Pechurina, 2020, p. 1). For many, material objects are not only a thing. They are "aide-mémoires, precipitating memory and facilitating the process of remembrance" (Marschall, 2019, p. 2).

It is impossible to understand human perceptions of the world they inhabit without understanding the prominence of culture and materiality, as these two concepts are densely connected. The term "material" in material culture refers to a "broad and unrestricted range of objects" (Schlereth, 1999, p. 2), and it is laboriously constituted by culture. Once objects signify things or establish social meaning, materialization occurs. Explicitly, materialization accentuates the physical object and represents aspects of social and cultural reality that form continuous and dynamic relationships between the individual self, objects, and society. Seemingly, through materialization, "a person is drawn into an object, effectively becoming it, or what it is seen to stand for" (Alexander et al., 2012, p. 687). Woodward (2007 p. 107) talks about the unity between object and human, and he believes in the "oneness between material and human, united by an emotional connection." Hence, the harmony between humans and nonhumans can lead people to understand cultural norms and discourses better. Such understandings enhance individuals' self-perception and allow them to negotiate their individuality within the collective.

The concept of culture in material culture is not easily understood. Culture is problematic and considered one of the most challenging concepts in the English language (William, 1981). In contemporary society, culture denotes several matters. People's understanding of the concept is associated with their beliefs and judgments based on their cultural experiences. Which means culture is neither solid nor fixed but rather a "liquid" (Bauman, 2004). This essay understands culture as an action—something we do ("a performance") rather than something we have ("a trait") (Holliday, 2013; Pillar, 2017, p. 10). By looking at culture in terms of performance, the essentialist belief of the culture concept, which was initially epitomized in the work of Greet Hofstede (1980, 1991) and Hofstede et al. (2010), can be circumvented.

It is naïve and unrealistic to avoid the role of a posthuman standpoint in studying material culture and materiality. Posthumanism highlights the relationship between humans and their surroundings (e.g., human vs. nonhuman, humans vs. artifacts, humans, and other living species). Otherwise stated, the main idea of posthumanism is "what it means to be human" (Pennycook, 2018 p. 445). According to Braidotti (2013, p. 12), posthumanism is "an opportunity to empower the pursuit of alternative schemes of thoughts, knowledge, and self-representation." By thinking about human and nonhuman relationships, we can become critical thinkers and reposition our being about who and what we are in the process of becoming and where to position our existence in the materialistic world.

In his book, Daniel Miller (2010) challenges the joint opposition between the "person and the thing," the "animate and inanimate," and the "subject and the object" (2010, p. 15). Miller (2010, p. 16) argues that the "best way to understand, convey and appreciate our humanity is through attention to our fundamental materiality." Hence, we appreciate our existence through the things around us; the more we value things, the more we appreciate and understand people. He also presents theories of material culture, starting with a view of objects per se, followed by the more esoteric theory of objectification and the idea that subjects and objects are interconnected (Miller, 2010, p. 25). Miller believes things make us just as much as we make things in many respects (Miller, 2010). For example, individuals can emotionally attach to their surroundings; the stuff they encounter develops their personal, social, and cultural identities. The underlined property also maps the person's emotional attachment to objects and places. In this regard, the material forms became repositories of affection and desire.

A study by Nägele et al. (2020) shows that tangible service objects like mugs, membership cards, and pens can help service providers establish an emotional connection with potential customers and strengthen the emotional bonds of existing customers. These little nonhuman objects can powerfully control one's thinking and influence feelings. Ahmed (2014, pp. 11–18) highlights the compatibility and integration between people, objects, and spaces. She argues that the robust relationship between these entities "invokes emotions," making the objects and places "sticky as sites of personal and social tension." In their article, Badwan and Hall (2020, p. 236) highlight the prominence of "inter/intra-action with different objects, places, and artefacts," wherein objects have the power to connect people to their surroundings and "enable the emergence of critical spaces."

Objects are potent symbols of migrant and diasporic belonging. They help individuals create their homes and establish their sense of their existence in the diaspora. According to Woodward (2007), even the most ordinary and nonconventional object can symbolize the most profound human consciousness and aspirations. Humans are defined by what they think and say and are influenced by the material things they interact with, use, and create. Based on Gell's (1998) and Harrington-Watt's (2014) argument, Marschall (2019, p. 254) delineates that personal objects have "agency ... they trigger emotional responses and stimulate social effects and actions." A similar argument was put forward by some posthuman scholars who believe that an object or "stuff ... creates us in the first place" due to their powerful existence and the unique characteristics of the owners (Miller, 2010, p. 10). In their study, Philipp and Ho (2010) found that South African migrant women in New Zealand express their sense of home through the objects they transported from South Africa. The objects held high emotional value for them and "helped them foster a sense of transnational belonging without traveling to their country of origin" (Marschall, 2019, p. 4).

Besides, the physical environment can trigger an individual's identity. People establish a sense of attachment to places (e.g., a city, neighborhood, educational establishment, home, or even a room inside a house) and identify with these places (Giuliani, 2003). Hence, the personal attachment to a site, for example, a town or a village, will reflect their self-definition of being a city or a village person. Also, places that people have lived can generate one's sense of belonging. According to Hauge (2007, p. 1), "[P]laces are also influenced by people's identities." Objects can help individuals implement decorations and personalize their spaces. Through those spaces, they "reflect and communicate who they are." In that vein, material things can shape or reshape individuals' and groups' desire to be identified as a particular sociocultural group member.

Studies have shown that migrants pay extra attention to material stuff. Because material objects can help establish an "imagined home beyond [a] home through physical, individual, social, and temporal belongings." In addition, they develop a spiritual relationship with their loved ones through material stuff and memories (Kreuzer et al., 2018, p. 335). In other words, *stuff* can create affection at different moments, help people establish a new sense of belonging, and form new personal and social identities.

Objects and Identity

While the study of identity has been the focus for many years, the concept itself is problematic. Identities come with labels. Accepting and applying different descriptions requires a thorough understanding of what identity might entail. Due to the complex and elusive range of inconsistency and variability of the phenomena, this essay attempts to highlight some definitions to provide the readers with a clear discernment of the concept. Strauss (1959, p. 11) remarks that identity is an elusive concept: "everyone's sense of his own personal identity." For (Woodward, 2007, p. 134), identity refers to people's socially determined sense of who they are, involving one's sense of self "with particular corporeal and emotional qualities." It also includes social actors' societal positions and roles across time and space. From the postcolonial, postmodernist, and nonessentialist standpoints, understanding identity is linked to belonging to multiple groups and performing various roles through engagement in the broader society and the ability to navigate between them without any glitches.

Identity has been considered at the personal, social, and cultural levels, and the type of identities that belong to these categories are primarily intersected. Meaning aspects of one's personal identity can also form social and cultural identities. For instance, one's marital status (a type of personal identity) might position the person into a particular social category (e.g., married person). Relatedly, one's wedlock is perceived idiosyncratically by distinctive cultures and defines the person in terms of cultural types. These personal, social, and cultural identity categories can be avowed by the persons or ascribed to them by others and their social and cultural groups. Although there is a comprehensive overview of the immense and diverse literature on the identity concept, beyond the scope of this essay, an attempt is made to extract the main issues of debates over identities with particular attention to the self-categorization theory (Turner, 1985; Turner et al., 1987). According to Turner and colleagues (1987), self-categorization involves personal and social identities in relation to material objects.

Personal and social identities are distinct and have well-defined features that make a person unique depending on one's personal and social positioning (Hewstone et al., 2002). While the former refers to the unique attributes (the "I") that individuals assign to themselves regardless of the influences of the surrounding society and social relations (Leaper, 2011), the latter is the individual's self-categorization based on their group membership (the "we") or "us" versus "them" (Tajfel & Turner, 1986). Components of one's personal identity are the various social identities one has attained due to different experiences. Individuals' identities are not static or fixed but continuously evolve and are materially and culturally situated (Zilliacus et al., 2017).

Identity has many characteristics; individuals have multiple ascribed and avowal identities. Individuals' ascribed identities are assigned attributes to the individuals based on the contingencies of one's birth. In some situations, the traits may involve stereotypes. The *avowal identities* are the presentation of self in demonstrating "who I am" to others (Martin & Nakayama, 2010). Each facet of a person's identity is molded and produced in multiple and complex ways during socialization. These attributes can be expressed verbally (e.g., through language, accent, and communication style) or nonverbally (e.g., through the food we consume, clothes, material, and personal objects) (Fong & Chaung, 2004). The ascribed and avowal identity traits can be described as the "normative significance" of the individual's membership in the group(s). They can provide agency and are the source of power when the dominant identities come into play; as a result, people treat you as a "source of authority" (Appiah, 2019, pp. 10–11).

Furthermore, the stuff individuals surround themselves with profoundly assists them in determining their personal and social identities. According to Woodward (2007, p. 135), Objects can do "social work," meaning they might denote aspects of one's social identity, such as "subcultural affinity, occupation, and social status," to name a few. In the case of migrants, objects and material objects are potent means of establishing and representing an individual's identity. By implementing various strategies, they showcase and express aspects of their identities.

Likewise, places can be considered material objects that influence and change people's identification perceptions. No matter what, places can control everyday actions and emotions (e.g., what you do and how you feel) since a place is not a "physical environment separated from people…, but rather indivisible" (Seamon, 2013, p. 11). A place is a location with meaning; it is just a space until people put meaning to it by accentuating a specific experience. Once people are attached to a site, they start collating memories based on particular familiarities with typical buildings, surroundings, and people. Because places control one's emotions, influencing the interface or boundary between the environment and an individual's psychological well-being. A physical environment can impact one's identity and signify specific emotional attachment (Prince, 2014). A person can establish affection for multiple places deliberately or instinctively because of personal (e.g., childhood memories), social (e.g., the feeling of inclusion in a particular neighborhood), and cultural (e.g., the relevance of cultural rootedness) factors. Nonetheless, individuals' sense of attachment to a place might upsurge or decline since a place attachment is not an inactive endeavor but evolves and fluctuate over one's existence.

Interviews as a Data Collection Technique

This qualitative essay employs a narrative interview as the primary data collection, drawing attention to Walter Fisher's (1987) narrative paradigm. Qualitative research can take on many forms; it is an approach that accentuates "words rather than quantification in the collection and analysis of data" (Bryman, 2016, p. 374). Interviews used to examine an individual's lived experiences, and gain insights into people's feelings and thoughts. Interviews are a conversation that takes place between two or more people (Saunders et al., 2009). The notion is broad that describes a wide range of interviewing styles, such as in-depth interviews, structured, semistructured, and unstructured interviews, focused group interviews, and narrative inquiry, to name a few. These methodologies are valuable for researching migrants and their communities because they acknowledge an in-depth exploration of their migration and resettlement journey.

Narrative inquiry is the most common everyday communication; it is an amicable data-collection technique that values individuals' stories. Moreover, it portrays its type's artistic quality, conscientiousness, and nonpedantic nature. Kim (2016, p. 1) describes narrative inquiry as a "perfect hybrid of research and art" that can help the researcher collect data and satisfy their predisposition and inclination. Narratives can come from varied places, periods, imaginations, and people. Humans are known as "homo Narran" (Fisher, 1987, p. 62). They contribute to narrating a handful of curious, estranged, shocking, engaging, and controversial storytelling traces. According to Fisher (1987, p. 24), human beings are inherently storytellers with a natural capacity to recognize the coherence—the degree to which a story makes sense—and fidelity—whether the story "rings true" of stories they tell and experience. In other words, humans can learn through storytelling rather than through a rational argument or explanation and justification.

In the narrative paradigm, the role of the story is highly appreciated. The story consists of respective and distinctive minutiae that depend entirely on the context. A story translates an experience into something that, when contemplated and pondered, can be passed on to others. Nevertheless, stories are not perceived as credible or valid if the content is false or does not make sense (Brown, 2003). Fisher's narrative paradigm is respected for studying migrants and their communities, especially in studying material culture and artifacts. The narrative paradigm permits the researcher to accumulate extensive data;

it is a naturalistic and representational approach and an interplay between the freedom of expression of the participants and the researcher's positionality. In other words, Fisher's (1987) narrative paradigm allows the participants to talk about their experiences coherently, to divulge and tell stories about their lives. It also permits the researcher to examine and reflect on the different aspects of the disclosed narratives by respondents.

The data for this study were collected by implementing different narrative techniques drawn from the Life Story Narrative (Atkinson, 1998) and Biographical Narrative Interpretive Method (Wengraf, 2001). These two approaches are pretty far apart in structure, yet they share a similar goal—collecting narrative data. Distinct narrative techniques were used to inspire the respondents and enunciate the vicissitudes of their migration experiences, give meaning to their life stories, and arrive at *narrative rationality* (Fisher, 1987). Narrative rationality is how "we evaluate stories as true" (Sellnow, 2010, p. 38).

During the interviews, three research participants, two male and one female, narrated their stories, and they shared personal items like a journal and photos of precious objects they had kept for some time. During the interviews, respondents reflected on their choices and explained the importance of those items concerning their identity. Giving participants time and space to reflect on the objects was necessary because it showed that objects are not just material things; they can be defining factors in establishing a person's social meanings.

Conducting Narrative Analysis

Analyzing narrative data is a challenging task, constituting several steps, as Foss (1996) explains. First, the narrative analysis must fulfill specific requirements, which is demanding and time consuming. Foss (1996) claims that the researcher must examine the narrative systematically and carefully by providing information about the character (the narrator), plot (the sequence of the events in a story), and setting (the time and place in which a story is told) on a selection of elements on which they have to focus.

This study used structural narrative analysis—how the story is told (Riessman, 1993; James, 2023)—and dialogic/performative narrative analysis approaches (Riessman, 2005).[1] Merging the two methods assists the reader in understanding the research participants' migration experiences precisely, while the former provides the reader with a clear picture of the character, plot, and setting in the narrative blocks or stories they tell. The latter links the words, images, or visual data coherently and views the narrative as multivoiced and coconstructed. To follow the demand of these approaches, the researcher selected relevant texts that offered two events and were organized by time. Next, she ensured that the earlier and later events were connected and presented a story. Then, she described the character and setting before interpreting the data regarding the story's morals (Sellnow, 2010, p. 41). After that, she evaluated the potential implications of the narratives by asking "what," "who," and "why" to answer the "so what" questions to arrive at a discussion point (see the sample analysis in the analysis section).

Finally, the researcher organized the data under specific themes to help identify cliché or essential and noteworthy patterns in the narratives. Before analyzing and discussing the data, the next section will introduce an in-depth background of the research participants to allow the reader to understand the narrative data comprehensibly.

Participants' Pen Portrait

The data presented in this study is drawn from three research participants: Lia, Kamo, and Alan (pseudonyms). The participants are all first-generation Iraqi Kurdish immigrants.[2] They were born in Southern Kurdistan or Iraqi Kurdistan. All the respondents have resided and lived in the United Kingdom for over 15 years.

Lia, female; 49 years old at the time of the study; arrived in England at age 32.

Lia arrived in the United Kingdom in 2000. She received refugee status shortly after she arrived in the United Kingdom, and since then, she has settled in London. Lia holds a bachelor's degree in psychology and education studies from Saladin University in Northern Iraq. She also completed several other short courses during the years she spent in London, such as accounting, administration, and family community. In addition, Lia is an active member of the Kurdish community in London; she established several Kurdish supplementary schools to help Kurdish families and children maintain their heritage language. Besides, she has been involved in voluntary work and helped several charity organizations support homeless people inside the United Kingdom and back in Kurdistan.

Kamo, male; 51 years old at the time of the study; arrived in England at the age of 30.

Kamo is a single man from Suleimani. He is educated to a diploma level, and at the interview, he introduced himself as a poet, a writer, and an actor from Iraqi Kurdistan. Kamo left his homeland when he was 29. After his father passed away, his family experienced hardship, and his mother could no longer support him in completing his education. Therefore, he had to leave his drama course at the university of Baghdad. As a result, he embarked on the migration journey to have a better future and help his family overcome poverty. On his way, he crossed many borders and worked in different countries to support himself while traveling. Since arriving in the United Kingdom in 1999, he has resided in Kent—in the Southeast of England. Kamo currently works in a repair shop.

Alan, male; 42 years old at the time of the study; arrived in England at the age of 29.

Alan is a single man from a working-class background originally from Erbil—the capital city of Iraqi Kurdistan. His father was a builder, and his mother was a stay-at-home parent. Like Kamo, Alan also experienced poverty; the lack of enough resources forced him to work at a young age while being in full-time education. He completed his architecture degree in Erbil, but soon after graduation, he decided to migrate and establish a better future for himself and his family. Upon arrival in the United Kingdom, Alan worked in different industries while studying for a master's degree at a university in London. He also completed his Ph.D. eight years ago, and since then, he has worked as a lecturer and researcher in London.

Findings

In the following pages, participants' data will be analyzed. Before that, it is essential to clarify that the analysis in this section and throughout this essay reflects the researcher's subjective views. People might disagree with how the data has been interpreted in different stories. However, due to the richness of the narratives, it is possible to assign different interpretations, which can vary based on the researcher's or interpreter's trajectories since narratives are producers and transmitters of reality (Heikkinen, 2002).

Reading Material Culture

Whether general or personal, objects have power over us, making us rethink specific experiences within a particular situation. They also influence our minds and, in some cases, conquer our thinking. Objects help us collate our memories into blocks of events and sequences; no matter how big or small, they affect our emotions and transcend us to past moments. In the following pages, I will present data concerning material objects and materiality and highlight the importance of objects in manipulating the personal and social identity of the research participants.

This essay is not intended to describe material objects only or judge the participants based on their narrative. Instead, it attempts to examine the meaning of those objects, observe the relationship between them to their owners, examine their emotional impact, and explain their role in the identity construction process. The following pages and paragraphs will present the research participants' experiences concerning material objects, the power of these objects in creating nostalgia, and shaping and reshaping their presence. For the transparency of the data analysis and discussion section, the data will be presented under two headings: (a) material objects, nostalgia, and identity, and (b) emotion, place and identity.

Material Objects, Nostalgia, and Identity

Once I read a blog by an Iranian writer, Nadia Nooreyezdan, who moved to New York in 2017. Upon arrival, Nadia began collecting objects that tied her to the past; she connected her emotions to those objects and explained their impact on her psychological well-being. For example, according to her, the displayed artifacts by her bedroom window can provide a feeling of her lost home (Nooreyezdan, 2018). While meeting the research participants, I remembered Nadia's writing, and I began to draw a link between her experiences with objects to the narratives that participants disclosed during the meetings. As a researcher, I wanted to know about participants' experiences with material stuff and materiality.

The first narrative data comes from Lia. She explained the importance of transporting some objects from her hometown, like clothing, home accessories, food, and books, to name a few. To her, the objects she transported told a unique story and disclosed information about her personal and social identities. She also discussed gifts' value and power in determining a personal and social relationship between herself and her intimate relatives. For example, she gifted a white jersey to her son. The shirt is a symbolic representation of the Kurdish football team. During the interview, Lia describes the shirt as cheap and low in price, yet she believes that the object fortifies the emotional bond between her and her son.

> The shirt does not mean anything to me, but he likes football. So, I thought buying him a shirt depicting the Kurdistan football team was a good idea. I know the shirt was not expensive, but to me, the value of a gift lies in the spiritual bond that the piece creates between two people, and I think the shirt did that.

Gifts are personal choices that reflect an individual's identity, and others can picture us in their minds through gifts. Based on Lia's narrative, gift-giving is not only an economic commodity but also a vehicle by which she establishes a bond with the people she loves (e.g., her children). Lia's gift choice (a jersey) reflects her son's spirit as interested in sports, especially football.

Likewise, a journal is a powerful object controlling an individual's sense of being. Traditionally, journaling is nothing more than writing down one's thoughts. Still, it can be perceived as a prevailing means of communication between the inner self and outer realities. It can cultivate an individual's thinking and helps clarify and refine thoughts and emotions. In other words, journal writing is a straightforward way to contact your identity. It is a way that assists people in "[tracking] their evolving identities" (Cooper, 2013, p. 40). During the first meeting with Kamo, he presented a small diary he had kept for over 22 years. At the time, I did not understand the value of the object. However, after reviewing the written records, I could see the richness of the data in my hand. The following pages are dedicated to Kamo's journal to (a) understand the object's value, and (b) recognize and analyze its contents concerning the objectives of this essay. Based on the interview, Kamo discussed the journal and explained its values as follows:

> The document [journal] is very close to my heart. Once I decided to…. The written records reflect on specific incidents, describe my feelings, and

define me.... Journaling has helped me to find inspiration and let my imagination run wild. It also helped me reduce stress and anxiety, and it helped
strengthen my memory.

Kamo's journal has multiple utilities. First, it functions like a medication con-
tainer that collates thoughts and emotions. Simply put, the notebook became
a safe space to clear his mind and record the emotional clutter on the empty
pages. Second, journaling helped Kamo express his feelings and brainstorm
his imagination in a very poetic way. He established a solid relationship with
his mind through written words and recalled stories. Third, he put his emotion
down to release the pain, trauma, and gloomy outlook through past experiences. Finally, journaling facilitated his establishment of better psychological
well-being, emancipated negative emotions, and avoided cynicism.

In his journal, Kamo wrote the texts and stories in his mother tongue
(Kurdish Sorani) mostly, meaning not the object only; still, the written texts
in the Kurdish language reinforce aspects of his personal, social, or even cultural identities. Furthermore, he has organized his journal into several sections
or chapters, which he calls *westga,* meaning "stations." He named and assigned
descriptions to each station based on his good and bad experiences across borders. For example, the first station is designated to stories of being in Tehran,
Iran—the land of "jejune" and never-ending.

The second station in Kamo's journal is Istanbul, Turkey. For Kamo, Istanbul was the land of "freedom" due to his opportunities in Istanbul despite
the differences in cultural norms and values. The third chapter is designated
for the stories in Athens, Greece. Due to the lack of resources like money
and food, Kamo called his third station the land of the "destitute." The fourth
destination he arrived at was Rome, Italy. Rome is labeled in Kamo's journal
as the city of beauty and architecture, and the center of civilization, followed
by his fifth destination, Paris. Kamo describes Paris as a fantastic, elegant, and
sophisticated city with a unique culture. Finally, London was Kamo's last destination. He marked London as the city of dreams and happiness due to its
community spirit and opportunities to develop skills.

Between each station, Kamo documented his struggles and feelings. He
also included a selection of poems from famous Kurdish and Persian poets.
The lyrics echo stories about losing past love, feelings of loneliness, and ad-
miration for the landscape and scenery of his homeland. The attitudes and
sentiments signify a shift in his character within the script. Each script tells a
unique story about him, revealing aspects of his personal and social identities

at specific moments. For example, he talked about the nights he spent in Calais as follows:

> I am here by the seashore for over a week, trying to cross the channel. Not to escape this town [Calais] but to skedaddle from a smuggler, those who cannot write their name correctly. … I am very annoyed at those bootleggers and traffickers who have no mercy on anyone…. Alas to these young boys, beautiful girls, and families detained under these smugglers' clemency.

Kamo's written records reflect his unambiguous experience while trying to cross the British channel. His language and word choice show the suffering and difficulties he has encountered to arrive at his chosen destination. This can be seen through his phrases, such as *skedaddling from smugglers* and *being under the mercy of some people*. In Kamo's narrative, the pronoun "those" in describing the human traffickers might indicate and demonstrate group exclusiveness or "out-group" derogation (Tajfel & Turner, 1986). In this context, Kamo's default position organizes the people in Calais into us versus them. He is hostile toward the smugglers by assigning the adjectives illiterate and ignorant, *those who cannot write their names correctly*. However, he repels and shows mercy to those like him, *these young boys, beautiful girls, and families*. He seems to victimize *young boys* and *beautiful girls* and accentuate in-group positionality (Tajfel & Turner, 1986) due to shared realities and mutual experiences.

He then raps his border-crossing experiences in the following narrative and discloses the difficulties he experienced in different locations. He indicates how his life has been threatened due to cold, lack of shelter, the problem of being foreign in Iran and Turkey, and his trauma due to the smuggler's attitudes and behavior.

London—the sixth station

> After a long journey and crossing multiple borders, I am ashamed of my days in Iran, homeless and working in cold weather. What about the fear and the blames I had from people in Istanbul, the distress and horror I encountered upon my arrival to Greece, and dealing with the ruthless smugglers…. I am finally here [London], now I can resume my hobbies and live my life. I hope this station helps me to achieve all my dreams and arrive at a stage where I can find contentment and serenity.

In the narrative above, Kamo highlights several interesting incidents about his migration experiences. He starts the story by discussing the pain and sorrow he encountered in diverse countries and locations. He then highlights his trauma from dealing with people (smugglers) who were supposed to help him ease his border-crossing journey. After, he shifts his narrative to something more positive by claiming *I am finally here*, denoting that the sorrow and pain have ended. He is finally ready to seek happiness rather than being stuck in the trauma of the past. Furthermore, *now I can resume my hobbies and live my life*, indicating aspects of his identity. Through practicing those hobbies, he reunites with his authentic self, tackling migration trauma and searching for his identity in the new place—the United Kingdom.

Upon arrival at his planned destination, London, Kamo's texts take a positive turn. It looks like the pressure of the migration journey no longer constrains him. However, he still seeks his true identity and evades two different realities. Kamo composed:

> UK—Dream
> I cannot believe what just happened; I was lost somewhere else in the world and where I am now. I see the silhouette of people I love dancing in the air. I wish I could return to those times and my childhood domicile.... It is not easy to be alone..., and I would not have been able to continue without seeing the dear birds flying above my dark roof.

The above narrative reveals the feeling of astonishment Kamo has experienced after being in the United Kingdom for some time. He is still shocked and cannot believe he has finally arrived in a safe Western country. Phrases like "where I was and where I am now" indicate the geographical division between before and after. It tells the story of self as a spatial trajectory and an identity transformation resulting from the border crossing and its outcomes. Kamo's dilemma emerged from being stuck between places and spaces, establishing in-betweenness and transnational identity.

Emotion, Place and Identity

Places, big or small, influence an individual's emotions, thoughts, behavior, and decisions. Even certain places might affect a person's identity, becoming significant and contested arenas of collective being and belonging, since places communicate and reflect people's attributes at certain moments in life. It signifies and preserves identity on social, personal, and cultural levels. Otherwise stated, places are "a component of diverse sub-identity categories, which makes the term 'place identity' difficult to operate" (Peng et al., 2020: 3). According to the research participants' stories, individuals' sense and understanding of place evolve based on different personal and sociocultural values. The following pages are dedicated to the participants' data about place and identity. The section sought to examine the role of place in forming, developing, and maintaining a participant's identity, how the meaning of place is constructed by social actors, and the impact of places on their emotions.

The Power of Place and Identity

From early childhood, humans establish an emotional bond with a particular place, people, and their constituted memories. Some locations somehow have the potential to influence our behavior, attitudes, and beliefs. Either the place itself or the memories attached to it have the power to affect our feelings, and as a result, our identities might be influenced and transformed. Seeing places like shops, streets, or even buildings might weave us back to the past, and by digging deep down, we are likely to find more complex emotional terrain about specific places. The power of place is a versatile and malleable idea with several uses. Therefore, we need to examine how our surroundings (places we live or have lived, buildings, streets, or even cities) shape our thoughts, emotions, and actions.

The first example is derived from Alan's narrative. Alan expressed his feelings about buildings and the surrounding environment. He explained how certain features in a building, such as color and design, influence his emotion and reflect his personal and social identities. Alan (interview 1) claims:

> I like vesting places with unique buildings and architecture because it relates to my field. But I love exploring historical sites too. Luckily, in the UK, many historical architectures are protected by the law, which I visit whenever possible. I also went to other places overseas. I love what I do; I always meet new people from different backgrounds and make new friends. When you step into any historical site, you visualize how people lived in the past and how they dealt with their daily routines.

Through visiting and exploring the historical sites, Alan delves into the history of these buildings and reconnoiters the lived experiences of those who used to own and live in these buildings years ago. As Qazimi (2014) indicates, places have tangible and intangible features, including people's associations and feelings upon exposure to a particular space. For Alan, traveling and exploring certain areas reflect his identity (an architecture and an explorer identity). His hobbies or desires to visit different historical places position him within a particular social group—the explorer community (people who travel and explore the world)—reflecting his social identity (Tajfel & Turner, 1986). Also, following his hobbies has assisted him in establishing a relationship with people with similar interests worldwide and provides him essential emotional and social resources (Doll, 1996). For Alan, making new friends based on similar interests is critical in developing his social identity and expanding his worldview.

He then talked about specific features that influence his views on different places and buildings, like color, the façade, or the appearance. During the follow-up interview, Alan took me on a delightful trip down his memory lane by showing me a picture of a house with a beautiful exterior. He took the picture in a village 50 miles from London a few months before the interview. The house in the photo features a blue door and windows covered by ivy, green plants, foliage, and flowers.

> [This building] is beautiful; it is beyond my imagination. The house with the blue door and the windows stuck in my head for a long time. The house and its features remind me of myself and connect me with some interesting memories of someone I absolutely loved. You know, when you are young, you engage in many things, they were good memories, then thinking about those memories, you realize that nothing is permanent [his relationship]. I am not the same person as 20 years ago. I have changed; my beliefs, hobbies, and dreams are different. But I still love the blue color; that has not changed. When I first walked into this area, I loved the outlook of the house, and I stood there for minutes. I still do not know why? It took me back to the past and reminded me of someone [his girlfriend]. I love that house and wish it could be mine.

In the above extract, Alan talks about a house. He talks about his relationship with blue and links it to his personal experiences. To him, blue is associated with a person (his girlfriend) and the memories around that relationship. Interestingly, he highlights the changes in his life, suggesting his identity has transformed. He demonstrates this in his narrative when he postulates that *I am not the same person as 20 years ago, I have changed*, and his *beliefs, hobbies, and dreams are different*. The changes in his identity go against the essentialist beliefs that perceive identity as a static phenomenon. However, Alan's narrative highlight that internal and external factors might play a part in one's identity formation and evolution, such as age, education, life opportunities, life experiences, and society, to name a few. Furthermore, *the house with the blue door and the windows* became a "sticky place" imbued with emotions and associated memories (Ahmed, 2014; Badwan & Hall, 2020).

Humans have the power to choose where to go and where to stay. By selecting specific locations, we give meaning to those places and assign different identities to sites based on our experiences. Therefore, there is a big chance that certain areas influence our perceptions and thinking. To some, finding the right place is vital in enhancing their self-respect and belonging, which can be revealed in Kamo's narrative:

> [The] pub is like any other place where the primary function is to make money, but to me, it is more than that. It is a place where I can meet people from diverse socioeconomic and sociocultural backgrounds.... After a long day at work, I needed to be where I could feel respected, wanted, or valued, and I found that location.... What I like about this place is the cultural and social events that occur three to four times a month. Those events allow me to express myself freely without thinking about people and their judgments. Because most people who arrive here are foreigners, they are like me, and with a small click, you can relate and connect with them. As a result, I feel free and can be who I want to be without pressure, so I regularly come here to be myself.

Kamo's attachment to one pub among many is demonstrative.[3] It is related to the place and the community defined by it (Giuliani, 2003). The physical and social aspects of the pub, the atmosphere, the food, and, most importantly, the people are a critical endeavor that fulfills his social and psychological prerequisites. Further, the pub defines Kamo's personal, social, and place-related social identity (Uzzel et al., 2002). Otherwise stated, Kamo developed personal and social identities by identifying himself as a part of the group, defined by the place—the pub, the people, and the social events. The pub is a social space where Kamo and others can experience diversity and inclusion without being judged for who they are and express multiple personal and social identities through participation in distinct activities. Likewise, being in a place with people from diverse backgrounds allows him to have a better adaptation experience and gain better social and psychological well-being. In this regard, the pub is a haven or a "place ballet".[4] It is a space where people come together, engage in interpersonal and intercultural exchanges, support each other, and gain emotional relief and support. In the follow-up interview, Kamo postulates that the pub shapes aspects of his social identity and that a particular seating area defines him as a writer and a poet. While waiting by the pub window, he suggested changing our table upon arrival. As a researcher, I respected his decision, and without any hesitation, he stated the following:

> I always sit here [at the back], calling it my magic table. I tried the other tables but did not like them. Although this table is positioned at the back, it is close to the stage area. Here, I can relax, socialize, and watch people perform. Or simply detach myself from everyone, where I can read and engage in writing.

The above narrative shows the power of place and material objects in shaping an individual's identity. For Kamo, the small pub and its products—the material objects (e.g., the table, the place, and the table's location)—manipulate his personal and social identities. Those objects have controlled his emotions and restrained his choices (where to sit). Due to life events and experiences, Kamo has experienced the self-reinforcing cycle, meaning his attachment to specific objects and space has increased. Also, his beliefs about the table and the production of better writing have reinforced his devotion and created a barrier to experiencing new things elsewhere. This finding is supported by Dozier and Ayers (2021), who claim that "life events may impact the way we view our possessions … over time" (p. 106). For example, Kamo might consider the table his own since he has visited the pub for years, and losing his seating position might generate a sense of loss or loss of aspects of his identity.

Unlike Kamo and Alan, Lia demonstrated a robust attachment to her town (her birthplace). Throughout the interviews, she highlighted her passion for her city and constantly linked the stories to where she came from. She also talked about her yearning to return to Kurdistan.

> I always see myself as a guest in this country. Although I lost my dad, I will one day lose my mom. However, I am optimistic that there is a place that I can go back to and call it home…. Even if I have sorrow and pain, I will not share it with anyone. Still, I can go to the top of the Goyzha mountain[5]— and release all the discomfort and agony by looking at my city.

Despite being in the United Kingdom for many years, Lia's emotional attachment to her birthplace did not subside. Based on her narrative, she projects a robust connection to her homeland, town, and surrounding environment (e.g., Goyzha Mountain). For her, Suleimani is a sticky place where she can release her emotions and those feelings that repressed her at some point in her life as a form of catharsis. As a result of the emotional connection, Lia developed a mental representation of her home, which contains a "mental map" that unites her memories and reality, reflecting on her identities.

While some studies have shown a clear relationship between objects and people's attachment to certain places, the attachment experiences vary from person to person. Unlike Alan and Kamo, for Lia, objects do not provide a sense of passion for a place, as she states in the following narrative.

> I often wake up in the middle of the night, and when I open my eyes, I ask myself, what am I doing here? Even though the position of my bed is the same as the one back home, when I look around, I realize it is not my home. Until this day, this feeling lives with me.

Lia has lived in the United Kingdom for a long time, but emotionally she lives in the past (e.g., her hometown). For her, being at home is not just about living in a place or occupying a physical space; it is also a feeling, emotion, imagination, and territory embedded with all her experiences before her migration journey. In other words, her birthplace is a "sticky place" of desire. Lia's stickiness is about emotions that shaped the "very surface" of her body "through the repetition of actions over time," and her feelings circulate between time and space (e.g., her hometown and the memories she established).

Discussion

Based on the data presented in this study, objects are a vital component for the research participants; however, understanding the value of these objects differs between them. Respondents see objects as material embodiments that envisage the individual's creativity and identity. Through the production, circulation, and consumption of objects, participants negotiated between different elements of their identities within their confabulated culture through their accumulated stuff. Their experience with material objects results in various physical and emotional attachments to what participants have collected or kept. They seem to influence and control their perception, emotion, and thinking. For example, Kamo's journal was negligible and inconsequential at first. Still, after many years, the document granted its value because Kamo made the journal meaningful by including past experiences and memories and revisiting those memories regularly. As a result, the objects formed social relations and forged diasporic imaginations and identities. The items participants kept functioned as nostalgia, creating social connections with the lost one, instigating participants' agency, and triggering responses toward their sense of existence. In this respect, we could argue that objects have "social lives" (Appaduari, 1986) or "biographies" (Kopytoff, 1986).

The data also reveals the significance of place concerning individual identities. Also, the physical environment can actively contribute to a person's identity. In this study, participants' sense of place or "stickiness" emerged from social and personal exchanges, and they established a mutually constitutive relationship between their sense of self and diverse places. As a result, their identities are enacted in part through repeated contact and experiences with those places, affecting the "accumulation of affective value" (e.g., see Lia's connection to her birth town or Kamo's attachment to a table inside the pub) (Ahmed, 2014, p. 92; Badwan & Hall, 2020). What appears to be important is that humans and nonhumans are intertwined and act together. Objects have power over the participants' emotions, which can be seen in some of the narratives by Alan and Kamo in describing their feelings about buildings and places. Both participants made these places and buildings meaningful by adding their experiences and trajectories. This finding aligns with Miller's argument when he postulates that "stuff creates us in the first place" (Miller, 2010, p. 10).

Nevertheless, places and objects can arguably affect people; they are futile and ineffectual until people give meaning to them. In this context, neither persons nor objects can withstand alone. The two function together and are intertwined in many respects. First, people create material artifacts, spending hours, days, even months to get the desired result. Then, these objects will concur with an individual's mind and emotions, and based on those objects, identity positioning might transpire and position each of us in certain societal situations. Finally, it is through the accumulated stuff, objects, and personal trajectories toward places and their constituted entities that our identities evolve, and we grow at individual, social, and cultural levels.

Conclusion

Multidisciplinary perspectives on material culture, materiality, and identity have influenced the current study. It aimed to show the dynamic relationship between humans and nonhumans and the interaction between people and objects by analyzing empirical data using structural narrative analysis and dialogic/performative narrative analysis approaches. Based on the data presented and its examination throughout the essay, it is viable to claim that objects are necessary assets in human life. It can help persons to understand their personal and social positioning better. Objects can be seen as a language whereby individuals make assumptions and position themselves by assigning meaning. The chosen object might carry personal and emotional implications for many, and they have physical existence—one determinant and characteristic of human cultural practice.

While the current study highlights the relationship between material objects and a group of Kurdish migrants in the United Kingdom, researching material culture and materiality in the Kurdish context is still at an elementary stage. Hence, more needs to be done to highlight the experiences of the unvoiced minority groups and show their unique relationships with material objects and materiality, because material objects migrants bring to the new country have a particular social and cultural meaning, representing an extension of their identity (Mahmud, 2023 [forthcoming]).

The data presented in this essay are based on three research participants, meaning the findings cannot be generalized to the entire Kurdish population or other groups. Hence, a more extensive and in-depth study on material objects is required across the Kurdish population regardless of the groups' cultural and linguistic differences. Also, there are opportunities to examine how different generations utilize entities and the role of those objects in easing one's adaptation experiences using the Photovoice and autoethnography methods. Finally, bringing my personal practices, history, and trajectories with things will allow a better engagement and add value to the existing literature on material culture, materiality, and identity.

NOTES

1. Storytelling is seen as performance by a "self" with a past who involves, persuades, and (perhaps) moves an audience through language and gesture, "doing" rather than telling alone.

2. First-generation Kurdish immigrants are those who gain citizenship or permanent residency in the country to which they immigrated.

3. According to Shumaker and Taylor (1983), attachment is "a positive affective bond or association between individuals and their residential environment" (p. 233).

4. Place ballet is a phenomenological concept introduced by David Seamon in his book *A Geography of the Lifeworld: Movement, Rest and Encounter* (1979), which describes the regularity of place founded, habit, routine, and supportive physical environment.

5. Goyzha Mountain is one of the two tallest mountains that overlook the city of Suleimani in Southern Kurdistan (Northern Iraq).

REFERENCES

Ahmed, S. (2014). *The cultural politics of an emotion.* 2nd ed. Routledge.

Alexander, C., Jacobs, R., & Smith, P. (2012). *The Oxford handbook of cultural sociology.* Oxford University Press.

Appadurai, A. (1986). Introduction: Commodities and the politics of value. In Arjun Appadurai (Ed.), *The social life of things: Commodities in cultural perspective* (pp. 3–63). Melbourne: Cambridge University Press.

Appiah, K. M. (2019). *The lies that bind: Rethinking identities.* Liveright Publisher.

Atkinson, R. (1998). *Life story interviews: Qualitative research method.* Series 44. Sage Publications.

Badwan, K., and Hall, A. (2020). Walking along in sticky places: Post-humanist and affective insights from a reflective account of two young women in Manchester, UK. *Language and Intercultural Communication, 20*(3), 225–239. https://doi.org/10.1080/14708477.2020.1715995

Bauman, Z. (1973). *Culture as praxis.* Routledge and Kegan Paul. https://doi.org/10.4135/9781446218433

Bauman, Z. (2004). Zigmunt Bauman: Liquid Sociality. In N. Gane (Eds.), The future of social theory (pp. 17-46). London: Continuum.

Braidotti, R. (2013). *The posthumanism.* Polity Press.

Brown, D. M. (2003). *Transformational preaching: Theory and practice.* Virtual Book Worm Publishing.

Bryman, A. (2016). *Social research methods.* 5th ed. Oxford University Press.

Buchli, V. (2004). *Material culture: Critical concepts in the social sciences.* Routledge.

Cooper, J. E. (2013). Keeping a journal: A path to uncovering identity (and keeping your sanity). *Journal of Educational Perspectives, 46*(1 and 2), 40–43. https://files.eric.ed.gov/fulltext/EJ1088286.pdf

Doll, B. (1996). Children without friends: Implications for practice and policy. *School Psychology Review, 25*(2), 165–83. https://doi.org/10.1080/02796015.1996.12085809

Dozier, M. E., & Ayers, C. R. (2021). Object attachment as we grow older. *Current Opinion in Psychology, 39,* 105–108. https://doi.org/10.1016/j.copsyc.2020.08.012

Eagleton, W. (1996). Kurdish rugs and kelims: An introduction. In P. Kreyenbroek & C. Allison (Eds.), *Kurdish culture and identity*. Zed Books Ltd.

Fisher, W. R. (1987). *Human communication as narration: Toward a philosophy of reason, value, and action*. University of South Carolina Press.

Fong, M., and Chuang, R. (2004). *Communicating ethnic and cultural identity*. Rowman and Littlefield.

Foss, N. J. (1996). Knowledge-based approaches to the theory of the firm: Some critical comments. *Organization Science, 7*, 470–476. https://doi.org/10.1287/orsc.7.5.470

Gell, A. (1998). *Art and agency: An anthropological theory*. Clarendon Press.

Giuliani, M. V. (2003). Theory of attachment and place attachment. In M. Bonnes, T. Lee, & M. Bonaiuto (Eds.), *Psychological theories for environmental issues* (pp. 137–170). Ashgate.

Greig, H., Hamlett, J., & Hannan, L. (2015). *Gender and material culture in Britain since 1600*. Palgrave.

Harrington-Watt, K. (2014). Photographs as adaptive, transitional objects in Gujarati migrant homes. *Crossings: Journal of Migration and Culture, 5*(2/3), 273–287.

Hauge, Å. (2007). Identity and place: A critical comparison of three identity theories. *Architectural Science Review, 50*(1), 44–51. https://doi.org/10.3763/asre.2007.5007

Heikkinen, H. L. T. (2002). Whatever is narrative research? In R. Huttunen, H. L. T. Heikkinen, & L. Syrjälä (Eds.), *Narrative research: Voices from teachers and philosophers* (pp. 13–25). SoPhi.

Hewstone, M., Rubin, M., & Willis, H. (2002). Intergroup bias. *Annual Review of Psychology, 53*(1), 575–604. https://doi.org/10.1146/annurev.psych.53.100901.135109

Hofstede, G. (1980). *Culture's consequences: International differences in work-related values*. Sage.

Hofstede, G. (1991). *Cultures and organizations: Software of the mind*. McGraw-Hill.

Hofstede, G., Hofstede, G. J., & Minkov, M. (2010). *Cultures and organizations: Software of the mind* (3rd ed). McGraw-Hill Ltd.

Holliday, A. (2013). *Understanding intercultural communication: Negotiating a grammar of culture*. Routledge.

James, W. (2023). Structural narrative analysis. In J. M. Okoko, S. Tunison, & K. D. Walker, (Eds.), *Varieties of qualitative research methods*. Springer Texts Education; Springer, Cham. https://doi.org/10.1007/978-3-031-04394-9_70

Khrenova, L., & Burrell, K. (2021). Materialising care across borders: Sent things and family ties between Sweden and Ukraine. *Nordic Journal of Migration Research, 11*(3), 250–264. https://doi.org/10.33134/njmr.399

Kim, J. H. (2016). *Understanding narrative enquiry*. Sage Publications.

Kopytoff, I. (1986). The cultural biography of things: Commoditization as process. In A. Appadurai (Ed.), *The social life of things: Commodities in cultural perspective*. Cambridge University Press.

Kren, K. (1996). Kurdish material culture in Syria. In P. Kreyenbroek & C. Allison (Eds.), *Kurdish culture and identity*. Zed Books Ltd.

Kreuzer, M., Mühlbacher, H., & Von Wallpach, S. (2018). Home in the re-making: Immigrants transcultural experiencing of Home. *Journal of Business Research*, *91*(C), 334–341. https://doi.org/10.1016/j.jbusres.2017.10.047

Leaper, C. (2011). More similarities than differences in contemporary theories of social development?: A plea for theory bridging. *Advances in Child Development and Behavior*, *40*, 337–378. https://doi.org/10.1016/b978-0-12-386491 -8.00009-8

Lynch, K. D. (2009). Objects, meanings, and role identities: The practices that establish association in the case of home-based employment. *Sociological Forum*, *24*(1), 76–103. http://www.jstor.org/stable/40210337

Mahmud, C. R. (2018). *A sociolinguistic study: Language identity among Kurdish immigrants in the United Kingdom* [unpublished master's dissertation]. University of Kent.

Mahmud, C. R. (2023). Objects are not just a thing: (Re)negotiating identity through using martial objects within the Kurdish diaspora in the UK [manuscript submitted for publication].

Marschall, S. (2019). "Memory objects": Material objects and memories of home in the context of intra-African mobility. *Journal of Material Culture*, *24*(1). https://doi.org/10.1177/1359183519832630

Martin, J. N., & Nakayama, T. K. (2010). *Intercultural communication in contexts*. 5th ed. McGraw-Hill.

McDowall, D. (2021). *A modern history of the Kurds*. 4th ed. IB TAURIS, Bloomsbury Publishing Plc.

Miller, Daniel. (2010). *Stuff*. Polity Press.

Money, A. (2007). Material culture and the living room: The appropriation and use of goods in everyday life. *Journal of Consumer Culture*, *7*(3), 355–377. https://doi.org/10.1177/1469540507081630

Nägele, N., von walter, B., Scharfenberger, P., & Wentzel, D. (2020). "Touching" services: Tangible objects create an emotional connection to services even before their first use. *Business Research*, *13*, 741–766. https://doi.org/10.1007/s40685 -020-00114-0

Nooreyezdan, N. (2018). The nostalgia of ordinary objects. *Asian American Writers' Workshop*. https://aaww.org/the-nostalgia-of-ordinary-objects/

Pechurina, A. (2020). Researching identities through material possessions: The case of diasporic objects. *Current Sociology, 68*(1). https://doi.org/10.1177/0011392120927746

Peng, J., Strijker, D., & Wu, Q. (2020). Place identity: How far have we come in exploring its meanings? *Frontiers in Psychology, 11*, 294. https://doi.org/10.3389/fpsyg.2020.00294

Pennycook, A. (2018). Posthumanist applied linguistics. *Applied Linguistics, 39*(4), 445–461. https://doi.org/10.1093/applin/amw016

Philipp, A., & Ho, E. (2010). Migration, Home and Belonging: South African Migrant Women in Hamilton, New Zealand Population Review36, 81-101.

Philipp, A., & Ho, E. (2010). Migration, Home and Belonging: South African Migrant Women in Hamilton, New Zealand: Official newsletter of the New Zealand Demographic Society. *New Zealand Population Review, 36*, 81-101.

Pillar, I. (2017). *Intercultural communication: A critical communication.* Edinburgh University Press.

Prince, D. (2014). What about place? Considering the role of physical environment on youth imagining of future possible selves. *Journal of Youth Studies, 17*(6), 697–716. https://doi.org/10.1080/13676261.2013.836591

Prown, J. D. (1982). Mind in matter: An introduction to material culture theory and method. *Winterthur Portfolio, 17*(1), 1–19. http://www.jstor.org/stable/1180761

Qazimi, S. (2014). Sense of place and place identity. *European Journal of Social Science Education and Research, 1*(1). https://doi.org/10.26417/ejser.v1i1

Ran, G. J., & Liu, L. S. (2021). Re-constructing reverse family remittances: The case of new Chinese immigrant families in New Zealand. *Journal of Ethnic and Migration Studies, 1*(19), 1–19. https://doi.org/10.1080/1369183X.2021.1999221

Riessman, C. K. (1993). *Narrative analysis.* Sage.

Riessman, C. K. (2005). Narrative Analysis. In N. Kelly., C. Horrocks., K. Milnes., B. Roberts & D. Robinson (Eds), *Narrative, Memory & Everyday Life* (pp. 1-7). University of Huddersfield.

Schlereth, T. J. (1999). *Material culture studies in America.* AltaMira Press.

Schlereth, T. J. (1982). *Material culture studies in America.* The American Association for State and Local History.

Seamon, D. (1979). *A geography of the lifeworld: Movement, rest and encounter.* Routledge.

Seamon, D. (2013). Place attachment and phenomenology: The synergistic dynamism of place. In L. C. Manzo & P. Devine-Wright (Eds.), *Place attachment* (pp. 11–22). Routledge.

Sellnow, D. D. (2010). *The rhetorical power of popular culture: Considering mediated texts.* Sage Publications Ltd.

Sheumaker, H., & Wajda, S. T. (2008). *Material culture in America: Understanding everyday life.* ABC-CLIO.

Shumaker, S. A., & Taylor, R. B. (1983). Toward a clarification of people–place relationships: A model of attachment to place. In N. R. Feimer & E. S. Geller (Eds.), *Environmental psychology: Directions and perspectives* (pp. 219–251). Praeger.

Strauss, A. (1959). Mirrors and masks: The search for identity. *American Sociological Review, 20,* 298.

Saunders, M., Lewis, P., & Thornhill, A. (2009). *Research methods for business students.* Pearson Publishing

Tajfel, H., & Turner, J. C. (1986). The social identity theory of intergroup behavior. In S. Worchel & W. G. Austin (Eds.), *Psychology of intergroup relations* (pp. 7–24). Hall Publishers.

Turner, J. C. (1985). Social categorization and the self-concept: A social-cognitive theory of group behavior. In E. J. Lawler (Ed.), *Advances in group processes: Theory and research,* Vol. 2 (pp. 77–122). JAI Press.

Turner, J. C., Hogg, M. A., Oakes, P. J., Reicher, S. D., & Wetherell, M. S. (1987). *Redis- covering the social group: A self-categorization theory.* Blackwell Publishing.

Ünver, H. A. (2016). Schrödinger's Kurds: Transnational Kurdish geopolitics in the age of shifting borders. *Journal of International Affairs, 69*(2), 65–100.

Uzzell, D., Pol, E., & Badenas, D. (2002). Place identification, social cohesion, and environmental sustainability. *Environment and Behavior, 34,* 26–53. https://doi.org/10.1177/0013916502034001003

Wengraf, T. (2001). *Qualitative Research Interviewing: Biographic Narratives and Semi-structured Methods.* London: Sage Publications.

William, R. (1981). *Culture.* William Collins Sons.

Woodward, I. (2007). *Understanding material culture.* Sage Publishing.

Woodward, S., & Fisher, T. (2014). Fashioning through materials: Material culture, materiality, and processes of materialization. *Critical Studies in Fashion and Beauty, 5*(1), 3–22. https://doi.org/10.1386/csfb.5.1.3_2

Zilliacus, H., Paulsrud, B. A., & Holm, G. (2017). Essentializing vs. non-essentializing students' cultural identities: curricular discourses in Finland and Sweden. *Journal of Multicultural Discourses, 12*(2), 166–180. https://doi.org/10.1080/17447143.2017.1311335

HAMDI ECHKAOU | Indiana University of Pennsylvania and
Al Akhawayn University in Ifrane

Moroccan Facebook *Influenceurs'* Online Environment as a Message and Massage Text

Abstract

In this essay, I address the social media influencers in Morocco. I specifically target Moroccan influencers who aim at political and social change. In this essay, I label them as *"mu 'ththirīn"* in Arabic and/or *"influenceurs"* in French interchangeably because these are terms by which activists were highlighted in the "post-Moroccan Spring" period of 2011. After the uprisings that swept the Middle East and North Africa, the Moroccan social media activists shifted their agency from fulminating their anger against the political elites and the status quo on the streets to making their pages and accounts spaces of resistant but sustainable activism. Moroccan *mu 'ththirīn*, or *influenceurs* as the word means in Arabic, connotes the possibility of leaving a trace and exercising an impact on their followers within their online territories and cognitive capacities. The *influenceurs* are using their online medium to sustain the drift of agency and the imaginary hope of change that has been displaced by mainstream mass media. It is a continuous clashing dichotomy between media of the youth and those of the past generation. Other dichotomies entail social media versus mass media, the publics and the masses, the framework in which the feedback is allowed and where the message is imposed, and finally the terrain of protest, reflection, and compromise. This essay starts from the framework argument of Marshal McLuhan that "Medium Is the Message and/or Massage." In other words, all of the above-mentioned aspects of electronic culture of the online space extended the possibilities of influence through propaganda, discussion, counterarguments, and rational criticism as well as unlimited satire and commenting, which are limited by other mass media tools such as TV, radio, and the press. Social media empowered the influencers and amplified their potential influence to reach a mass number of followers through the synchronization of face-to-face communication. Using Joshua Meyrowitz's term highlighted by

McLuhan, the medium "retribalized" the influencers' followers by assembling them around political and social causes but with separate and distinct backgrounds and perspectives. The medium then is not only a projecting tool of the claims of influencers but is an image of their followers' struggle by which the activists and *influenceurs* created their identity.

Keywords: medium, environment, message, massage, *influenceurs*, social media

Introduction

Utilizing social media (e.g., Facebook) as a platform in Morocco, including all of the other social media platforms such as Twitter and blogs, allows the political influencers to take current topics happening and elaborate on them. They contribute with as many comments and critiques as possible. Taking the Moroccan case, various social media platforms differ in their influence conveniences. Twitter in Morocco is not celebrated as a tool for people to interact with individuals from different ideological segments of society. This is due to the fact that other social networking sites such as Facebook have always been that space for political and ideological deliberation that allows for the creation and sharing of content in a way that is easily accessible to a broad Moroccan audience. Similarly, blogs did not reach the same level of accessibility and interaction as Facebook. However, it offered a number of influencers the space to report their views and critiques in a significant and elaborate way that allows only like-minded followers to join and continue the reflection over those shared ideas.

Thus, in this essay, I will address the social media influencers who address the social and political debates in Morocco. Specifically, I will target the social media influencers who aim at political and social change. They were labeled as "*mu 'ththirīn*"[1] in Arabic and "*influenceurs*" in French, which became popular in the Moroccan national public discourse in the "post-Moroccan Spring" period. Those terms circulated extensively on Moroccan social media platforms when the prime minister of the government, led by the Islamist party of Justice and Development (PJD), scheduled a meeting with some digital savvy youth bloggers on June 13 of 2015 (Roudaby, 2015). The local media and activists from the country agreed to refer to them as "*influenceurs* and *mu 'ththirīn*." Critics of the meeting, multiple social media activists who in most cases are aligned with the February 20th Movement, questioned the criteria by which certain digital savvy youth are addressed as *influenceurs*.

The social media activists shifted from fulminating their anger against the political elites and the status quo on the streets to making their pages' spaces of peaceful but sustainable activism. The Arabic term *mu'ththirīn* is a derivation from the root words *mo'athir*, *'ththara*, and *'athar*, which denote an influencer, a person who leaves a trace and exercises an impact on the followers within their circles, and a trace such as footprints, respectively.

Moroccan *influenceurs* favor social media as the tool that "massages" their messages to the audience. It used to be that the topics discussed in media outlets favored one-sided views about events, which avoided clashing with mainstream opinions. Now, the sociopolitical stances are as varied as the populations, and the *influenceurs* distribute, contribute, and allow these perspectives to flourish in order to represent society from different angles.

In Morocco, Facebook is still the most widely used social media platform (Dekker & Engbersen, 2014). It characterizes a form of extension to the critical voices and minds. It also enables individuals to rely on various connections and multitudes of networks, exploit the surrounding technological dynamism to create messages of new structures, and protect the borders of gained freedoms of expression within social media. The Moroccan *influenceurs* are aware of the determinant nature of technological platforms that make their voices and messages impossible to undermine or ignore; now they have an effect in the offline society and no longer surrender to the status quo. In addition, *les influenceurs* contribute with their daring commentary, with their articulate linguistic competencies, and with their critical-thinking capabilities to merge all of that with the unlimited possibilities of social media to distribute the new media message. This is the type of message that was in the past undermined, attacked, and silenced. In this era, *influenceurs* shifted to new media messages that are different from the mass media ones and even oppose the mass media messages in terms of rating, audience feedback, and possibilities for reflection. The messages of the new media are critical in nature, but they aim to revitalize a conscience and a society of critical views. In addition, the structure of social media promotes commenting in order to recruit more followers and reestablish a resistant environment shaped by the ability to access technology and reach a mass number of followers.

In the Moroccan political and social public debates, it is relevant to consider the social media tools of *les influenceurs* as a "massage," as they have a "therapeutic" influence on them as activists who post resisting content in the first place. The influence is also extended to their immediate society and acts from the dominant structures of the policy makers. In my primary discussion with one of *les influenceurs*, namely Hicham Charm, he insisted that his contributions are ways that "help him discharge his inside burden and tiredness" from the status quo. The "massage" effect of the new medium is reinvigorating the spirit of change with a new wave of demands, and seeks achievements that correspond to those in the world beyond the border of Morocco. The "massage" effect of the *influenceurs'* social media imposes demands reinforced by the "global village" reality, which is shaped by the aspiration to enjoy what other communities in other regions are enjoying, as well as the willingness of those followers of influencers' content within that spectrum to call for achievements and accountability. For sociopolitical influencers, social media provided new possibilities that altered shedding light only on the center and brought the peripheries and marginal demands into focus. Thus, these new social media influencers of the political space managed to bring the marginal corner under their followers' spotlight. In addition, the engaging nature of social media makes inhabitants of participants from the disregarded corners as effective mobilizers within the technological framework.

The influencers' followers within social media are filling the drift of agency and the imaginary hope of change displaced by the weakened activism offline and by the consistent influence championed by traditional mass media. Sociopolitical influencers then challenge the numbness of traditional mass media, which are still dominating the Moroccan sociopolitical discourse, and engage themselves and their followers in the process of consumption and distribution of resisting content. This participation in social media for influencers is a continuous exhibition of the dichotomy between the medium of active users and the medium of passive consumers. Other dichotomies entail social media versus mass media, the publics and the masses, the framework allowing feedback and where the message is imposed, and finally the terrain of protest, noise, reflection, and compromise.

Noise is a significant point that characterizes the technological dynamism in favor of the Moroccan *influenceurs*. The "noise" in social media plays against the flow of mainstream media. Wells (2011) emphasized the notion of "noise" as articulated in Shannon and Weaver's model of communication. In their contribution from 1948, they developed two types of noise, namely physical and semantic noise. For Moroccan *influenceurs,* this medium adapts to play both roles effectively. A physical noise disrupts the flow of the news shared on mainstream media by criticizing it and producing numerous updates about the current state policies to counter its narrative. Other instances of such physical noise appear in the emergence and reemergence of many pages that pop up, updating the local political and social conditions of Moroccans in every corner of the country. The second type, namely the semantic noise, now belongs to the youth generation and social media tools backed by switched-power position in regards to the state media machine. These *influenceurs* used the provided tools and their ability to reach various types of followers and audiences locally and internationally to erode the state manipulation of information.

Theoretical Background

Two theories frame the foundational background of this essay. The first one is of Marshal McLuhan et al.'s perspective of technological determinism (Mc-Lauhan et al, 2001). I start with the possibilities that the technological venues opened for the oppositional, diverse, and critical discourses pushed forward by young Moroccans. The second principal base in this research is the "artic-ulation" formation advocated by Stuart Hall. By articulating here, I mean the potentiality enhanced by the possibility of encoding and decoding messages in ways that adapt with the technological sophistication. Both of these theo-ries, I believe, state the extent in which social media as a contemporary form of technology from the McLuhanian point of view and as a cultural product from Hall's perspective redefine our understanding and engagement of the social and societal realities. Social media users today produce numerous content that one cannot control and that intervenes within the process of encoding and decoding novel messages.

Another interesting connection between McLuhan and Hall emerges in their crossing points about the floating textual consideration of technology. For McLuhan the form outweighs the content, as mentioned earlier, and for Hall, when it comes to the process of "representation," what is not said and/ or the silences in the media in most of the cases matter more than what is said and pictured. The form then is endowed with technicalities that affect the message and either empowers it or, on the contrary, pacifies it. For Hall (1980), the stages of "production, circulation, use and reproduction" are steps he developed from the effects of television as a mediating platform of messages. He conceives that that possibility of "circuit" (another term that combines McLuhan and Hall) replicates structures of hegemony (p. 507). Both perspectives again meet at emphasizing there is a specificity effect in the message exchange process defined by the medium. It is what Hall calls "the determinate moments." These moments are the instant in which every concept and ultimately every message is loaded with the meaning those behind the medium aim to spread and consequently exert hierarchy and dominance.

Among the elements I pursue to elaborate on the connections between both McLuhan and Hall is the concept of the signified and/or "message form" in Hall's terms. He termed it as the "form of appearance of event in its passage from source to receiver" (Hall, 1980, p. 508). Both theorists meet in addressing the connotations as exercising tremendous impacts in the process of transmitting the information. During this process emerges the importance of noise effects. I assume that the noise that the medium is carrying changes the perspective and policies influenced by mainstream media to take into consideration what is involved, commented on, and advanced by the new media. This noise is rather a healthy process from the perspective of *les influenceurs*, and is therefore a reality that currently imposes itself as a force that no one can eliminate or neglect.

In addition to all of the above-mentioned aspects of electronic culture, the media also extended the possibilities of discussion, debates, and rational criticism as well as unlimited satire allowed by other media tools, such as TV and newspapers. Social media empowered the youth and amplified their potential to reach the synchronization of face-to-face communication. Using Joshua Meyrowitz's term highlighted by McLuhan, this medium "retribalized" the youth by assembling them around clear, legitimate causes, but with separate and distinct backgrounds and perspectives (as cited in Katz et al., 2002, p. 196). The medium then is not only a projecting tool of the claims of youth, but is an image of their struggle by which the activists and *influenceurs* created their identity.

Interestingly, however, we cannot take for granted that there exists an elitist nature of both forms, be it technological or content based, especially when discussing the "medium" as being the "message." Among the aspects that distinguish form and content are the varied languages used, and the ways ideas are organized and articulated. Let us take as an example the nature of language each *influenceur* chooses as their channel to the audience. In most cases,

Standard Arabic and Darija are the major two languages utilized, with aims to counter mainstream journalistic and audiovisual sets that use very specific language to maintain power, prestige, and/or address the masses in a way that affects their decisions. This type of combining both the form and the content can influence more effectively than one of them can do separately. Nevertheless, it is true that the form, which in most cases nowadays incorporates certain new media outlets as an advancing and marketing form of content, ends up exerting a power and an influence on the audience.

McLuhan et al. (2001) made a distinction between social drama and electric drama as if the dichotomy represents the past generation and the current generation. Each of these groups approaches the life "environment" in very distinctive ways depending on their focus. The former generation focuses mainly on the content and the latter reshaped their message to include the technological tools as the focus, which raises different ways of dealing with life. As an example, the former reproduces similar ways of maintaining the status quo and the latter exhibits rebellion.

For *les influenceurs* in Morocco, Facebook plays a major role in their existence; it is a decisive medium in their daily activities due to its hooking nature and promotional aspect of their messages and struggles. It defines their lives. Take, as an example, the technological advancements implemented in our environment: they significantly speed up the swiftness of our lives and make them more comfortable. Some examples of these are clocks at the university departments and in waiting rooms and/or at the bus stop, smart phone applications, and every technological material. They all replace and threaten the social contact and the interpersonal relations that were dominant factors in bringing people together before the major social media communication tools shaped our current environment. Therefore, these technological advancements ease our life intricacies, but do so at the expense of our social and dialogic capacities (Peters & Simonson, 2004).

The social media medium in other cases is a trap. It spreads passivity among participants, and one of these confining limitations is excessive slacktivism. For McLuhan et al., however,

the road to recovery ... is to recognize that electronic media are subtly and constantly altering our perceptual senses. The serial logic of print is fading out before the intuitive "mosaic" of instantaneous communication. Books "contain," TV "involves." The new vision is mythic, tribal, decentralized.

Man now lives in a global-sized village, and is returning. (Aden, 1969, p. 362)

Being able to utilize the medium in ways that lead to the betterment of the social, political, cultural, and economic life can help in switching its control into humane directions.

Sukarno, the president of Indonesia, made a telling simulation about the power of pictures that mobilized the colonized nations to turn their conditions upside down (Kusno, 2013). New mediums of communication liberated nations from living under suppression into pushing their revolts mainly due to being exposed to different nations outside their spectrum who enjoy certain benefits that the oppressed were deprived of. Therefore, materialistic aspects of television, refrigerator, and motorcar images projected via Hollywood can and did cause revolts. Of course, that is not the only driving force for uprisings, but there is a force of seeking freedom, joy, and stability under a rule. The combination of both incentives, namely technology and the peoples' determination, will create unprecedented shifts (McLuhan et al., 2001, p. 131).

Methodology

I have always been interested in working on *les influencers* who appeared out of the Moroccan uprisings of 2011. Their contributions created a movement strong in its discourse, analysis, interpretation, and judgment about domestic, social, cultural, and economic conditions of Moroccan policies. In addition, they are very much aware of the external challenges and use social media to transmit a unique message that projects the inner pains of those silenced in impoverished and disenfranchised areas. Due to a medium that connects them with other publics, they can adapt to the external, foreign challenges of the establishments beyond the power of the national state. So, they do not get their feedback from the mass media; instead, they develop their own points of view but based on lived realities. I now see the usefulness of the "medium is the message" point approach, and I am investigating to what extent that might be helpful to me. I aim to address the specific platforms that *les influenceurs* have created for themselves on social media to provide unique discourses that counter the mass media discourses and would like to see to what extent I am right in selecting that approach. There is a concern that the "medium is the message" is undermining the social, psychological, and relational realities of the users while it raises the importance of the medium as a form. So, does that fit? In this analysis, Harold Adams Innis's concept of monopoly of knowledge is important to use as the starting point in investigating the relevance of the medium as the message (Innis, 2008).

The focus of this essay will address what I call here Moroccan *influenceurs* for political and social change. My focus will address four *influenceurs*. First is Hicham Charm, who writes in Darija, or Moroccan dialect, and whose focus is addressing current social, political, and economic issues from a satirical and critical point of view. Second is Mayssa Salama Ennaji, who writes in Standard Arabic and who uses her page to attack the state public policies and political formations as illustrations of dominance. The third is Mina Bouchkioua, whom I interviewed earlier on her involvement with the youth movement, and now she uses literary writing as an expressive method to voice her disgust with the status quo. Finally, I will address the page of the journalist Ismail Azzam, whose page reports about events in a professional manner to guarantee the lay citizens access to reliable and truthful information. The content they share on their Facebook pages defined the majority of these activists. Thousands of Moroccans follow their statuses and contributions across the country as they reflect on daily struggles and work as passionately as they possibly can to mirror what they view as the real Morocco, far from the cosmetic televised and mediatized one portrayed by the state media.

In this essay, I focus mainly on the potentialities that combined the fervor these activists have and the medium, namely Facebook in this case, that created their raison d'etre within the Moroccan politicized environment. The medium shaped their image to the extent that they identify their affiliation to *sha'b al-faysbūk*, or "the people of Facebook." For McLuhan et al., every aspect of life characterizes what they call "environment"; in this environment, everyone is bound to certain influences that shape their attitudes and form their thinking (McLuhan et al., 2001, p. 142). The medium therefore allowed the politicized environment to prosper due to the technical possibilities of the tool that among the aspect of synchronization, feedback, and large audience managed to alleviate the potentials of their message to create effects and impacts on the ground.

Technology Disturbance and Its Reverse Effects

The overall assumption of this essay aims to qualify the importance of the technological content to the one of form. The "anti-text" (Katz et al., 2002, p. 191), which comprises the image, the sound, and the visual and sensory effects of videos and text, are crucial attributions that determine and strengthen the message reception as well as its effect. Referring to the cases at hand, *les influenceurs* mentioned above switch their reliance on texts to posting videos and images depending on the topic they tackle and the effect they seek to arouse in their audience. Although the text's content and the reaction of the commenters are ephemeral, the effects created and supported by the technological device remain durable. That fact explains the association between the pages and the ideological stance of *les influenceurs* behind articulating the causes of their contributions.

For McLuhan et al. (2001), because technology is endowed with potentialities of "electric circuitry," we end up being immersed in a space without even having to rethink its effect; we just live by its flow (p. 63). Information, therefore, acquires certain power over those producing it and those on the receiving end. It enacts engagement and novel thinking processes of a nonlinear nature such as criticism, creative mobilization, campaigning, and sarcastic assessment of events and state actions.

To break into the sphere of dominance used by the state's technological sophistication, *les influenceurs* exploited the electric and electronic technology to reduce the monopoly of their nation states over media apparatuses. Take as an example the forms of images and the democracy of the facade, which the contemporary state's forms of communication are advancing among the population of the inside and outside world. Through their careful but creative use of technological tools, messages of *les influenceurs* embarrassed and resisted the local state's conduct in alleviating the structural types of violence such as poverty and underdevelopment.

The technological dynamism made it possible for *les influenceurs* to uncover corruption camouflaged by mega-festivals and formal conventions. The state narrative aims at sending a message of prestigious conditions, which shapes the reality of the content, disregards the deep reality of the margins, and only highlights the center, which in this case focuses on the state's media coverage of events and works so hard on the make-up rather than displaying the true reality. Similarly, but in contrast, *les influenceurs* utilized technology as an electronic drain that absorbs the mythical narratives of state media tools. They consider it a tool that covers the larger picture and allows the underprivileged and the uneducated to benefit from their chances of joining the stage of participation. For Papacharissi (2015), "[M]edia do not make or break revolutions, but they do lend emerging publics their own distinct mediality. Mediality shapes the texture of these publics and affect becomes the drive that keeps them going" (p. 308). The "conduit" effect that the medium has brings its "affective" trace over the audience and leads to extraordinary transformation.

The risk, however, and from McLuhan et al.'s point of view, is that technology applies various forms of manipulation based on eroding away the old forms of communication, and ultimately exerting new effects on both the users and the audience (McLuhan et al., 2001, p. 138). Thus, electronic media characterize violent effects, which substitute the street's active demonstrations and sometimes reduce the efficacy of direct face-to-face interaction. The technological tool allows *les influenceurs* and their followers to voice their anger and frustration. But the forms of electronic media construct a subtle conflict and attack on the human emotions by downgrading the volume of their outloud effects. By prospecting the future, this research is skeptical about the instantaneous possibilities of undergoing change. The medium as a form seems to be decisive in valuing the necessity of change and in controlling the speed in which transformations takes place.

NOTE

1. Transliteration according to the International Journal of Middle East Studies. https://ijmes.chass.ncsu.edu/docs/TransChart.pdf.

REFERENCES

Aden, M. J. (1969). The state of letters. McLuhan: Pro and con man. *The Sewanee Review, 77*(2), 357–369.

Dekker, R., & Engbersen, G. (2014). How social media transform migrant networks and facilitate migration. *Global Networks, 14*(4), 401–418.

Hall, S. (1980). 'Encoding/decoding'. In Centre for Contemporary Cultural Studies (Ed.): Culture, Media, Language: Working Papers in Cultural Studies, 1972–79 London: Hutchinson, pp. 507-517.

Innis, H. A. (2008). *The bias of communication.* University of Toronto Press.

Peters, J. D., & Simonson, P. (Eds.). (2004). *Mass Communication and American Social Thought: Key Texts, 1919-1968.* Rowman & Littlefield.

Katz, E., Peters, J. D., Orloff, A., & Liebes, T. (2002). *Canonic texts in media research. Are there any? Should there be any? How about these?* Polity.

Kusno, A. (2013). *After the new order: Space, politics, and Jakarta.* University of Hawaii Press.

McLuhan, M., Fiore, Q., & Agel, J. (2001). *The medium is the massage. An inventory of effects.* Gingko Press.

Papacharissi, Z. (2015). Affective publics and structures of storytelling. Sentiment, events and mediality. *Information, Communication & Society, 19*(3), 307–324. https://doi.org/10.1080/1369118X.2015.1109697.

Roudaby, Y., (2015). Receit de la rencontre de Benkirane et El Khalfi avec les influenceurs du web. *Tel Quel.* https://telquel.ma/2015/06/15/recit-rencontre -benkirane-elkhalfi-les-influenceurs-du-web_1452059

Simonson, P., & Durham, J. P. (Eds.) (2004). *Mass communication and American social thought: Key texts, 1919–1968.* Rowman & Littlefield Publishers.

Wells, R. (2011). *Weaver's model of communication and its implications.* Retrieved May, 11, 2020. http://www.mrc.uidaho.edu/~rwells/techdocs/Weavers%20 Model%20of%20Communication%20and%20Its%20Implications.pdf

SACHIYO M. SHEARMAN, EWA RUSEK | East Carolina
University, State University of Applied Sciences in Krosno

The Impact of International Virtual Exchange on Students' Intercultural Sensitivity and Global Identity

A Narrative Analysis of Students' Accounts

Abstract

The International Virtual Exchange (IVE) refers to the sustained, technology-supported interaction among students in different regions of the world. The IVE creates opportunities for students to interact and collaborate with those who have different backgrounds from their own. Students' participation in experiential learning, such as an IVE, can help students to be more self-reflective, globally aware, and comfortable in interacting with diverse others. In this study, we examined students' experiences of the IVE using the theoretical frameworks suggested by experiential learning process (Kolb, 1984), identity negotiation (Ting-Toomey, 2005, 2010), and identity-based motivation (Oyserman, et al., 2017). A series of semistructured in-depth interviews were conducted among students who have participated in the course that has the IVE modules. We interviewed a total of 35 students (57% female, 37% male, and 6% nonbinary) who participated in the IVE modules led by the authors. All the students' narratives were transcribed and analyzed through thematic analysis. Students' narratives were analyzed in terms of possible evidence for developing global identity and intercultural sensitivity after their IVE participation. The authors examined students' narratives and identified five themes in terms of challenges (language barrier, cognitive cultural differences, communication styles differences, group dynamics, and procedural challenges) and five gains (language learning, confidence/comfort, global awareness, moving to ethnorelative states, and facilitating cultural understanding and empathy) from their IVE participation. The analysis of students' narratives using theoretical understanding and possible future directions for the effort such as IVEs are discussed.

Keywords: experiential learning, international virtual exchange, language, communication styles

International Virtual Exchange

The International Virtual Exchange (IVE) refers to the technology-supported sequential interaction among students in different world regions. The IVE creates opportunities for students to interact and collaborate with those who have different backgrounds from their own. Students' participation in experiential learning, such as an IVE, can help students be more self-reflective, globally aware, and effective in interacting with diverse others.

In order for colleges and universities to prepare students for a globalized and interconnected world, educators have been emphasizing the importance of an international curriculum (Kreber, 2009). One of the clear-cut indicators is the increased number of students who have been participating in the international student exchange and study abroad programs. According to the Institute of International Education *Open Doors* report, the number of students who participated in study abroad and exchange programs consistently increased until the 2018–2019 academic year (Institute of International Education, 2021).

Similarly, in Europe, the Erasmus program was established in 1987 to facilitate student exchange within participating nations to foster awareness and appreciation of other nations and cultures. The acronym Erasmus came from "European Community Actions Scheme for the Mobility of University Students" but was also named after the philosopher and humanist from the Netherlands, Erasmus of Rotterdam, who lived and worked in different parts of Europe during his lifetime (European Commission, 2013). In 2014, the Erasmus+ program started combining various programs for education, training, youth, and sports. Since the start of the Erasmus program, followed by Erasmus+, over 10 million students have participated in it to increase awareness and appreciation of other nations and cultures (European Commission, 2022). The program is now more inclusive, more digital, and greener, as its latest slogan goes, and it provides opportunities to study, gain experience, and volunteer abroad. This new program offers automatic recognition of credits earned abroad and fully digitalized administrative processes.

Due to the COVID-19 pandemic, the number of students who participated in study abroad or exchange programs in the academic year 2020–2021 dropped significantly. The disruption caused by the pandemic has rendered the continuation of student exchange programs impossible in many nations around the world. Students and educators learned to use virtual conferencing tools such as Zoom and Teams to continue their education domestically as well as internationally. Given this context, the IVE proved to be the best alternative to in-person study abroad programs.

The IVE had been a popular experiential learning tool even before the pandemic since many students could not join in the study abroad programs, the reasons being time constraints, disabilities, job or home-related responsibilities, and financial issues (Cairns, 2017; O'Dowd, 2013). As we move on to postpandemic societies, we may start more in-person exchange programs, as we have found that the IVE is a viable option for many individuals who may not be able to join in person.

The authors of the current study jointly conducted the IVE sessions over multiple semesters. The sessions involved students from the United States, Poland, Spain, Turkey, and other nations. We decided to examine students' narratives regarding their experience participating in the IVE sessions, according to the theoretical frameworks suggested by the experiential learning process (Kolb, 1984) and the identity-based motivation framework (Oyserman et al., 2017).

IVE as Experiential Learning

The IVE creates opportunities for students to interact and collaborate with those who have different backgrounds from their own. When it is combined with other course content, students not only learn academic details but also build comfort and confidence in communicating with diverse others. Various studies have highlighted the positive learning experiences and learning outcomes after participating in the IVE, such as TPACK skills, or technological, pedagogical, specific academic content skills (e.g., Dooly & Sadler, 2013; Rienties et al., 2020). Others have emphasized examining students' outcomes such as foreign language proficiency (Tian & Wang, 2010) and intercultural communication competencies (O'Dowd & Lewis, 2016) after participating in the IVE.

The IVE refers to the technology-supported and continued interaction between students in locations that are geographically separated. The EVALUATE Group (2019) defined the virtual exchange as "student-centered, international, and collaborative approaches to learning where knowledge and understanding are constructed through interaction and negotiation with students from other cultures" (pp. 8–9). In the current essay, we are using the term IVE to mean international virtual exchange, but other terminology has been used to refer to similar experiential learning. Scholars and teachers have used the terms such as collaborative online international learning (COIL) and online cross-cultural exchange (O'Dowd & Lewis, 2016). Regardless of the term, the IVE as experiential learning consists of key elements such as (1) collaborative effort across cultures or nations that are geographically separated, (2) continued interaction among members so they establish rhythm of interactions, and (3) virtual or online interaction that is technology-supported to overcome geographical separation. Frequently, the IVE emphasizes student-centered learning since the emphasis is placed on students' engagement and interaction with their international partners in cross-cultural exchange.

The experiential learning provides a framework to understand online intercultural interaction. An important premise of experiential learning is that experience plays the central role in the learning process. In the experiential learning literature, learning is defined as "the process whereby knowledge is created through the transformation of experience" (Kolb, 1984, p. 38). Drawing from the traditions of experiential learning, Kolb (1984) identified four stages of learning, which he called the learning cycle theory. Kolb (1984)'s learning cycle theory includes four stages: "concrete experience," "reflective observation," "abstract conceptualization," and "active experimentation."

In the context of the IVE, students engage in "intercultural interaction" in an online environment. They are applying various theories and research discussed in intercultural communication classes as they engage in interactions and communication with people who have geographically and culturally different backgrounds. Students go through "concrete experience" when they are linked with international student partners. They communicate and exchange ideas. Then the students make "reflective observations" when they share their views about their specific experience. In this process, they must be reflective as to how they are modifying their regular communication styles to fit the

IVE's intercultural communication contexts. The students, then, go through the stage of "abstract conceptualization" where they form hypotheses about the experience with help of previous intercultural communication theories via teachers' lectures or textbooks. In this study, students have to make sense of their experience referring to the course concepts. In the next stage, students engage in "active experimentation." They can choose to apply and experiment with their newly gained hypotheses as they engage in the intercultural communication interactions with their international student partners.

For example, an American student may experience miscommunication in an online conversation with a Turkish student in Poland during the IVE session. He or she then reflects on such an observation and shares what they consider as possible reasons for the confusion. In the third phase, the instructor explains possible causes of the miscommunication in communicating interculturally, such as differences in cultural values and expected communication styles. Knowing these causes, the student then attempts to follow up with asking a question. In the fourth phase, he or she can figure out a way to experiment with the newly gained knowledge and skills in another interactive situation via new media. In this context, students are not passive learners, but they are actively engaged. They gain more knowledge and develop motivational, affective attitudes toward students in other countries as they learn how to function effectively in communicating with those who are culturally different.

Language, Culture, and Cognition

Naturally, the participants need a shared language when they participate in the IVE. In the case of our IVE sessions, we used English. This choice seems natural in our current state of use of English as a global language (Crystal, 2003; Northrup, 2013) and for our partnership since English is the first language for participants from the United States, and second or foreign for Polish, Erasmus, and other international students. Although the choice of using English is a reasonable one, we need to be aware of the challenges that come with it. Some obstacles are obvious, while others are not. The challenges include not just English proficiency among students who use it as a second language, but also the impact of language on their cognition. Additionally, this choice of using English for the IVE naturally creates power differences between the native speakers of English and those who speak English as a second/foreign language. Tsuda (2007) raised the issue with this unquestioned use of English as an international language calling it linguistic hegemony. The use of English creates linguistic and communicative inequality between native and nonnative speakers.

In the IVE, one of the most obvious challenges is the lack of English-language proficiency among some students who speak English as a foreign language. The English-language fluency of the participants is crucial, so students can engage in communication. Many international students have studied English for years, and they welcome the opportunity to speak English during the IVE sessions. Even though some of those who participated in the IVE are moderately proficient in English, they still faced some challenges. It can be difficult to express one's thoughts through concepts and phrases that may not be present or shared in their first language. Keysar et al. (2012) introduced the term foreign language effect (FLE) to refer to this difficulty. When native speakers presented a problem in their language, they were more likely to be influenced by its wording whereas nonnative speakers did not pay much attention to the "framing" of the problem—they were less sensitive to how the problem or question was formulated but focused on the issue itself (Keysar et al., 2012).

The studies of language and cognition prove that languages have their distinctive cognitive legacies, which shape people's thoughts (Bloom, 2014; Boroditsky, 2011). The cognitive process of an individual's reflection on the specific qualities of a particular language is often unique and not easily transferable. This distinctive processing and associated linguistic qualities can inform us about the culture of a particular nation (Deutscher, 2011). It is often the case that the particular linguistic and cultural experiences shared by the speakers of one language may not be shared by those who speak another language, or those who speak the same language as a second language. Although students may not fully understand the true depth of cultural or linguistic impact that it has on our perception and cognition, they do need to deal with these perceptual differences while they engage in intercultural communication. The FLE influences other cognitive aspects such as moral judgment. Speakers of two languages judge moral transgressions and social norm transgressions less harshly in their nonnative language than they do in their native language, at least when those transgressions do not involve significant negative consequences (Geipel et al., 2015). Students may be perceiving the opinions presented by their international partner students without realizing the potential cultural and linguistic impact. To make matters more complicated, intuitively, teachers tend to assume that people would make the same choices regardless of the language they are using, the wording just might be clumsy in a foreign language.

Besides this challenge presented in the cognitive process while communicating in a second/foreign language, the nonnative speakers of English have to deal with added stress in the international encounter when it comes to their anxiety and insecurity. The nonnative speakers of English can be articulate in their native language, but they need to manage the fact that they are not as fluent or comfortable in expressing themselves in English. Horwitz (2010) noted that anxiety inhibits second-language engagement. If students fail to deal with their anxiety in speaking English as a second/foreign language, their level of English proficiency will go down. The nonnative English speakers in the IVE should deal with the possible psychological stress, anxiety, or insecurity that they may feel.

Intercultural Communication Competence and Intercultural Sensitivity

In this postglobalized society, students are expected to be globally aware and comfortable communicating with diverse groups of people. Students in colleges and universities are expected to gain intercultural communication competence and learn how to be an effective communicator in an intercultural setting. Intercultural competence is defined as "the ability to communicate effectively in cross-cultural situations and to relate appropriately in a variety of cultural contexts (Bennett & Bennett, 2004, p. 149)". This definition has its emphasis in behavioral aspects, yet it also entails cognitive and affective elements.

The intercultural communication competence has three components: affective, behavioral, and cognitive (Bennett & Bennett, 1993, 2004). For a person to demonstrate ability to communicate effectively and relate with others in an appropriate manner, individuals need to achieve both affective and cognitive components. An individual proficient at intercultural communication should be able to have their own cultural awareness as well as objective understanding of cultural values and their impacts. At the same time, individuals need to do that without a bias in favor of their own cultural standard and without unfairly judging the other, while not overly generalizing.

Bennett (1986) and Bennett and Bennett (1993, 2004) proposed a framework to understand one's development of cultural sensitivity in the Developmental Model of Intercultural Sensitivity using students' reactions in intercultural workshops, classes, and exchanges. This model explains the individuals' reaction in confronting cultural differences and their process of becoming interculturally competent communicators. The development model of intercultural sensitivity is organized into six stages on one continuum: denial, defense, minimization, acceptance, adaptation, and integration. The first three stages are categorized as ethnocentric and the latter three are categorized as ethnorelative states. In the ethnocentric stages, we use our own cultural standard, while in ethnorelative stages, others' cultural standards are adopted. In the denial stage, an individual believes in his or her own cultural beliefs and denies the presence of cultural differences by taking psychological or physical distance. In this stage, an individual is content to believe in his or her own cultural presuppositions as the only one and main standard. In the next stage, individuals may be exposed to cultural differences but in the defense mode, which means they see their own culture as the only correct one and the one that is to be protected. In the minimization stage, individuals attempt to diminish the cultural differences by seeing other cultures essentially similar to their own. It means they are aware of the cultural differences but they attempt to see the surface level differences only with an assumption that at the core all the cultures are similar to the ones that they believe in.

The next three stages are ethnorelative, where one's own culture is viewed and understood in the context of other cultures. In the acceptance stage, other cultures are understood as having a different reality than your own and considered as equally complex and valuable. In this stage, individuals accept cultural differences as they are, while showing equal respect to their own cultural values and beliefs. In the adaptation stage, individuals are able to take the perspective of another cultural worldview. They can shift perspectives from using their own cultural views into using the perspectives of others' cultural views. Lastly, in the integration stage, individuals can combine their self-concept with the cultural values and beliefs of their own as well as those of other cultures. In this stage, individuals have a global identity, where they are aware that people's self-concepts are not just characterized by the views of one culture. In the integration stage, a person's self-concept is impacted by both his or her original cultural views and the views of other cultures.

Theory of Identity Negotiation and Identity Motivation

In order for an individual to be an interculturally sensitive communicator, he or she should function in a globalized context. We often communicate in a way determined by our identity and negotiate our identity through our communication (Ting-Toomey, 2005, 2010). Identity negotiation theory (Ting-Toomey, 2005, 2010) explains to us that the identity is oftentimes not just about individuals' own self-perception but also about perceived sociocultural group membership identity. People may have a social identity related to a social club, a local community, or region. In the context of the IVE, we often perceive each other's national-level identity as salient. Therefore, it becomes important for individuals to be able to negotiate each interactant's identity through interaction, while balancing sociocultural membership identity and personal identity features.

Thus, the question is: Can we see ourselves as members of this globalized society? It is crucial as our level of global identity could impact our behaviors in various contexts. If we perceive ourselves not as a part of this globalized society, we may not feel comfortable in the diverse and global context. If we see ourselves as a part of this globalized community, we may feel comfortable connecting with international others. Global identity is defined as one's tendency to view self as an entity of the global community, as opposed to simply identifying with smaller local groups.

Studies report that the global identity impacts consumer behaviors (e.g., Wang et al., 2021), technology readiness and technology use (e.g., Westjohn et al., 2009), and also sustainable behaviors (Ng & Basu, 2019). Wang et al. (2021) proved that people exhibit the tendency to donate to the beneficiaries that are geographically close rather than those who are distant. The study reported that the individuals with high mobility tend to exhibit global identity, and those with global identity are more likely to donate to the distant beneficiaries. Ng and Basu (2019) examined the association of one's global identity and their preference for using environmentally friendly products. As they predicted, individuals with more dominant global identity exhibited stronger personal responsibility in acting in an environmentally friendly manner, thus preferring to engage in proenvironmental behaviors.

Oyserman and colleagues' (2017) identity-based motivation theory helps us understand the link between global identity and behavior. The theory explains how one's identity or self-concept can impact one's motivations for actions or self-regulations. Oyserman and her colleagues (2017) explain that one's motivation is impacted by one's identity where self-concept is considered not stable but fluid, and is impacted by situation. Identity-based motivation theory starts with the assumption that identities have value—people prefer to act and make sense of situations in identity-congruent ways. It is implied that people are motivated to regulate their behavior, to work toward desired and away from undesired future identities, and to act in ways that fit who they are now and want to become. Although identities have value in that people prefer to act (action readiness) and make meaning (procedural readiness) in line with their identities, which identities come to mind and what these identities imply for action and meaning-making are not fixed and depend on features of the immediate situation (dynamic construction) (Oyserman et al., 2017, pp. 140–141).

Oyserman et al. (2017) emphasize the importance of a situated approach in understanding our identity. Specifically, Oyserman et al. (2017) explain three premises for a situated approach: flexibility in our thinking, situational-based tendency of our thinking, and our lack of awareness about the impact of contexts to our thinking. We tend to be flexible in the way we think. Our thinking process is often impacted by the situation, while we may not be aware of the contextual impact it has on our thinking process. Given this premise, it is predicted that small changes in contexts can impact how people see themselves and consequently how they behave.

This approach can be applied to the analysis of identity negotiation processes discussed in the field of communication. Our identity is formed through the interaction with others, while the communication process influences one's identity. Ting-Toomey's (2005, 2010) identity negotiation theory explains how communicators' identities intersect in the process of communication. When we communicate, different elements of our identity (e.g., gender, age, nationality, ethnicity, race, social class, disability) become salient. Individuals engage in identity negotiation through interaction since the particular domains of identity become salient at times. People who are communicating may jointly form a shared identity, while others may work to elicit a desired identity. One individual may support or challenge the other's suggested identity through their interactions.

Ting-Toomey's (2005, 2010) identity negotiation theory and Oyserman and colleagues' (2017) identity-based motivation theory help us understand one's motivation given dynamic construction of identity, action readiness, and one's interpretation of experience. When applied to the IVE, students may perceive themselves as representing their own cultural background. At the same time, each student may develop a global or international identity as a person who engages in interaction in a global context. Given the context where their regular classroom is now the IVE, students have to accept the fact that they are someone who functions well in a globalized context, and that they should be effective in communicating with their classmates in this global environment.

Goals of the Current Study

Students' participation in the IVEs can be considered as experiential learning where students have a chance to view themselves as active members of a global society. Drawing from Ting-Toomey's (2005, 2010) identity negotiation theory and Oyserman and colleagues' (2017) identity-based motivation theory, we examined the impact of the IVE on students. We would like to understand students' narratives of their experiences and search for the challenges that they faced in participating in the IVE modules, and possible gains that they had.

Knowing that their identity is impacted by the contexts, does participation in the IVE change how they see themselves? Do they consider themselves as part of this large global community as opposed to someone who operates in a local community with a local mindset? Specifically, we would like to examine how students' level of intercultural sensitivity is impacted by their experience of being a participating member of the IVE modules. Therefore, we put forward the following research questions.

Research Question 1: Given the narratives of students' experiences of participating in the IVE sessions, what are the students' perceived (a) challenges and (b) benefits?

Research Question 2: How does the IVE experience differ for the students who use English as a first language and those who use English as a second language?

Research Question 3: What types of impact did the students who participated in the IVE sessions report in the narratives of their experience participating in the IVE sessions?

Methods

Participants

We interviewed a total of 35 students (57% female, 37% male, and 6% non-binary or third gender) who participated in the IVE modules we taught. Fifteen participants were from the United States, including two international students: 1 Czech and 1 Nigerian. Twenty participants studied in Poland: 13

Polish, 4 Turkish, and 3 Spanish students on the Erasmus + exchange program. The participants ranged from 19 to 59 years old with a mean of 24 years old and a standard deviation of 7 years. The majority of participants (85%) indicated that they had already traveled abroad, while 15% never had. Additionally, 68.5% had participated in some type of international curriculum in the past prior to the IVE module employed in this study, while 31.5% never had.

Procedures

A series of semistructured, in-depth interviews were conducted among students who had participated in the course with the IVE modules. The students were contacted after the IVE modules were completed—some after the semester had finished, others during the semester, right after the completion of the IVE modules. The students were asked about their perceived challenges and benefits as well as their perceptions of cultural similarities and differences. The authors transcribed the interview responses and conducted thematic analyses (Braun & Clarke, 2006, 2012). We analyzed them in terms of challenges and gains, possible evidence for intercultural sensitivity, and some signs of their global identity emerging after the IVE participation.

Measures

The survey included some demographic questions and several open-ended questions regarding students' experiences of the IVE sessions and their perception of their global identity. The demographic questions included age, sex, ethnicity, and their experiences in international traveling and international curriculum, such as the IVE or study abroad program. The questions concerning their IVE experiences were meant to find out what they enjoyed most and least, what they considered challenging and fun, and also what they believed they had gained from participating in the IVE modules. Also, students were asked to report their views on globalization and their identity and what impact, if any, their participation in the IVE sessions had on their attitudes or views.

Results

In the participants' narratives of challenges or difficulties, many similar issues were commented on and shared by students both in the United States and Poland. Research Question 1a and 1b examined students' perceived challenges and gains. The following six key themes emerged as challenges: language barrier, cognition/cultural difference, communication styles, stress and anxiety, group dynamics, and procedural difficulties. We also identified six areas of possible gains reported in the narratives. They include benefits of gaining global awareness, comfort and confidence, language learning, moving to ethnorelative states, facilitating culture understanding and empathy, and strength of joint sessions.

Research Question 2 asked whether students who use English as a first language differ from those who use English as a second/foreign language in engagement and learning. We provide some answers to this question, as we report "challenges that students" faced, since students who speak English as a second language had significantly more mention of linguistic and psychological challenges that they faced. On the contrary, students who speak English as a first language highlighted other issues of being misunderstood or technological/procedural challenges.

IVE Challenges

Language barrier. Many Polish, international, and Erasmus+ students indicated that they were comfortable communicating in English most of the time. It must be pointed out that a few Erasmus+ participants in Poland were students of pedagogy, not English philology, and so they had every right not to be proficient while discussing different issues with native speakers of English. One such frustrated student wrote: "What I liked least was that I couldn't communicate at all as I find it difficult to speak English, especially American English, as they spoke very fast, and we are taught British English from a very young age."

Even for some students whose major was English, and who had participated in similar types of virtual exchange classes before, it was the first encounter with American students speaking at a regular pace and using idiomatic expressions. Although some challenges with language barriers were mentioned, many Polish, Spanish, and Turkish students mentioned the linguistic benefits of the IVE sessions they participated in, however hard to follow they might have been initially. American students did not mention much about language issues as their own challenge, but they noted that they should be understanding of international students who are speaking English as their second language for the IVE session.

Cognition and cultural differences. The differences between phonological, lexical, and grammatical systems of English and Polish, Spanish, or Turkish sometimes led to confusion. Fortunately, as one of the nonnative speakers of English said, "I could understand at least 90% of the conversations. If I couldn't understand, I used my partner politely and he/she always repeated or spelled what he/she was saying." In numerous cases, however, students noted the challenges due to the cognitive and cultural differences. This challenge was not caused by a single word or phrase but by different experiences, dissimilar linguistic concepts, or incompatible interpretations of a seemingly unambiguous term. One student wrote, "While we were talking about COVID-19 and lockdown, their faces were so upset. They had some mental and psychological issues. Because I live in a small city in Turkey, it was not such a complicated situation for me." The term "lockdown" is not so emotionally charged for native speakers of Turkish, nor is it associated with oppressiveness.

This is partially due to the cultural interpretation of an experience such as lockdown, but also due to the different use of facial expressions in communication. The observation seems to prove that the ability to speak a new language is a gateway to a new culture and it allows nonnative speakers to appreciate cultural differences they would otherwise never access. What it does is give them exposure to these cultural and cognitive differences in interpretations of the words and diverse perspectives.

Communication style differences. Some students noted communication style differences in terms of openness and perception toward communication. One Polish participant noted that "the students from our nation (Poland) were probably a little more restrained in terms of openness, but as the class progressed throughout the weeks, most of us felt more relaxed." Another student observed that "students in that culture were somewhat more ready to open conversations than us." This difference in the communication style coincided with the language issues discussed earlier and created a compounded challenge for some of our students.

During the class discussion, one American participant mentioned that "I did not enjoy it when some of the other students were silent during discussions. I felt as if they were unsure of how to communicate since English was not their first language." He proved to be sympathetic to the other student's language issues, but still not happy about the fact that this person was silent during the discussion. One Turkish student observed that "Polish people are more distant compared to Turkish and American" but also noticed that "they [Americans] were really relaxed while we were talking about some topics. However, I was a bit under stress." One Polish student summed up the differences in communication styles by briefly saying that "some people are different from others." Still, another said, "I think students who attend the class are open and sincere. We could talk about everything. I find American students more talkative and it's because they probably feel more comfortable with their own language than us Polish students." It cannot have been easy for Polish and international students, as well as Americans, to communicate effectively across cultures. Several Polish students were unnaturally shy and confused by the colloquialisms they heard for the first time; two of the Spanish girls, otherwise very sociable, were frustrated about their English not being good enough; and some Americans became slightly impatient with prolonged silence they had to cover up in the breakout rooms. However, the general feeling was very positive, and everybody seemed to be understanding toward culturally and linguistically motivated communication style differences.

Stress and anxiety. As we discussed in the earlier section, nonnative speakers of English have to deal with stress, anxiety, and insecurity when they communicate. Many students noted the sense of frustration from not being able to come up with certain expressions quickly. They reported the sense of fear and anxiety making mistakes or not being able to get their point across during the IVE interactions. Several nonnative speakers of English felt uneasy about not speaking correctly when they had no time to organize their thoughts. One Turkish student wrote: "I have a fear of making mistakes," and added that "sometimes I couldn't find enough time or conditions to express my opinion." One Polish student commented, "I was able to talk to the students calmly, without fear" thanks to their knowledge of English. Some observed that they had a good enough command of English to worry about causing "misscommunication." However, several students noted the discomfort, difficulty, and a bit of stress not always being fully comfortable communicating in English. A Spanish student mentioned feeling overwhelmed by the topic, stating that "in some moments I was good because I knew how to communicate and I had knowledge about the topic given that day and in other moments I was bad because I didn't even know how to express myself and I was overwhelmed because I couldn't speak."

Group dynamics. From several nonnative speakers' narratives, it transpired that it definitely takes confidence to be sociable in the presence of native speakers. As has already been mentioned in the previous paragraphs concerning language proficiency and communication styles, students focus on what is being said rather than expressing their thoughts. It's a common observation that it is easy to be social in one's mother tongue, when practically no time is needed in order to construct sentences. But in a second language, one has to figure out what to say and how to say it. It means that the IVE participants in Poland had to think twice as hard to make a conversation interesting. In such situations, the conversation dynamic suffers. Consequently, any nonnative speaker needs to accept the fact that they will stumble sometimes but at the same time they will feel an overwhelming sense of achievement when they realize they are improving. This is precisely what the participants in the IVE who are nonnative speakers of English experienced. Such ambivalent views can be found in their narratives. Statements like "I felt insecure, had to avoid awkward silence, I had a few hard times," etc. were very common.

Several students noted that the most enjoyable part of the IVE experience was the small group discussion, since they felt comfortable discussing in a smaller group rather than the joint session with the entire group of students. In our IVE sessions, we used Zoom breakout sessions multiple times. When we did, we simply used the Zoom feature, so that groups were created automatically. In case adjustment was needed, so that we could balance out the Polish and American students in our sessions, we attempted to adjust that after the automated breakout sessions had started. Unfortunately, we could not always balance out the number of students representing each nation. Students mentioned that there were different group dynamics depending on the groups and that at times they were uncomfortable. One student mentioned the anxiety associated with being a minority member within a breakout session stating, "Whenever I was the only Polish student in a breakout room, I kind of felt overwhelmed." Although some students felt uneasy, they noted that as time went by, they felt more comfortable speaking in the breakout sessions. One student observed that the partner students "didn't criticize my English accent" and "seemed happy to meet/know me." Some students reported that they felt the sense of welcome and the feeling of acceptance, even though they had problems with the proper wording. This indicates to us that students who use English as a first language should show encouragement, understanding, and acceptance for those who do not. The narratives give us an insight as to the balance between the big joint class time and breakout sessions, and the balance among the students representing different cultures in each group.

IVE procedural challenges. Instructors needed to overcome many procedural challenges such as time differences and academic year discrepancies in setting up the IVE sessions. There also was a situation during one of the meetings that one of the instructors got shut out of the Zoom session and the other had to take over. Some students faced technical difficulties of not having a good enough internet connection to share their video, while other students had issues of audio quality and other incompatibility issues. Naturally, since we were in different time zones, when they did interact, half of the class was in the morning, while the other half was nighttime. This simple fact impacted some of the interactions among students. It was the Polish/Turkish/Spanish students that complained about sessions starting after 6 p.m. They claimed they would have been more productive in the morning, but different time zones cannot possibly be leveled out.

IVE Gains

In this section, we share our analysis of benefits that are discussed within the students' narratives. Our Research Question 3 asked, "Given the narratives of students' experience participating in the IVE sessions, what types of impact did the students who participated in the IVE sessions experience in terms of their global awareness and cultural sensitivity?" Three benefits of participating in the IVE that we have reported here can answer this research question. Some of our students reported evidence of increasing their global awareness, facilitating cultural understanding, building empathy for others, and moving from an ethnocentric to ethnorelative state.

Benefits of language learning. Naturally, the Polish and international students noted that the mere fact of communicating in English during the IVE session helped them in practicing their English skills. Most of them shared their enthusiasm: "If your level of English allows you to express your opinions it is good, talking with other students was fun, I have improved my English-speaking skills." They reported that they had learned a lot from being exposed to various types of American English, since several participants from the United States spoke English with a southern accent and not in standard American English. Several students mentioned that they were happy to be able to overcome fears of using English as a second language toward the native speakers of English.

American students also experienced the benefits of communicating with international students who used a variety of "global Englishes" (Crystal, 2003). American students may perceive American English as the standard English. In fact, however, in the global setting, a variety of Englishes are employed and accepted. The mere exposure to these varieties is a huge learning experience for American students who may not have had a chance to travel internationally in the past. They also understood that it was important to choose words and phrases that could be understood by the international partners even though they were used to using certain idioms, slang, or expressions that were shared by their classmates. Yet during the IVE sessions, these students needed to be fully aware of their word choices and how each word they used could be interpreted or misinterpreted by their international partners. American students may not have had the fear of speaking English, but instead, they had the anxiety of not being understood. Several students noted that they did not want to look as if they did not care about the others by speaking fast, but at the same time, they did not know how much to slow down and not look as though they were patronizing. Through IVE participation, students are expected to be aware of their word choices, and their own communication behaviors while taking the perspectives of international students.

Comfort and confidence. Generally speaking, the opinions were enthusiastic. Some students reported feeling very comfortable communicating with people from various nations. A Polish student noted that "I also became more open to communication with people from abroad." Another student said that "personally I try to be braver right now. I should be less afraid and unsure of [sic] the contact with foreign people." Several Polish students, not only those who thought highly of their linguistic abilities prior to the IVE experience, emphasized how it boosted their confidence. One female participant said: "For the first time [I] spoke to American students—it was a great experience; I should be less afraid and ashamed of the contact with foreign people." And still another said, "I gained more courage to interact with people from different cultures."

Global awareness. In Research Question 3, we inquired about the types of impact the students who participated in the IVE sessions experienced in terms of their global awareness and cultural sensitivity. Based on the narratives we received, students' perceptions of globalization were carefully analyzed. For most of them it was an exciting opportunity and example of globalization. They said that globalization helps create "the opportunity to make new friends, get to know foreign cultures and traditions." An American student noted that "as we link and connect more with people in other countries, we develop a sense of responsibility" as a member of the world. Another student from the United States noted that he feels that "the borders between countries and cultures seem disappearing" and social media such as "Instagram, Facebook, Twitter and TikTok show us how we should live and what we should eat, which is making people more similar." Thus, from students' perspective, the IVE participation is an extension of their daily experiences of current interconnectedness.

Several students indicated various impacts that the IVE participation had on them, including the global awareness, familiarity, awakened curiosity, and confidence in communicating in global contexts. One student from the United States noted that "I gained a different and wider view of the world." A student from Poland observed that "I have gained more confidence." Still another noted that learning more about other cultures should be useful in the future. Another Polish student related to globalization in the following way: "We learn about each other ... but it does not come without any work put into it."

Facilitating understanding and empathy. The students mentioned numerous positive aspects of participating in the IVE. These included deeper understanding of each other, appreciating differences, and discovering similarities among participants. In the courses such as Intercultural Communication, the instructors often discuss cultural variabilities and how cultures differ in various ways (Hofstede et al., 2010). Given this knowledge and our exposure to the stereotypical views of each other, we tend to expect and accept cultural differences.

Some students noted that through the IVE participation, they found similarity with the international partner students that they had not expected. Although the differences seemed to be more evident at first, many students noted that they found similarities. Several students got involved in the interpersonal communication and interaction, which helped them have a better understanding of each other. A Polish student mentioned that it was interesting to learn "how American universities work, how people perceive reality, and how they act in everyday situations." One student not only got interested in learning about American culture but also indicated his interest in visiting the country someday. "Now, I know more about other cultures and for the first time I spoke with American students—it was a great experience. Yes, I would like to visit the USA in the future, because I really want to see this interesting country." A Turkish student wrote: "I could make new friends who I still talk to nearly every day."

Several students noted that successful interaction and global cooperation should come with not just tolerance but also empathic understanding of each other. One American student noted that "we always feel more empathy to the other country, when we actually know someone from there," and that programs like the IVE help connect students in such a way that they can get to know each other at a personal level. Given the fact that our identity is built during the interaction with others, we can claim that this type of interaction helps students view themselves as individuals who contribute to better understanding in a global context.

Moving to ethnorelative states. We have noted some signs of students being self-reflective of their preconceived perceptions about people from other cultures. Some students noted that it is easy to perceive others through stereotypes, but that is not what one should do. One student indicated clearly moving from an ethnocentric to an ethnorelative state and being perceptive about preconceived notions.

> Yes, I stopped perceiving people from other countries just through stereotypes and prejudices. It had a very positive impact on me. I am grateful that I've met so many new friends from other countries. It has given me the opportunity to become more open towards other people and have some knowledge about the American people. It was a great time.

A student from the United States indicated that they felt the emotional connection and "empathy" fostered through the understanding of shared goals and values in life. One participant noted as follows:

> It truly changed my perspective on someone who lives so far away being different. I was pleasantly delighted to discover that what matters most to us is spending time with family and friends, eating delicious food with friends and family, and studying hard. I believe that experiences like this assist to foster empathy between two different nations. It is no longer just a distant place for me. It's almost like if I were there on a visit, being able to identify with that location with friendly people and names.

This student indicated an awareness of interdependence and a sign of global identity. A Polish girl observed:

> I consider myself a very open person. Nowadays people are not so focused on their own country; they share many things together. There are people who don't feel they belong to any particular country because they perceive the whole world as their motherland. That's why we are interdependent.

These students shared positive results from the IVE sessions. Each one is meaningful for their learning. Students learned to suspend judgment given the preconceived notions and to stay open, as they felt some level of interconnectedness through discussions.

IVE procedural gains. Earlier, we mentioned the difficulty in matching course content and scheduling given differences in time zone and academic structure between partners. We also encountered a few technical difficulties during our synchronous IVE sessions. Let us mention some of the positive experiences that we had through the IVE sessions. Students are not just learning from one instructor, but from two instructors in these joint IVE sessions. Some students commented that they enjoyed learning from both instructors and learned from the interactions among the instructors. Additionally, this type of joined class rescued us from technical challenges. For instance, when one of the instructors got kicked out from the synchronous IVE sessions, the other instructor took over and continued class because we had a shared teaching plan. When one of the instructors was faced with a technical difficulty during an IVE session, the other instructor could continue class. The IVE synchronous sessions essentially provided us a backup plan for both students and instructors. This not only provided physical and technical support but also emotional and psychological support in conducting this type of technologically supported class meeting, which could inevitably face some challenges at times. The joint class provides intellectual stimulus and broadening of viewpoints by having two instructors and students from diverse backgrounds.

Conclusions

In this study, we examined students' narratives after their participation in the IVE sessions. Experiential learning such as this should help students expose themselves to diverse perspectives and help them prepare to live and work in an increasingly diverse world. We analyzed the narratives of students who participated in the IVE sessions and identified five challenges (language proficiency issues, impact of language on cognition, communication style differences, stress and anxiety, group dynamics, and procedural difficulties) and five gains (language training, comfort and confidence, cultural understanding, global awareness, and intercultural sensitivity). Those challenges and gains are not mutually exclusive, and carefully analyzed, they have provided meaningful concepts for us to understand the students' experiences and insights as to how to improve the IVE modules for the future.

We believe that the students' participation in the IVE sessions has contributed to their development of intercultural sensitivity. Bennett (1993, 2001) and Bennett and Bennett (2004) proposed the Developmental Model of Intercultural Sensitivity to explain the process. The narratives demonstrate to us that students are exposed to diverse perspectives and cultural differences in communication styles. They need to readjust their prior knowledge about international students in order to engage in the interaction. They also have to devise what they say and how they speak. Several students reflected on their preconceived notions and stereotypical information that they had been exposed to in the past, prior to participating in the IVE. Students realized that they had to get past these preconceptions about others, and to find similarities with their international partners. Their comments indicate to us that our students have moved from an ethnocentric to ethnorelative mindset.

We build our identity through our interaction with others. In the IVE, students gain the opportunity to interact with people in different nations. As Ting-Toomey (2005, 2010) noted, students had to negotiate their individual identity labels as they built shared identity as students or global individuals. Drawing from Oyserman et al.'s (2017) discussion on the importance of the situated approach in understanding our identity and the assumption that the identities have values, we can say that the students who participated in the IVE are forced in the situation where global identity is required. While students engage in global interaction with international partners, they are exposed to diverse cultural perspectives. They have the chance to reflect on these cultural differences and similarities and feel obliged to value these globalized contexts. They are often asked to talk about national culture and its impact. They also make national comparisons as they interact with international students. Given this process, the students' sense of identity as global citizens, or as people who engage well in a globalized context, is highlighted. Many students note that they have gained deeper cultural understanding, and the differences they discuss with their partners can be juxtaposed with the individual challenges that they encounter. The narratives that we analyzed present some evidence that students who participated in the IVE became more comfortable and confident in interacting with international students.

Limitations and Directions for Future Study

We are only presenting qualitative narrative analysis given the in-depth interviews with the participants of the IVE sessions. In the future, we should examine the impact of the IVE quantitatively, examining various indicators of intercultural sensitivity of intercultural communication competence. The students who participated in our shared IVE sessions are limited to students from the United States, Poland, and other nations that happened to be represented due to them being international students in the United States or the Erasmus+ programs. The cultural distance of participants impacts their perceptions and interactions (Shenkar, 2001). The intercultural interaction between American and European students may differ greatly from the interaction between American and Turkish students. The cultural differences may be represented as a psychological distance among the participants and hence students' experiences of the IVE may differ greatly depending on the cultural difference (Sousa & Bradley, 2006). In the future, we can consider comparing the students' IVE experiences when there are different degrees of cultural distance. Moreover, the current study examined students' perceptions after they had participated in the IVE sessions and did not include pre- and postcomparisons of their perspectives, which can also be included.

The authors believe that experiential learning helps students be exposed to diverse perspectives and prepared to be effective in a diverse and global workplace. The instructors of the IVE could consider issues associated with language proficiency, psychological stress, and cultural differences in cognitive and communication styles. Additionally, the IVE instructors can educate native speakers of English regarding linguistic inequality and work to equalize the power in the IVE discussions while preparing the nonnative speakers for the possible stress that they may feel. Our hope is that we can provide more experiential learning opportunities like the IVE so that students can not only develop global awareness and intercultural competence but also foster global identities.

REFERENCES

Bennett, M. J. (1986). A developmental approach to training for intercultural sensitivity. *International Journal of Intercultural Relations, 10*(2), 179–196.

Bennett, M. J., & Bennett, J. (1993). Intercultural sensitivity. *Principles of Training and Development, 25*(21), 185–206.

Bennett, M., & Bennett, J. (2004). Developing intercultural sensitivity. An integrative approach to global and domestic diversity. In D. Landis, J. Bennett, & M. Bennett (Eds.), *The handbook of intercultural training.* 3rd ed. Sage.

Bloom, A. H. (2014). *The linguistic shaping of thought: A study in the impact of language on thinking in China and the West.* Psychology Press.

Boroditsky, L. (2011). How language shapes thoughts. *Scientific American*, *304*(2), 62–65. https://www.jstor.org/stable/10.2307/26002395

Braun, V., & Clarke, V. (2006). Using thematic analysis in psychology. *Qualitative Research in Psychology*, *3*, 77–101. https://doi.org/10.1191/1478088706qp063oa

Braun, V., & Clarke, V. (2012). Thematic analysis. In H. Cooper, P. M. Camic, D. L. Long, A. T. Panter, D. Rindskopf, & K. J. Sher (Eds.), *APA handbook of research methods in psychology, vol. 2: Research designs: Quantitative, qualitative, neuropsychological, and biological* (pp. 57–71). American Psychological Association.

Cairns, D. (2017). The Erasmus undergraduate exchange programme: A highly qualified success story? *Children's Geographies*, *15*(6), 728–740. https://doi.org/10.1080/14733285.2017.1328485

Crystal, D. (2003). English as a Global Language (Second Edition). Cambridge University Press. https://doi.org/10.1017/CBO9780511486999

Deutscher, G. (2010). Through the language glass: Why the world looks different in other languages. Metropolitan Books, Henry Holt, and Company.

Dooly, M., & Sadler, R. (2013). Filling in the gaps: Linking theory and practice through telecollaboration in teacher education. *ReCALL*, *25*(1), 4–29. https://doi.org/10.1017/S0958344012000237

Eguchi, M., & Shearman, S. M. (2017). Use of new media in intercultural communication instruction. *Global Partners in Education Journal*, *6*(1), 1–21. http://www.gpejournal.org/index.php/GPEJ

European Commission. (2013). *History of the Erasmus programme*. European Commission. https://web.archive.org/web/20130404063541/http://ec.europa.eu/education/more-information/reports-and-studies_en.htm

European Commission. (2022). *Erasmus+: Enriching lives, opening minds*. European Commission. https://erasmus-plus.ec.europa.eu/

The EVALUATE Group. (2019). *Evaluating the impact of virtual exchange on initial teacher education: A European policy experiment*. Research-publishing.net. https://doi.org/10.14705/rpnet.2019.29.9782490057337

Geipel, J., Hadjichristidis, C., & Surian, L. (2015). The foreign language effect on moral judgment: The role of emotions and norms. *PLoS ONE*, *10*(7), Article e0131529. https://doi.org/10.1371/journal.pone.0131529

Hagley, E. (2020). Effects of virtual exchange in the EFL classroom on students' cultural and intercultural sensitivity. *Computer-Assisted Language Learning Electronic Journal*, *21*(3), 74–87. http://callej.org/journal/21-3/2020.pdf

Hammer, M. R., Bennett, M. J., & Wiseman, R. (2003). Measuring intercultural sensitivity: The intercultural development inventory. *International journal of intercultural relations*, *27*(4), 421–443. https://doi.org/10.1016/S0147-1767(03)00032-4

Hofstede, G., Hofstede, G. J., & Minkov, M. (2010). Cultures and Organizations: Software of the Mind (Third Edition). McGraw-Hill.

Hook, J. N., Davis, D. E., Owen, J., Worthington, E. L., Jr., & Utsey, S. O. (2013). Cultural humility: Measuring openness to culturally diverse clients. *Journal of Counseling Psychology, 60*(3), 353–366. https://doi.org/10.1037/a0032595

Horwitz, E. K. (2010). Foreign and second language anxiety. *Language teaching, 43*(2), 154–167. https://doi.org/10.1017/S026144480999036X

Institute of International Education. (2021). *Study abroad all destinations: Historical data.* https://opendoorsdata.org/data/us-study-abroad/fields-of-study/

Keysar, B., Hasegawa, S., & An, S. G. (2012). The foreign language effect: Thinking in a foreign tongue reduces decision biases. *Psychological Science, 23*(6), 661–668. https://doi.org/10.1177/0956797611432178

Kohli Bagwe, T., & Haskollar, E. (2020). Variables impacting intercultural competence: A systematic literature review. *Journal of Intercultural Communication Research, 49*(4), 346–371. https://doi.org/10.1080/17475759.2020 .1771751

Kolb, D. A. (1984). *Experiential learning: Experience as the source of learning and development.* Prentice-Hall.

Kreber, C. (2009). Different perspectives on internationalization of higher education. *New Directions for Teaching and Learning, 118,* 1–14. https://doi.org /10.1002/tl.348

Lenkaitis, C. A. (2021). Virtual exchanges for intercultural communication development: Using can-do statements for ICC self-assessment. *Journal of International & Intercultural Communication, 14*(3), 258–274. https://doi.org /10.1080/17513057.2020.1784983

Ng, S., & Basu, S. (2019). Global identity and preference for environmentally friendly products: The role of personal responsibility. *Journal of Cross-Cultural Psychology, 50*(8), 919–936. https://doi.org/10.1177/0022022119873432

Northrup, D. (2013). How English became the global language. Palgrave Macmillan.

O'Dowd, R. (2013). Telecollaborative networks in university higher education: Overcoming barriers to integration. *The Internet and Higher Education, 18,* 47–53. https://doi.org/10.1016/j.iheduc.2013.02.001

O'Dowd, R. (2018). From telecollaboration to virtual exchange: state-of-the-art and the role of UNICollaboration in moving forward. *Journal of Virtual Exchange, 1,* 1–23. https://doi.org/10.14705/rpnet.2018.jve.1

O'Dowd, R., & Lewis, T. (2016). *Online intercultural exchange: Policy, pedagogy, practice.* Routledge.

Oyserman, D., Lewis, N. A., Jr., Yan, V. X., Fisher, O., O'Donnell, S. C., & Horowitz, E. (2017). An identity-based motivation framework for self-regulation.

Psychological Inquiry, 28(2–3), 139–147. https://doi.org/10.1080/104784
0X.2017.1337406

Rienties, B., Lewis, T., O'Dowd, R., Rets, I., & Rogaten, J. (2020). The impact
of virtual exchange on TPACK and foreign language competence: Reviewing
a large-scale implementation across 23 virtual exchanges. *Computer Assisted
Language Learning, 35*(3), 577–603. https://doi.org/10.1080/09588221
.2020.1737546

Shenkar, O. (2001). Cultural distance revisited: Towards a more rigorous conceptualization and measurement of cultural differences. *Journal of International Business
Studies, 32*(3), 519–535.

Shearman, S. M., & Eguchi, M. (2018). "I have to text my classmate in China!": Use
of new media in intercultural communication classes toward multidimensional
learning. In N. Bilge & M. I. Marino (Eds.), *Reconceptualizing new media and
intercultural communication in a networked society* (pp. 140–169). IGI.

Sousa, C. M., & Bradley, F. (2006). Cultural distance and psychic distance: Two
peas in a pod? *Journal of International Marketing, 14*(1), 49–70.

Tian, J., & Wang, Y. (2010). Taking language learning outside the classroom:
Learners' perspectives of eTandem learning via Skype. *Innovation in Language
Learning and Teaching, 4*(3), 181-197. https://doi.org/10.1080/17501229.2010
.513443

Ting-Toomey, S. (2005). Identity negotiation theory: Crossing cultural boundaries.
In W. B. Gudykunst (Ed.), *Theorizing about intercultural communication*
(pp. 211–233). Sage.

Ting-Toomey, S. (2009). Identity theories. In S. Littlejohn & K. Foss (Eds.),
Encyclopedia of communication theory (pp. 493–496). Sage.

Ting-Toomey, S. (2010). Applying dimensional values in understanding
intercultural communication. *Communication Monographs, 77*(2), 169–180.
https://doi.org/10.1080/03637751003790428

Tsuda, Y. (2007). The hegemony of English and strategies for linguistic pluralism:
Proposing the ecology of language paradigm. In M. K. Asante, Y. Miike, & J. Yin
(Eds.), *The global intercultural communication reader* (pp. 187–198). Routledge.
https://doi.org/10.4324/9780203934982

Wang, Y., Kirmani, A., & Li, X. (2021). Not too far to help: Residential mobility,
global identity, and donations to distant beneficiaries. *Journal of Consumer
Research, 47*(6), 878–889. https://doi.org/10.1093/jcr/ucaa053

Westjohn, S. A., Arnold, M. J., Magnusson, P., Zdravkovic, S., & Zhou, J. X. (2009).
Technology readiness and usage: A global-identity perspective. *Journal of the
Academy of Marketing Science, 37*(3), 250–265. https://doi.org/10.1007
/s11747-008-0130-0

MARIELLA OLIVOS PH.D | ESAN University

Perspectives on the Phenomena of Social Media Use by Leaders and Social Media Influencers

Findings From an Online International Collaborative Project Among Students in Peru, the United States of America, and North Macedonia

Abstract

There has been an increasing interest in social network communication among young students worldwide. In that sense, this explorative study aims to understand students' perspectives on social media use by leaders and the current phenomena of social media influencers (SMI). The research was set within an international university venture module that employs tools of information and communication technologies. The data collection came from a project among students in Peru, the United States of America, and North Macedonia in which students worked through Zoom meetings. The purpose of this course was to deliver a group presentation that identified how some leaders use social media in their cultures. As a result, students produced a report with content, images, and pictures of the leaders previously selected in a common area in each country. One topic that inductively emerged was that despite cultural differences among the groups, most students identified social media influencers as leaders and emphasized female influencers' advocacy of women's empowerment. This study provides a further understanding of the impact of social media on the concept of leadership for young people despite cultural differences like being more individualist or collectivist, with high-context or low-context styles of communication. Finally, this study confirms the existence of a new SMI industry with direct implications for our society.

Keywords: social media, social media influencers, leadership, communication, cultures

Introduction

One of the most valuable aspects of the COIL (Collaborative Online International Learning) programs is the possibility for students to interact with their peers in other countries and, thus, discover and extend cultural and communication differences, and acquire new capabilities and skills. It is also a sustainable strategy supported by technology to promote the benefits of "internationalization of the curriculum" on campus. However, it is very challenging for instructors to design discussion topics and propose relevant themes for collaborative projects that allow students to discover and to learn from these differences.

The Global Partner in Education (GPE Network) has organized the Global Understanding course each semester since 2006. The secretariat of GPE at East Carolina University supports the connection of faculty and students in different countries who interact twice a week for four weeks using a synchronic platform to communicate. The aim of the course is to learn about other cultures, acquire intercultural competence, share information, and work on joint projects.

For these reasons, one topic that offers those possibilities is the study of leadership in cultures. For instance, what do young people think the definition of a leader is? How do they define them, and in what spaces is it possible for them to identify them? Based on the students' analysis, it is possible to find similarities and differences that will improve the students' intercultural competency. In this regard, social networks are currently used by young students and leaders of all political, religious, business, and sports areas, among others. Moreover, as pointed out by Matthews et al. (2022), there is a wide use and growth of social media (SM), including most traditional leaders' positions. Therefore, this common denomination of the leader's adoption of SM enables comparisons across contexts and is an additional method for assessing leadership. In addition, it is exciting and valuable to understand how young people perceive leaders' roles in SM.

Context

According to Momen (2019), at present SM are more dominant than traditional media since the internet as a platform encourages people to express opinions, debates, and discussions on any topic. In other words, young students are present, observing and selecting the voices they empathize with on SM.

Moreover, when referring to young students' use of sources of information, it is crucial to consider some facts. From a study, results applied to young students in Spain (Herrero, 2022); 64% of young people between 18 and 24 years old globally consider digital and social media as their primary source of information. Young people are not interested in traditional media such as newspapers, radio, or television; they prefer influencers and YouTubers as referents. Current adolescents are a "visual" generation since they use narratives (short videos, photos, and pictures) and spend long hours on various websites and streaming platforms. In addition, a gender bias was reported in Herrero's study since more male influencers were identified compared to female influencers. The female influencers that were mentioned were usually partners of famous male celebrities.

Furthermore, according to Chambers et al. (2018), in developed countries, children aspired to have careers around celebrity culture, which nowadays is gaming, SM, and sportspeople. The report showed that being a social media star is the fourth most wanted career by children (ages 7–11) worldwide.

Theoretical Background

Social Media and Freedom of Expression

Thanks to globalization and the internet, which play a fundamental role in freedom of expression, people share their opinions on different social networks. Thus, this gives rise to a more attentive and informed world in real time with issues worldwide and constant communication. According to Kushin and Yakamoto (2010), social networks have become a medium in which people, apart from seeking information, can give different opinions on different topics, such as political issues.

Social networks and new technology are also giving importance to human connectivity, thus generating an impact on political issues. In that sense, young people are exposed to different news, and they use that information to form their own opinion, in addition to sharing it (Vogels et al., 2020).

Furthermore, social networks have a more significant impact when mobilizing the attention of the community or a specific country toward a fact (Loisau & Nowacka, 2015). A clear example is the women's rights or the Black

Lives Matter movements, where social networks played a fundamental role in the propagation of news and comments by many artists and people who supported the cause. Regarding women's rights, the #MeToo hashtag was particularly relevant as it was used all around the world as a tool for online activism, mainly on Twitter. In five months, nearly three million tweets were related to this topic; in other words, not only victims were retweeting, but also supporters, which means that this hashtag contributed to creating a culture of solidarity. It is also interesting to mention that although a well-known actress started the movement in 2017 (Alyssa Milano), the research found that most of the tweets with this hashtag came from personal accounts, which means that a celebrity encouraged people to speak out about their own experiences with abuse (Martínez et al., 2021).

Eriksen (2020) argues that "freedom of expression" is associated with human rights and cosmopolitan thinking to the need for respect and recognition, and almost all countries have introduced a system for regulating freedom of expression (Momen, 2019).

In that sense, it is highly relevant to understand freedom of expression laws by country: in the United States, the government protects freedom of expression. According to the First Amendment to the US Constitution,

> Congress shall make no law respecting an establishment of religion, or prohibiting the free exercise thereof, or abridging the freedom of speech, or of the press; or the right of the people peaceably to assemble, and to petition the Government for a redress of grievances.

This gives the right to petition the US government to make a complaint or seek assistance without fear of reprisal or punishment.

In Peru, the constitution and legal context guarantee freedom of expression. Peru follows the Universal Declaration of Human Rights that established that freedom of expression does not permit any expression of discrimination regarding national, racial, or religious aspects, nor violence against a vulnerable group, known as "advocacy of hate."

However, in North Macedonia, freedom of expression has to do with the liberty of expressing personal convictions, conscience, and thoughts, and public expression is guaranteed.

Momen (2019) argues that the internet is a platform that provides power to people so that they can express their different opinions without classifying them as good or bad. The freedom of expression that social networks encourage is shown in the form of debate or discussion of different topics, in different discussion forums or on platforms such as Twitter.

Aziz (2021) mentions that "there exists a corrupt nexus between media and political parties," which has put press freedom at risk. Moreover, with the access to information provided by the internet, "social media and smartphones are now transformative agents" (i.e., with the use of social networks and digital transformation, there is greater access to information, which also has an impact on democracy). In other words, nowadays, the population takes influencers as role models.

Social Media Influencers

Social media influencers (SMIs) are online personalities who influence their followers across one or more SM platforms (Rundin & Colliander, 2021).

Influencers are transforming how to communicate with target audiences (Booth & Maltic 2011). SMIs represent a new type of independent third-party endorser who shapes audience attitudes through blogs, tweets, and other SM (Freberg et al., 2011). SMIs are shapers of public opinion who persuade their audience through the conscientious calibration of personae on SM (Abidin & Ots, 2015).

SMIs are produced, not born; each is identified and constituted by various SM intelligence analytics and social scoring companies (Hearn & Schoenhoff, 2017). Since SMIs depend on getting as much attention as possible, they learn to understand the public while shaping their representations, which also works as a personal brand in the audience's mind. In that way, these people take advantage of global trends, such as taking selfies and making themselves part of the saleable objects. To put it another way, they use their public image to sell products and services. An interesting case is the example of the Cavinder twins, who went from being professional basketball players to SM stars with more than four million followers on TikTok in less than three years (Hamilton, 2022). Nowadays, the 21-year-old millionaire girls have partnered with different companies since, in June 2021, Supreme Court Justice Brett Kavanaugh made it possible for college athletes in the National Collegiate Athletic Association to capitalize financially on their name, image, and likeness (NIL). Initially, it was their father, a former CEO, who contacted the right people at the right time, and due to the lack of regulations, the NIL industry has become a complex market that generates about $19 billion a year (Moses, 2022).

This situation reflects an impact on the country's economy and entrepreneurial activities and taxation. In the case of Peru, the national agency of taxes SUNAT (Super Intendencia Nacional de Administración Tributaria) has recently announced that influencers must act as any other company and therefore pay the corresponding taxes (Estudio Echecopar, 2022).

What is more, Khamis et al. (2017) stated that the common factor between influencers and traditional celebrities is that they have a unique selling point and a charismatic public identity, which is also affected by the preferences of the core audience.

According to the definition by Gräve (2017), an SMI is perceived as an opinion leader who communicates to an unknown audience through digital platforms. Therefore, not only should they be communicators but also their appeal must keep up with global news, authenticity, and engagement with their created image.

Furthermore, gratification is vital when it comes to fulfilling the role of an influencer. As it was seen, influencers feel gratification by creating new content, making a difference with their actions, or just the happiness from helping people while giving them advice for a healthier way of life.

Keller and Berry (2003) mention that influencers can convince the public to use or not use the products or services they promote by giving their advice or suggestions. They are perceived as trustworthy people. Some of these SMIs work full-time creating content of quality and live with this, working with companies in paid collaborations called sponsored content (De Veirman et al., 2017). However, there still needs to be more knowledge of this phenomenon when referring to freedom of expression in students and whether to quote influencers' opinions.

Methodology

The study of Matthews et al. (2022) explains the nature of SM data. SM allows individuals to share content through SM platforms such as Instagram, Facebook, Twitter, WhatsApp, and TikTok. The Big Data gathered describes the anatomy of SM, high in volume, velocity, variety, and veracity, and the strength provided by the accessibility. Matthews et al. (2022) provide researchers with methodological recommendations for SM use in leadership studies as content analysis and computer-aided content analysis. For the students' collaborative project, they were requested to focus on the leaders' SM content. This essay analyzes the content of the students' projects at an explorative level.

The project was part of the Global Understanding Course, which connects students in different geographical locations. In this case, we report the experience of the collaborative project that represents a mandatory task that is graded independently by the instructors. The students participated in the Global Understanding Course in the year 2021. They were located at Universidad ESAN in Lima, Peru, at East Carolina University (ECU) in Greenville, North Carolina, and at Skopje in North Macedonia, the University American College. Students discussed topics that allowed them to discover and learn the characteristics of each culture, understand how they affect society, and identify behavioral values and norms in each location.

For this collaborative project, instructors in the three countries agreed on the topic of "Leaders and Communication through Social Media." Twenty students participated in Peru, 19 in the United States, and 16 in North Macedonia. Students from Peru and the United States worked for four continuing weeks, divided into 10 teams, at the beginning of the semester, connecting for 50 minutes twice a week. Afterward, the students from Peru worked with the students in North Macedonia for three continuous weeks, connecting for 50 minutes twice a week. Instructors organized eight international teams in pairs or groups of three people from the participants' institutions. Students had to connect through the Zoom platform during the sessions but could choose any other platform to discuss ideas outside the lessons.

The general theme of the collaborative project was "Culture and Social Media Usage," the specific topic "Project Leaders and Social Media: How Do They Use Social Media to Communicate?"

The main goal was to analyze how a leader, previously selected by each student in their native country, uses SM to communicate. Each team had to agree on and select the leader from the same professional field, sector, or industry.

The specific goals were: first to compare and contrast communication characteristics through SM and identify similarities and differences, and second, to create a "Best Practices Checklist for Effective Social Media Use."

The students needed to organize their time and resolve the challenges of the time zones between countries as well as the different styles of communication. They had three weeks to meet virtually outside the class to discuss the main findings. Finally, each team reported their comparisons in a PowerPoint presentation to their instructors.

Findings in the Collaborative Project on Leaders and Social Media: How Do They Use Social Media to Communicate?

The first team, formed by students from Peru and North Macedonia, found a similar characteristic of leadership: the student from Macedonia argued that no matter how complicated the situations a leader may go through, they must know how to handle the comments with serenity and remain firm in their position. For both students, the content creator must be responsible for the quality of their content. In other words, they cannot share untruthful information, as this can cause conflicts between different groups of people, regardless of the creator's initial intention.

In the second team, Peruvian students presented the "Best Practices Checklist for Effective Social Media Use." In their opinion, the essential qualities to consider in a leader were: a clear identity, good relationships, and honesty. The same Peruvian students showed how his North Macedonian peers perceived the same best practices. In this case, they presented the following "rules": honesty, integrity, calmness, appropriate tone, and understanding.

The third team, formed by students from the United States and Peru, chose two female athletes, Simone Biles and Alexandra Grande, who endured hardships while growing up. The students showed photos of the athletes' achievements and a short biography. They claimed their current success inspires others to never give up and keep trying to achieve their goals. They pointed out how "Simone Biles is a leader in the athletic industry due to the fact that she is considered the most decorated American gymnast." In turn, "the Peruvian athlete in karate Alexandra Grande, born in Lima in 1990, won several gold medals in international events and received the highest distinction in Peru for an athlete sport: "La Gran Cruz." In that sense, resilience was a key factor mentioned by both students in their presentations. For American students, leadership is related to being resilient, in students' words: "[A] good leader must be able to bounce back from hardship and persevere." Moreover, being influential is essential: "[T]hey should inspire others and be a role model, someone to look up to, non-problematic," and "they should be able to give back to the community and speak up for others." Leaders should be positive: "[T]hey should be a beacon of hope and smile in the face of adversity," and "no one should bring them down and they should know that they are doing."

For the fourth project, students selected female representatives of leadership. The student from Peru mentioned a congresswoman, Sigrid Bazan, and the student from the United States, an American television model and author, Chrissy Teigen. One common factor is that both women talk about politics and human rights and have a TV space. Moreover, both Sigrid and Chrissy are involved in proabortion movements and undocumented immigrants' rights, which, in the students' opinion, makes them "modern" and "trustworthy." In addition, the photos chosen for the students' presentation showed them wearing very fashionable clothes, which could suggest that the students also admire them because of their ability to be activists while remaining feminine. In this case, the students agreed that the essential characteristics of a world leader are being able to handle criticism, having good communication skills, and being honest and dedicated.

Finally, the fifth project found that the most striking characteristic of leadership is creating awareness while talking about their life improvement. In the students' example, influencers have the common characteristic of empowering other women. In addition, it is vital to notice that these influencers or leaders have a large number of followers, so in this way, they can promote different products, and their speeches and opinions reach many people. For instance, Peruvians Isadora Lange and Marisol Benavides and American Oprah Winfrey have their own TV programs where they can spread the word about women's empowerment. Isadora's activism is through her blog and podcast on Spotify, Instagram, and Facebook. Marisol uses the same social networks to post funny videos, give motivational messages, and run workshops related to creativity, wellness, and women's disinhibition. Moreover, the three of them are writers who have published books meant to improve women's lives.

In essence, all the students chose SMIs as leaders. Peruvian and American students considered that an influencer must be able to manage massive amounts of information. This characteristic can also be associated with the attribute the Macedonian student mentioned in his presentation, which was "being calm and collected."

Conclusions

Based on the students' collaborative work, a leader can model or influence people's actions to make things happen, which is the case for SMIs. In other words, SM has directly affected the meaning of "leadership." Moreover, the examples of the leaders chosen by the students have shown how SM can effectively amplify women's voices and identify strategies to facilitate their impact on decision-making processes better, as stated by Loiseau and Nowacka (2015). In addition, Miller, (2018) pointed out that the participation of women in social media has helped create a community of support for women.

Two athletes, the American Simone Biles and the Peruvian Alexandra Grande, are examples of leaders in the United States and Peru, respectively. The content on their SM is related to their personal life, which can be associated with what students in Peru and Macedonia attribute to a leader. It is important to note that both athletes belong to minority groups. Simone is a Black woman who is a survivor of abuse, and Alexandra is a Mestiza woman from a poor background.

However, what happens when these female leaders are less resilient than the public thought? For example, in July 2021, Simone Biles withdrew from the Olympics to prioritize her mental health. Even though the immediate response was positive and understanding, later, many people considered her decision as not being able to deal with adversity. Some called her a "quitter," and one male presenter even accused her of being selfish (Niesen, 2021). Would the public have reacted differently if Simone had been a privileged White man? For instance, the well-known swimming champion Michael Phelps was arrested more than twice for drinking and driving, which in 2009 led to a three-month suspension by USA Swimming, and one sponsor, Kellog Co., dropped him. However, Michael was not censored or judged by the public and continued his career. In 2014 he was chosen as the male athlete of the year by USA Swimming (Associated Press, 2014).

In this regard, it is essential to address the problem of the misrepresentation of women in the media. Are they considered people or bodies that must perform at all costs? Are they seen as influential leaders or victims? Unfortunately, according to Mavin et al. (2016), women leaders worldwide have higher probabilities of being represented sexually, in a negative light, or as wives of significant figures in the media.

In this sense, students considered that "being able to take criticism" is associated with confidence since it requires "the influencer" to handle various comments without affecting their content and personal life. In their view, influencers must be self-confident people that provide truthful content.

Regarding geographical and cultural differences, based on the students' examples, it was observed that in the United States, SMIs use humor to make the viewers laugh and relax. In contrast, women influencers in Latin America use public emotions to persuade their viewers and make them feel empathy. Worldwide, content about personal life is a relevant trend, regardless of culture. Other factors such as gender, age, and background might influence the decision to follow an influencer.

Furthermore, when comparing cultural traits, one fascinating difference is that the United States is a country where individualism, achievement orientation, and assertiveness are promoted from a young age. This characteristic is expressed as well in SMI communication. Evidence can be found on SM posts by Biles or the Cavinder twins that encourage excellence in all life aspects, not only in sports but also romantically, familiarly, and aesthetically.

On the other hand, Peru scores high in collectivism according to Hofstede's (1994) dimension model. Grande's posts, for example, show her holding a Peruvian flag, and most posts are related to the sport she practices. In addition, a common situation that most sports athletes face is that even though they demonstrate ambition and make a great effort to achieve their goals, they need to be supported by family and friends to succeed, due to the lack of support provided by the Peruvian government, sports clubs, sports associations, or colleges, in contrast to the American situation. Additionally, Peruvian athletes do not have as many followers as American athletes, which suggests that they are not as influential as their American peers. Similarly to Peru, North Macedonia scores highly on the collectivism metric, indicating that its citizens value high interpersonal connections for decision making. Consequently, for their project, Macedonian students emphasized the importance of organizations and groups that encourage civic and political engagement, activism, and improvement of the education system.

For instance, "Youth Can" and "AED EKVALIS" are associations that promote equality and stimulate reflection on how to alter social dynamics for both individual and group well-being.

Moreover, organizations such as "KRIK" post educational content on their social media profiles to incentivize youth involvement in the creation of public policies. The Macedonian word "KRIK," which means "screech" or "outcry," represents a collective feeling toward the current system.

As Khamis et al. (2017) pointed out, the contemporary democratization of media production and freedom of expression facilitates self-promotion and self-branding; further investigation should be done on the students' differentiation of leadership and self-branding.

Social networks are more relevant now, and the literature remains fragmented and incipient (Litterio et al., 2017). In addition, as Herrero suggests

(2022), education at all levels should offer students "media literacy" and not just "digital literacy." This means not just teaching them to use platforms, software, and SM in general, but learning to be critical on the information they are exposed to. The educational models that imply international collaboration are valuable since they allow students to share ideas and values while acquiring intercultural competency.

Finally, in contrast to the findings by Herrero (2022), who reports more male influencers in Spain, more female influencers were reported in this collaborative project rather than men.

Limitations and Future Research

The present study is an explorative and observational analysis based on a small international sample of students' collaborative projects. The findings of this study, while not generalizable, demonstrate the relevance of SMIs in terms of defining a leader among young people. Through the appearance of SMIs, it is evident that a new type of leadership has arisen with a distinct pattern of communication-mediated technology. Finally, the study results have revealed the lack of regulations in an emerging industry with direct implications on a country's economy, culture, and society, allowing for more research in various fields.

Acknowledgments

We would like to thank the students for allowing us to share their content reports, and Andrea Garcia, research assistant at Universidad ESAN, for her assistance with the edition.

REFERENCES

Abidin, C. (2016). Aren't these just young, rich women doing vain things online? Influencer selfies as subversive frivolity. *Social Media + Society*, 2(2). https://doi .org/10.1177/2056305116641342

Abidin, C., & Ots, M. (2015). *The influencer's dilemma: The shaping of new brand professions between credibility and commerce*. Presentation, AEJMC, Annual Conference, San Fransisco, CA, 6–9. https://wishcrys.files.wordpress.com /2019/03/abidin-ots-2015-the-influencere28099s-dilemma-the-shaping -of-new-brand-professions-between-credibility-and-commerce.pdf

Associated Press. (2014, December 19). Michael Phelps pleads guilty and admits alcohol problem. *The New York Times*. https://www.nytimes.com/2014/12/20/sports/michael-phelps-pleads-guilty-admits-alcohol-problem.html

Audrezet, A., de Kerviler, G., & Moulard, J. G. (2020). Authenticity under threat: When social media influencers need to go beyond self-presentation. *Journal of Business Research, 117*, 557–569.

Aziz, A. (2021). Digital pitfalls: The politics of digitalization in Bangladesh. *Communication, Culture and Critique, 14*(3), 529–533.

Booth, N., & Maltic J. (2011). Mapping and leveraging influencers in social media to shape corporate brand perceptions. *Corporate communications: An International Journal, 16*(3), 184–191.

Brooks, G., Drenten, J., & Piskorski, M. J. (2021). Influencer celebrification: How social media influencers acquire celebrity capital. *Journal of Advertising, 50*(5), 528–547. https://doi.org/10.1080/00913367.2021.1977737

Chambers, N., Kashefpakdel, E. T., Rehill, J., & Percy, C. (2018). *Drawing the future: Exploring the career aspirations of primary school children from around the world. Education and Employers*. https://www.educationandemployers.org/wp-content/uploads/2018/01/DrawingTheFuture.pdf

De Veirman, M., Cauberghe V., & Hudders, L. (2017). Marketing through Instagram influencers: The impact of number of followers and product divergence on brand attitude. *International Journal of Advertising. The Review of Marketing Communications, 36*(5), 798–828. https://doi.org/10.1080/02650487.2017.1348035

Eriksen, T. (2020). *Globalization: The key concepts*. Routledge.

Estudio Echecopar. (2022, September 6). Los nuevos abogados (The new lawyers). *Estudio Echecopar*. https://www.echecopar.com.pe/publicaciones-la-sunat-y-los-influencers-por-que-actividades-deben-pagar-impuestos.html

Freberg, K., Graham, K., McGaughey, K., & Freberg, L. A. (2011). Who are the social media influencers? A study of public perceptions of personality. *Public Relations Review, 37*(1), 90–92.

Gräve, J. F. (2017). Exploring the perception of influencers vs. traditional celebrities: Are social media stars a new type of endorser? *Association for Computing Machinery*, 1–5. https://doi.org/10.1145/3097286.3097322

Hamilton, B. (2022, November 10). Miami's millionaire Cavinder twins are avatars for a new age of athletes. *The Athletic*. https://theathletic.com/3779314/2022/11/10/cavinder-twins-miami-nil/?smtyp=cur

Hearn, A., & Schoenhoff, S. (2016). *From celebrity to influencer*. In P. D. Marshall & S, Redmond (Eds.), *A companion to celebrity* (194–212). John Wiley & Sons.

Herrero, E. (Host). (2022, January 4). Hay que contar hasta 10 antes de compartir algo en tus redes sociales [You have to count to 10 before you share something on your social media] [Audio podcast episode]. Banco Bilbao Vizcaya Argentaria (BBVA). https://www.bbva.com/es/podcast-eva-herrero-hay-que-contar-hasta-10-antes-de-compartir-algo-en-tus-redes-sociales/

Hofstede, G. (1994). The business of international business is culture. *International Business Review*, 3(*1*), 1–14.

Keller, E., & Berry, J. (Eds.). (2003) *The influentials: One American in ten tells the other nine how to vote, where to eat, and what to buy.* Simon and Schuster.

Khamis, S., Ang, L., & Welling, R. (2017). Self-branding, micro-celebrity and the rise of social media influencers. *Celebrity Studies*, 8(2), 191–208.

Kushin, M. J., & Yamamoto, M. (2010). Did social media really matter? College students' use of online media and political decision making in the 2008 election. *Mass Communication and Society*, 13(5), 608–630. https://doi.org/10.1080/15205436.2010.516863

Litterio, A. M., Nantes, E. A., Larrosa, J. M., & Gómez, L. J. (2017). Marketing and social networks: A criterion for detecting opinion leaders. *European Journal of Management and Business Economics*, 26(3), 347–366. https://doi.org/10.1108/ejmbe-10-2017-020

Loiseau, E., & Nowacka, K. (2015). *Can social media effectively include women's voices in decision-making processes?* OECD Development Centre. https://www.oecd.org/dev/development-gender/DEV_socialmedia-issuespaper-March2015.pdf

Martínez, F., & Pacheco, C., & Galicia, M. (2021). The #MeToo movement in Twitter: Fighting gender-based violence. In *International Conference on Information Technology and Systems: Information Technology and Systems* (Vol. 1330, pp. 36–44). Springer VS. https://doi.org/10.1007/978-3-030-68285-9_4

Matthews, M. J., Matthews, S. H., Wang, D., & Kelemen, T. K. (2022). Tweet, like, subscribe! Understanding leadership through social media use. *The Leadership Quarterly*, 33(1), 101580. https://doi.org/10.1016/j.leaqua.2021.101580

Mavin, S. A., Elliott, C., Stead, V., & Williams, J. (2016). Women managers, leaders and the media gaze. *Gender in Management: An International Journal*, 31(5/6), 314–321. https://doi.org/10.1108/gm-05-2016-0105

Miller, C. C., & Somaiya, R. (2011, May 22). Free speech and privacy rights collide on Twitter. *The New York Times*. https://www.nytimes.com/2011/05/23/technology/23twitter.html

Miller, C. C. (2018, February 14). How Social Media Gives Women a Voice. The New York Times. https://www.nytimes.com/interactive/2018/02/09/technology/social-media-gives-women-a-voice.html

Momen, M. N. (2019). Myth and reality of freedom of expression on the internet. *International Journal of Public Administration*, 43(3), 277–281. https://doi.org/10.1080/01900692.2019.1628055

Moses, L. B. S. (2022, August 26). NIL after one year: A free-for-all of "free-market capitalism." *Bally Sports*. https://www.ballysports.com/national/news/nil-after -one-year-a-free-for-all-of-free-market-capitalism

Niesen, J. (2021, July 28). In a divided US, it's no surprise some see Simone Biles as a villain. *The Guardian*. https://www.theguardian.com/sport/2021/jul/28 /simone-biles-withdrawal-olympics-gymnastics-tokyo-media-reaction

Rundin, K., & Colliander, J. (2021). Multifaceted influencers: Toward a new typology for influencer roles in advertising. *Journal of Advertising, 50*(5), 548–564. https://doi.org/10.1080/00913367.2021.1980471

Vogels, E. J., Rainie, L., & Anderson, A. (2020). *Experts predict more digital innovation by 2030 aimed at enhancing democracy*. Pew Research Center. https://www .pewresearch.org/internet/2020/06/30/experts-predict-more-digital-innovation -by-2030-aimed-at [1] enhancing-democracy

MARIUSZ MARCZAK | Jagiellonian University in Kraków

Across Borders in the Digital Era
Challenges of Contemporary Translation

Abstract

Contemporary translation is a challenging activity that involves what has traditionally lain at its core (i.e., the transposition of a text originally produced in one context into another context) (Bassnett, 2014), while simultaneously transcending well beyond it. Due to increased globalization and international-ization (Orlando, 2016; Pietrzak & Kornacki, 2021), which have been induced by the rapid development of information and communication technology at the turn of the last two millennia, language service providers must deal with increased volumes of multimedia and multimodal content (Hofmann-Delbor & Bartnicka, 2017; Snell-Hornby, 2012) e.g., hypertext or social media posts (Desjardins, 2017). As a result, today's translators need to mediate interper-sonal communication in intercultural settings where they interact not only with representatives of different languages and cultures but also with multiple stakeholders in the translation process (European Commission, 2021; Risku & Dickinson, 2009), and—even more intricately—with the digital tools and resources that facilitate translation and the related workflow management (Massey, 2021). This essay tackles the challenges caused by the aforemen-tioned multitier interaction and identifies the competences indispensable for overcoming them.

Keywords: intercultural communication, intercultural mediation, collabora-tion in the translation process, translator competences

Since the turn of the 1980s and 1990s, translation hs been perceived—inter alia—as a form of intercultural mediation, where the translator acts to ensure mutual understanding between representatives of different languacultures—the term coined by Agar (1994) to denote the inseparability of language and culture—and reconciling cultural disparities between them (Bassnett & Lefevere, 1990; Snell-Hornby, 2006). However, due to advances in technology, which mean that today's communication formats involve the use of multiple media and modalities (Desjardins, 2017; Hofmann-Delbor & Bartnicka, 2017) and increased demand for the translation of varied content types in the wake of globalization and internationalization (Orlando, 2016; Pietrzak & Kornacki, 2021), contemporary translation involves other forms of mediation where translators interact not only with source text producers and target text recipients. Additionally, they also engage in mediating intercultural differences while collaborating with multiple stakeholders in the translation process (European Commission, 2021; Risku & Dickinson, 2009), negotiate communication enhanced by various media formats, and handle human–machine interaction while using a range of digital tools and resources with which they facilitate the translation process and workflow (Massey, 2021). As a result, translators face a number of challenges that need to be resolved with the use of adequate competences and 21st-century skills.

Translation as Mediation Between Disparate Languacultures

The 1980s and 1990s saw the rise of what is frequently referred to as the *cultural turn* in translation studies (Bassnett & Lefevere, 1990; Snell-Hornby, 2006), which drew attention to the fact that translation is not only a bilingual activity but also a bicultural practice. Prior to that time, translation was mostly perceived in purely linguistic terms as the manipulation of language forms and structures for the purpose of rendering the meaning of the original (source) text, written in one language, in the target language (i.e., the language of the recipients, or users, of the translated version). That conceptualization of translation was emblematic of the *linguistic turn* in translation studies, represented by Nida (1964), which in turn had been inspired by Chomsky's model of transformational generative grammar (Chomsky, 1957). In Nida's (1964) view, the underlying meaning of particular sentences, identifiable irrespective of the language in which a sentence had been produced, could be translated using appropriate target language structures. At the same time, Nida and Taber recognized that "[i]ntelligibility is not to be measured merely in terms of whether the words are understandable and the sentences grammatically constructed, but in terms of the total impact the message has on the one who receives it"

(Nida & Taber, 1969, p. 22), thus promoting the concept of dynamic equivalence rather than word-for-word translation.

The cultural approach to translation emphasized the need to recognize in translation the inseparability of language and culture, which—as Baker and Saldanha (2019) state—calls for translators to be able not only to shift perspectives between the languacultures involved in the translation process but also mediate between them and compensate for the refraction between the two realities at hand. In other words, translation is viewed as a form of intercultural mediation, "a cross-cultural event" (Snell-Hornby, 1988, p. 26), "communication across cultures" (Quale, 2003, p. 154), or a "relatively high-effort high-cost mode of mediated cross-cultural communication" (Pym, 2004, p. 7).

In congruence with that, the translator is by many (Katan, 2012; Liddicoat, 2016) positioned between cultures and attributed with the power to mediate between languages and cultures (Hatim & Mason, 1997; Taft, 1981)—or languacultures, in Agar's (1994) terms. By and large, the intercultural mediator could be defined as:

> a person who facilitates communication, understanding, and action between persons or groups who differ with respect to language and culture. The role of the mediator is performed by interpreting the expressions, intentions, perceptions, and expectations of each cultural group to the other, that is, by establishing and balancing the communication between them. In order to serve as a link in this sense, the mediator must be able to participate to some extent in both cultures. Thus, a mediator must be to a certain extent bicultural. (Taft, 1981, p. 53)

As Taft's (1981) definition reveals, the primary task of the intercultural mediator is to promote communication, mutual understanding, and interaction between representatives of disparate languacultures by reconciling cultural difference at explicit (expressions) and implicit (intentions, perceptions, and expectations) levels using their bicultural experience and the resulting competence. With regard to translation, in very much the same way, Katan (2012) talks about translation as a process in which the translator "attempts to mediate or reconcile differences" (Katan, 2012, p. 1), while Hatim and Mason (1990) view the translator as one who mediates communication between parties that otherwise would find it problematic and add that it is true regardless of what exactly is being translated, be it "patents, contracts, verse or fiction" (Hatim & Mason, 1990, p. 223)—or simultaneously interpreted, for that matter.

Taft (1981) posits that the mediator (translator) needs to be able to not only shift their cultural orientation but also display the kind of intercultural sensitivity that would permit them to decide on the most optimal translation solutions in specific cultural settings. This perspective on the role of the translator as an intercultural mediator is congruent with that of Hatim and Mason (1990), who maintain that the translator needs to be able to critically read the source text, identify potential disparity at sign (semiotic, textual) and value level, and subsequently produce a clear translation of the original whereby they would resolve any of the problematic disparities identified. Thus, in Hatim and Mason's (1990) view, to mediate between cultures the translator needs to be a critical reader with a degree of bicultural vision.

The conceptualization of translation as intercultural mediation additionally highlights a critical issue related to the impact that the translator may potentially have on how the source text is processed and what message(s) the target text ultimately carries. In very much the same way that the source text authors and target text recipients represent disparate languacultures, with their inherent intricacies, the translator is a carrier of their own languacultural load. Thus, as Hatim and Mason (1990) observe, it is only natural that the translator inevitably brings their own knowledge, beliefs, and attitudes not only to the translation process but also to the translation product (i.e., the target text), regardless of their best efforts to retain impartiality. The same issue was raised by Hewson and Martin (1991/2018), who highlighted the effect that the translator's sociocultural identity is most likely to exert on translation.

Consequently, it is necessary that translators act with caution and ensure that their intervention in the communication process between the parties involved does not exceed the boundaries of what is ethically acceptable, which finds reflection in professional documents, such as *The Code of Ethics and Code of Conduct,* issued by the Australian Institute of Translators and Interpreters (AUSIT, 2012), the *Code of Ethics and Professional Practice* by the American Translators Association (ATA, 2010), the *ITI Code of Professional Conduct* by the UK-based Institute of Translation and Interpreting (ITI, 2013), or the *Professional Sworn Translator's Code* by Poland's TEPIS (2019), to name a few. All these documents emphasize that the translator needs to focus on message transfer and remain impartial while facilitating communication.

In practical terms, it is imperative that the translated text carries the message intended by the author of the source text and has exactly the emotional effect on the audience that was intended by the author(s) of the source text. The translator must not intervene (e.g., to smooth objectional language or imprint the conventions of their own languaculture in the target text only because of what they deem desirable in the face of their own sociocultural background and identity). Nor are they supposed to engage in the provision of advocacy, guidance, or advice to those involved in the communication at hand.

It could be stated that while on the job, the translator needs to occupy a neutral vantage point in order to approach the mediation task in an unbiased fashion (i.e., neither to favor any of the parties involved in the translation, nor to feed their own sociocultural load into the process and its product). For that purpose, they need to step aside and look at both the languacultures in question from what Kramsch refers to as the "third place" (1993, p. 181). While her proposition aimed at facilitating the development of intercultural competence in foreign language learners, the very concept of the *third place* seems to adequately reflect the position from which the translator is to approach their role as an intercultural mediator.

Interestingly, Katan (2016) perceives intercultural mediation as a means by which translators can secure their jobs in a market where computer technologies are being extensively used to deliver translation services. In other words, he sees mediation as a distinguishing feature of human translators, very much in congruence with the views most recently expressed by Massey (2021), who underlined the human translator's contribution to machine translation as added value, which manifests itself in the use of intuition and deliberation, as well as rationality and embodied, embedded, enacted, or extended cognition.

Translation as Interaction With Stakeholders in the Translation Process

The translation process is a complex endeavor that only seemingly boils down to the translator mediating communication between source text producers and target text audiences, as it is not—and it has never quite been—as solitary an activity as it is often, rather romantically, believed. In fact, the concept of intercultural mediation in translation needs to be extended to cover other parties in recognition of two key facts. First, translation usually involves interaction with various stakeholders in the translation process (Cordingley & Manning, 2017; European Commission, 2021), which by no means is a *signum tempori* in contemporary translation profession; even in the Antiquity and the Renaissance (Cordingley & Manning, 2017; Jansen & Wegener, 2013) translators often collaborated with others to complete their translations jobs. Second, as Byram (1997) underlines while discussing his seminal model of Intercultural Communicative Competence, each culture is a complex entity that cannot be delineated by nationality only and which is intrinsically heterogeneous. Bolt (2001) elaborates on that, stating that the heterogeneity of culture stems from the fact that multiple identities can be distinguished both between and within individuals, as demarcated by a range of factors, including age or occupation.

In the fast-growing translation market of today (Chan, 2015; Ehrensberger-Dow & Massey, 2022; Klimkowski, 2015), where translation projects require numerous actors to team up in order to handle the ever-increasing volumes of content that requires translation (Orlando, 2016; Pietrzak & Kornacki, 2021), it all means that translators also mediate in-project communication to warrant efficient progression through the project workflow steps and the successful completion of the project per se. When Tipton and Furmanek (2016) talk about "professional intercultures generated between interpreters and institutional service providers" (2016, pp. 8–9), they refer exactly to what could be labeled as an example of an occupational culture, which is accessible only to those who are involved in it. By the same token, translators and any other individuals (e.g., domain experts or project managers) or groups (e.g., publishers, former clients, or audiences) involved in the translation process can be regarded as representatives of specific professional cultures whose successful interaction needs to be mediated to ensure effective collaboration.

In a paper examining the adequacy of degree, closeness, and betweenness as concepts of centrality in various translation settings, Risku et al. (2016) provide examples of translation networks that were formed by the stakeholders in translation projects administered in three different scenarios: (1) one where an experienced full-time freelancer translated content for author clients, (2) another, where translation of varied text types (e.g., a user guide or an advertising text) was delivered by a team of five in-house translators employed by the translation department of a technology company, and (3) a third, where mostly amateur translators were involved in online collaborative translation of varied content, via an open-access internet-based translation platform.

Although Risku et al. (2016) discuss only three translation projects, the data they provide suffice to demonstrate the proliferation of actors involved in the respective translation networks and the complexity of the interdependence between the network members, irrespective of the scale of the project and its initial setup. The latter is best illustrated by the project completed within the first scenario. Although seemingly dyadic in that it most apparently engaged the freelancer and the author client at the onset, the project actually involved a whole network of stakeholders, comprising the sponsor and head of the project, the controlling department in the client's firm, a reviewer/reviser, a proofreader, a graphic designer, and members of an online translation platform, because the freelance translation constituted a part of a broader project that had been commissioned by the client's organization. Evidently, this scenario confirms that, as O'Brien (2011) reported, even freelance translation may involve collaboration of various parties, mostly due to freelancers' collaboration with translation bureaus.

The second project involved a translation network, consisting of translators, the project manager, the research and design department, the technical writer, marketing professionals, the purveyors of the service portal, and the client, whose complexity and dynamics of member interaction varied from one text type and respective client to another (Risku et al., 2016).

In the third scenario, where the translation service was delivered by amateurs via a dedicated online translation platform, the network involved a huge number of translators (250,000), who were registered users of the aforementioned platform and also acted as translation requesters, feedback providers, and contributors participating in discussions related to the different strands of the project on an online forum, as well as online platform administrators (Risku et al., 2016). The data collected in connection with the last example reveals that even the professional versus amateur status of the translation project does not affect the complexity of the respective stakeholder network.

Overall, the networks that were created to facilitate the workflow in each of the three translation projects discussed above demonstrate the myriad potential communication paths and interaction patterns involved in contemporary translation, which tends to be a team effort. The multiple roles that Risku et al. (2016) identified while examining the translation process within all three scenarios reveal that translators need to negotiate collaboration across multiple occupational cultures (e.g., those of domain experts, project managers, reviewers, revisers, marketing departments, research and design departments, or technical writers). When one is cognizant of the fact that—very much like the source text authors and target text recipients—each of the stakeholders brings to the translation process their own disparate set of explicit and implicit cultural elements that need to be negotiated and reconciled for the greater good (i.e., the successful completion of the translation project), one must realize the enormity of the task that translators face when providing language services. The level of potential challenge is even better illustrated by the complexity of each occupational culture, which—as modeled by Hall's (1976) iceberg metaphor of culture—will comprise a range of behaviors, including the specific use of professional language (jargon) and related terminology, traditions, and customs at the explicit level and perceptions, assumptions, values, beliefs, and attitudes at the implicit level.

Interaction With Digital Content

The rapid development of digital technology, including the introduction and expansion of the internet, the rise of social media, and the appearance of computer-mediated communication tools, has exerted an enormous influence on the nature of translation services required in the contemporary language service provision market (Desjardins, 2017; Doherty, 2016; EMT, 2022; Rodríguez de Céspedes, 2019).

The wide marketing of personal computers (PCs), which began in the 1980s (Hutchins, 2015), induced the emergence of digital content, including digitized versions of general-purpose and domain-specific reference sources, such as (domain) encyclopedias and dictionaries, operating systems (e.g., Microsoft Windows), generic computer tools, business software (e.g., text processors), and entertainment products (e.g., computer games), which with time began to be delivered in multiple languages to serve user needs in various geographical settings.

However, the factor that intensified the proliferation of translatable digital content was the appearance of the internet, particularly in the 1990s, when it started to network individual households rather than academic, research, or military centers, to which it mostly had been confined before. The internet in itself quickly underwent rapid changes, which were caused by growing connection bandwidth and computer processing power. As a result, three major developmental stages, Web 1.0, Web 2.0, and Web 3.0, can be distinguished in the history of the internet, each characterized by specific forms of human–human or human–machine interaction and content types.

Web 1.0, often referred to as the Syntactic Web, spanned the 1990s and was based on the World Wide Web (WWW), which in general terms comprised websites and internet pages (Vanas, 2022). The WWW mostly featured textual content, enriched with a wide range of multimedia, including still and animated images, audio bites, and video clips. As Desjardins (2017) reports, content was also often delivered as hypertext, where the aforementioned multimedia and text were interconnected via hyperlinks, which permitted users to access specific fragments of text and the accompanying audio-video content in a nonlinear fashion. At the same time, Web 1.0 was highly undemocratic in that, as Vanas (2022) puts it, it involved one-way media consumption, with internet users falling into two disparate categories: content producers and content recipients (readers), hence the term *read-only Web*, which has also been used to define the first generation—so to speak—of the internet.

Web 2.0 (Boyd, 2009), in turn, was different in character, as it was largely dominated by user-generated content. It may be stated that Web 2.0 democratized the power relations between its users, by promoting the provision of content by all. In other words, on Web 2.0 users could act interchangeably as both content providers and readers, hence the terms *read-write Web*, *Social Web*, or *people-based Web*, which are frequently used to reflect the nature of the second-generation internet. This kind of Web permitted real-time interaction, largely facilitated by social networking sites and social media, as well as dedicated applications installable and operatable not only from personal computers but also handheld devices, especially smartphones.

Web 3.0, also known as the Semantic Web (Jat, 2022), differs from Web 2.0 in that it is powered by machine-generated, personalized content, which is automatically fed to individual users by algorithms—often supported by artificial intelligence (AI)—on the basis of users' preferred content choices or online habits. Thus, it is sometimes called the *read-write-execute Web*, where users function as both content producers and readers and where operations often executed in an automated fashion, thanks to the implementation of sophisticated technologies such as virtual reality (VR), augmented reality (AR), and intelligence amplification (IA) solutions. Thanks to the advent of broadband connectivity and considerably increased cloud-based storage space, Web 3.0 is also driven by big data, which—when processed and mined properly—facilitates the effective provision of user-customized content.

As Cronin (2013) observes, the instantaneity and accessibility of digital media—or multimedia such as those distributed over the internet—has contributed to the widespread dissemination of translations, which additionally often involve what Kress and van Leeuwen (2001) refer to as multimodal texts based on a range of semiotic resources such as—inter alia—language, image, music, color, or perspective. These, in turn, are often part of larger products such as online content (e.g., websites) or software. The proliferation of digital content has triggered the rapid development of the localization industry, which—as Esselink (2003) observes—established itself on a larger scale and underwent full professionalization in the 1990s. It entails not only the translation of content and software but also, increasingly, elements of programming and publishing. As O'Brien and Rodriquez Vazquez (2020) state, initially localization mostly involved the adaptation of software to the needs of target locales through the translation of the textual elements of user interface (UI), software documentation, online help content, as well as packaging and marketing. However, with the growth in popularity of cloud-based tools and applications, it was extended to cover the adaptation of Web content and applications.

At its simplest, "localization revolves around combining language and technology to produce a product that can cross cultural and language barriers" (Esselink, 2003, p. 4). As Pietrzak and Kornacki (2021) explain, it is a process that involves the use of translation as a means of the adaptation of digital content (i.e., software) for a particular locale, which can be a culture, language, or geographical region.

GALA (2020) elucidates that localization is a complex process that aims to adjust the visual aspects of a product and the related user experience so that the target audience believes it was created specifically for them, but it is by no means limited to translation. The nature of digital content, which usually needs localizing, also necessitates other modifications of the original product, including the adaptation of design and layout so that the target text fits in and displays correctly; adaptation of the sorting functions to the alphabetical order appropriate for the target locale; modification of various elements such as date and time, addresses, numbers, or currencies so that they match the notation systems used in the target locale; adaptation of graphic elements to meet the expectations and tastes of the audience; as well as the modification of content in congruence with the tastes and consumption habits of the target locale.

Localization breeds a number of challenges due to the nature of the content that it involves and the mode in which it is performed. The content is problematic when elements of UI that need to be localized are delivered as fragments of programming code which contain the so-called code strings (i.e., series of characters with variables and corresponding values encoded in a given programming language). As the values usually feature fragments of text, only they need to be translated. For instance, in the string *auth.singinButton* = *"Sign In,"* the variable *auth.singinButton* has the value of *Sign In* in the source language (English here) and it is only the latter that requires translation. As Hofmann-Delbor and Bartnicka (2017) explain, translating string values may be problematic because strings that are delivered by software developers (e.g., in an Excel file) may be very complex and they are usually not accompanied by visuals illustrating which part of UI exactly they encode. As a result, if strings are not annotated with comments, it is difficult to decide how to translate the values that they contain properly. It is demonstrable when the string value of *Edit* in English as the source language is considered. If the localizer cannot establish clearly whether the word is the name of a tool ribbon in a computer program or a clickable button that permits editing, it may be difficult for them to decide whether to translate the word into the target language as a noun or verb, respectively. Strings are often delivered in *.string* format files, which can be translated with CAT tools. However, while a CAT tool may filter out the string fragments that must not be altered in any way so that the programming code is not compromised, and display only translatable values as the source text, it nevertheless will not provide the localizer with a preview of what exactly is being translated, unless the client appends the source code with illustrative materials (e.g., screenshots). Consequently, in their translation choices, localizers need to rely either on their own programming skills, experience, or even intuition. As Hofmann-Delbor and Bartnicka (2017) observe, this kind of self-reliance is often necessitated by the *agile* mode, in which contemporary localization projects are completed due to market pressure for fast product release and programming costs. In this mode, source content (i.e., strings) is delivered to the localizer and returned to the client via online localization management platforms in real time, with the caveat that localizers usually deal with only chunks of content at a time without ever seeing the final product.

Another problem may stem from the actual design of the UI of the software being localized (e.g., the size of particular UI elements) such as buttons. Given that each button is a graphic element of specific size, while translating button captions, localizers must usually observe a specified character limit, which depends on button size. Failing to do so will be disastrous, because if the button has a rigid size, the caption will either overflow its boundaries or part of it will not display at all. Alternatively, if the button expands dynamically depending on caption length, it will not line up with others (e.g., when it is part of a virtual menu). Either way, the product (i.e., the localized UI) will be corrupt.

Yet another issue in the localization of digital content relates to the need to adapt the design and layout of digital source content to the target locale, which was highlighted by GALA (2020). The simplest example of that is the need to redesign the layout of a Web page that was originally designed in a left-to-right (LTR) language when it is being localized for a right-to-left (RTL) language. In that case, text direction is only the most obvious modification that will be required, as the entire page layout will need to change to respond to the reading habits of the users. The desired changes might be introduced by the web developers, in consultation with the localizer(s), but they might as well need to be introduced by the localizer themselves, which would require desktop publishing and web mastering skills.

Last but not least, translating digital content may require what GALA (2020) refers to as the modification of content with the tastes and consumption habits of the target audience in mind. Mooij (2004) illustrates this problem stating that while in advertising in China the use of transcription, calligraphy, and logo designs proves most effective in enforcing the written word, in English-speaking countries the same effect will be achieved by totally different means, such as the use of jingles and onomatopoeic object names. In such a case, localization will be a matter of transcreation rather than translation. Vale de Gato (2020) defines transcreation as a form of literary translation that involves criticism and creativity, but in the translation of digital content, the term has acquired a new meaning to denote the rewriting—so to speak—of the original content to suit the target locale. Munday (2009) exemplifies transcreation by discussing the need to rewrite the original soundtrack, including the language register, in video games to create target-culture appropriate effects of humor, while Chiaro (2009) reports that transcreation may also entail resubbing and redubbing in order to introduce references to popular culture so that the final product is enjoyable for users in a given locale.

A perfect example of the transcreation of websites is provided by the translation service Bubbles (bubbles.com), which demonstrates how the Nescafé homepage for the US customers dramatically differs in design from its equivalent addressed to Japanese customers. While the American version tends to be plain and static, with the product logo in the center and a background video reflecting the popularity of video advertising in the target location, the Japanese version is modular in design and provides product images and descriptions to reflect consumer interests in the target locale; it also additionally bears the logo of the parent company, which is more recognizable to Japanese customers.

Interaction With Technology

Traditionally translated texts were produced in what could be referred to as the pen-and-paper mode, or quill-and-parchment mode (i.e., with the use of now rather obsolete technologies such as reed pens (in Classical Antiquity, between 800 B.C. and 400 A.D.), quill pens (between the 6th and 19th centuries), and conventional Biro pens (from the 19th century onward)). Coupled with the invention of print in 15th century, it meant that up to the 20th century translators had basically relied on hardcopy documents, like scripts and printed texts.

With the advent of computer technology in roughly the mid-20th century, the face of translation began to change toward the increased use of digital technologies with which to augment the translation process. As soon as the first mainframe computers were built in the 1940s–1950s, mostly in academic centers, research was launched into the possibility of harnessing them to perform automated translations, which gave rise to the concept currently known as machine translation (MT) (Somers, 2003). However, research into MT was relatively soon suppressed by the findings of the 1966 ALPAC report (ALPAC, 1966), produced by the Automatic Language Processing Advisory Committee (ALPAC), which had been established at the National Academy of Sciences in the United States. On the basis of research into the effectiveness of translation performed by the machine (computer), the report deemed MT an unfeasible concept, with little prospect for future development. Instead, it recommended that efforts be made to facilitate and accelerate the translation process, thus shifting research toward the development of computer-assisted translation (CAT) tools, which would enhance rather than replace human translation. Simultaneously, despite the negative recommendations of the ALPAC report and severely diminished state funding, MT development projects were commercialized and continued resulting in the release of the first commercial MT system (DeCamp & Zetzsche, 2015), which was made available on a framework computer. Yet, due to infrastructural requirements and excessive cost, MT technology was mostly used by corporate buyers and language service providers.

It was the arrival of the personal computer in the 1980s that changed the situation, thus giving momentum to the introduction of computer technology to translation on an unprecedented scale. With desktop computers increasingly available to individuals and smaller businesses, the 1990s became the golden age of CAT tools, which were to help translators not only deal with increased demand for language services but also ensure consistency between and within texts. What is more, the internet made it possible to distribute CAT tools in a software-as-a-service (SaaS) mode (i.e., in the cloud) without translators needing to install software on the hard drive or use MT systems on optical discs (CD-ROMS). The SaaS distribution mode has not only increased efficiency and improved the availability of translation tools but also helped to draw together the two major developmental strands of translation technology—which had been running somewhat separately up to that point—as MT functionalities were integrated into CAT tools, thus making the latter even more powerful (Garcia, 2015).

Since then, the offer of translation technology has expanded exponentially. As the *Atlas of Translation Technology* (Nimdzi, 2022) illustrates, 800 technology solutions are currently available to translators, including a plethora of software types such as translation management systems, marketplaces and language service provision platforms, business management tools, quality management tools, audiovisual translation tools, speech recognition tools, and the new generation of elaborate, trainable MT systems.

In the fully computerized environment in which most translators work today (European Commission, 2020), they need to be able not only to mediate between source and target languacultures and professional cultures but also interact with the technologies and resources that they implement to facilitate the translation process and workflow management (Massey, 2021). What is more, as the content that requires translation is also digital, translators need to be involved in data curation and management. The integration of digital technologies in the translation process is so great now that increasingly human-in-the-loop systems (Evans, 2021) are being used to deliver high-quality translation, where the translator interacts with the machine and datasets. As Evans (2021) reports, it is the case with adaptive MT, where an MT engine, which is based on deep learning mechanisms, is initially trained with baseline and customer-provided translation data to provide translation suggestions. Subsequently, a human linguist needs to review the raw MT output and provide the MT engine with feedback that updates the MT engine database, so that it can produce better-quality translation suggestions. As the process occurs cyclically in a number of rounds, it interlocks the linguist (translator) with the technology turning the former into but a cog in the wheel. At the same time, the outcome of the process is accelerated and higher-quality translation.

Another dimension of human–machine interaction relates to the cleaning, anonymizing, annotating, domain classification, and bias management of datasets that are used to train MT engines, and ultimately to translate. One of the challenges related to this realm of translation activity is gender bias in MT data. At its simplest, gender bias is the skewness of MT data and MT output toward a specific gender. Mêchura (2022) explains that gender bias is evidenced by a situation where an expression that is gender-neutral in the source content becomes gender-specific in the target content (e.g., when the English word *doctor* is translated into German as Arzt (male form) or Ärztin (female form)). The problem with this kind of biased MT output is that if an MT engine persistently makes false assumptions about which gender form is supposed to be used in the target language, the human translator (posteditor) will need to identify gender-biased words and expressions and decide on what the desirable form is. Although based on AI technology, MT engines fail to recognize correctly what the intended gender form is, which affects the speed and quality of the translation process. As a result, the data with which MT engines are trained needs to be debiased, so that it permits the generation of unbiased translation suggestions.

To understand the debiasing process, one needs to take a closer look at how MT engines are trained and how they produce translation suggestions. Contemporary MT systems represent a technology referred to as neural machine translation (NMT), which is modeled on the complex network of neural connections in the human brain. As computers operate on numbers, NMT engines encode source sentences as sequences of numbers (meaning vectors) out of which target sentences are decoded. Individual words are encoded into sequences of 0s and 1s, but to mark similarities between words, additional vectors are also assigned to each of them. As a result, the neural network that constitutes an NMT engine can compute relations between words and the meaning spaces in which particular words are likely to be embedded, but it does so by recurrently computing and refining vectors for word meanings and embeddings based on the training data that are fed into it. Hence, the need for big data (Yamagata, 2018).

Gender bias—like any other possible bias, for that matter—derives from the nature of the training data that an NMT engine is fed with, which brings to mind the famous line by the English linguist John Rupert Firth, who once wrote, "You shall know a word by the company it keeps" (Firth, 1957/1969, p. 11). If on the basis of the training data an MT model establishes that particular words (e.g., adjectives) tend to appear in the vicinity of words denoting male gender, it will tend to generate translation suggestions accordingly. Simply put, it means that if the training data is gender biased, translation suggestions generated by an the NMT system will be too (Suresh & Guttag, 2019). That gender bias exists is an easily verifiable fact that can be tested by entering a gender-neutral sentence in a selected source language into an NMT system and analyzing the target sentence that the system generates. The following source sentences in English, which all feature gender-neutral nouns as sentence subjects or verb objects (underlined), are most likely to be translated into various languages with the use of gender-biased forms: *The* doctor *told the* nurse *that she had been busy. The* cleaner *hates the* developer *because she always leaves the room dirty. The* engineer *finished work.* and *The* teacher *will be running a parents' meeting on Tuesday.* For instance, if the sentences are machine-translated into Polish, they will all contain the gender-biased equivalents of the originally gender-neutral nouns: *lekarz/doctor* (male), *pielęgniarka/nurse* (female), *sprzątaczka/cleaner* (female), *deweloper/developer* (male) and *nauczycielka/teacher* (female).

The bias is also identifiable elsewhere. As Vanmassenhove et al. (2018) report, in the Europarl dataset, which comprises records of the proceedings of the European Parliament (EP) in 21 European Union (EU) languages, gender representation is highly biased, with the data strongly skewed toward the male gender. When one is cognizant that only 30% of EP speakers are women (Savoldi et al., 2021), one realizes that the bias simply reflects the issue of glass ceiling, which Schluter defines as "a powerful metaphor for the unethical, invisible, and yet virtually impenetrable barrier that prevents highly achieving women and minorities from obtaining equal access to senior career opportunities" (2018, p. 2793). Consequently, TM models trained with the Europarl dataset, due to the gender-biased word embeddings that they involve, will tend to produce automatic translations with the use of male forms for source sentences, including words such as *superb, astute, brilliant, impressive,* and *humble,* and with the use of female forms for source sentences containing words such as *sassy, sexy, cute,* or *beautiful.*

The bias is problematic in that it increases postediting effort, which will be necessary to correct the target text, but, as the above-cited Europarl-based translations indicate, it may also promote and solidify socially unjustifiable and potentially harmful biases. It breeds ethical concerns, especially when it is realized that the issue potentially relates to other kinds of bias, be it age- or profession-related. Therefore, to avoid such problems, those in charge of data curation need to debias the training dataset (e.g., by diversifying the language data that fall into it or annotating the already-existing data with meta-tags carrying gender-related information with regard to gender-neutral elements. It means that linguists (translators) engage in interaction with data while also counteracting gender bias as a social phenomenon by eliminating it—wherever unwarranted—from translated texts.

Competences Indispensable in Negotiating Barriers to Translation-Mediated Intercultural Communication

As it has been demonstrated above, contemporary translation involves communication across four major types of culture: (1) source and target languacultures, (2) the occupational and professional cultures represented by the stakeholders in the translation process, (3) the culture of the digital media, which relates to the multimedia and multimodal nature of translator-mediated communication, as well as (4) the culture of computerized translation technology, which involves interaction with translation tools and resources.

First, translators need to mediate cross-cultural communication by facilitating understanding and action between the producers of the source texts and the recipients of the target texts. Toward that end, they need to be able to critically read the source text, identify potential disparities (expressions, intentions, perceptions, and expectations) between the respective languacultures, and produce a translation that will provide an adequate resolution of the aforementioned disparities. To translate effectively they need to use and manipulate appropriate language structures to mediate and reconcile languacultural differences, and participate in the relevant cultures to develop bicultural vision, which will permit them to shift cultural perspectives. They also need to be able to remain impartial in the process, and distance themselves from the languacultures involved, lest they should add their own sociocultural load to the task at hand, as well as occupy a neutral position not to exceed the boundaries of intercultural mediation withdrawing from advocating, guiding, or advising to either of the parties involved.

Second, translators need to negotiate multiple communication paths through which they will be able to function in multiple professional occupational intercultures, represented by the stakeholders in the translation process with whom they collaborate. While interacting with clients, experts, revisers, and project managers, to name a few, translators need to deal with disparities pertaining to explicit (behaviors, traditions, and customs) and implicit (perceptions, assumptions, values, beliefs, and attitudes) dimensions of the stakeholders' varied cultures.

Third, translators need to interact with multimedia and multimodal digital content that they translate, which takes more advanced technology skills, such as programming, desktop publishing, or web mastering. While negotiating their path through digital content, translators need to adapt the design, layout, and functionalities of software or websites, modify UI elements to match the conventions of the target locale, but also transcreate and build content anew (e.g., by resubbing, redubbing, recording new soundtracks, or creating new graphics) to respond to the tastes, habits, and preferences of the target audience. To do so effectively, they may even need insight into issues relating to areas outside translation per se such as public relations or marketing.

Fourth, in the digital era, translators need to negotiate their own interaction with material resources such as computerized translation tools and resources that they use to facilitate the translation process. They need to know not only how to perform computer-assisted translation and workflow management, but also how to manage and curate data and interact with machines (MT engines) (e.g., in the human-in-the-loop scenarios).

Concluding Remarks

In light of the above, it can be stated that contemporary translation is a multitier and multistrand activity, which in many ways requires the translator to be the jack of all trades, so to speak. What constitutes a challenge is equipping translators with adequate competences that would permit them to function as one and deliver adequate language services in response to the dynamic demands of the professional translation market. To effectively cross borders between source and target languacultures and the occupational and professional cultures represented by the stakeholders in the translation process, and deal with multimedia and multimodal content, translators need to develop what the EMT translator/translation competence framework (EMT, 2017) defines as the language and culture, as well as translation, components, whereas to interact with translation tools and resources, they need to foster the technology component, as delineated by the aforementioned competence framework.

The language and culture competence will help translators develop transcultural and sociolinguistic awareness, as well as communicative skills that are indispensable for intercultural mediation. The translation competence will equip translators—inter alia—with the ability to tackle translation across various domains, on and for different kinds of media, and mediate in a range of intercultural contexts (e.g., while performing website/video-game localization or video-description), whereas the technology competence will permit translators to handle media, file formats, and web resources, as well as implement relevant translation technologies such as CAT tools or machine translation engines.

However, what poses difficulty is to envisage all the desirable competences being developed in academic translator education courses or professional training sessions. The volatility of the contemporary professional translation market seems to call for the development of a set of soft, transferable skills, which will help translators effectively monitor market trends and catch up with the latest changes. To do so, they need to be able to search efficiently for information, evaluate and select most relevant translation tools and resources, further their self-development (e.g., by participating in training offered as part of continuous professional development schemes or via self-learning), as well as display an attitude of openness to challenges and readiness to act flexibly. As a result, what gains particular importance is the personal and interpersonal component of translator competence, which, according to the EMT framework (EMT, 2017), entails—inter alia—planning and time management skills, teamwork skills relevant to multicultural and multilingual collaborative environments, self-learning, and self-evaluation skills. That, in turn, foregrounds the role of metacognitive awareness and skills, which translators can improve "through activating their personal resources and empowering them to meet the market demands of the postpandemic economic future" (Pietrzak, 2022, p. vi).

ADAM NOWAKOWSKI | **CRACOW UNIVERSITY OF TECHNOLOGY**

The Translator's Voice

Introducing the Vvedensky Continuum of
Free Translation Techniques

In loving memory of my sister,
Anna Poniewierska (1981–2023)

Abstract

The following essay focuses on free translation in general, and on a 2002 Russian translation of Timothy Zahn's *Heir to the Empire* in particular. The latter was completed by a prominent translator, Yana Ashmarina, with help from a group of anonymous collaborators, under a collective pseudonym, T. Karrde. Ashmarina was famous among fans of Star Wars in Russia for her overly free translations, abundant with pieces of her own writing inserted in the target text. To refer to this practice, the term *ashmarism* was coined. The essay discusses the curious phenomenon of *ashmarisms*, based on a comparative analysis of *Heir to the Empire* and the novel's Russian rendition, in order to present the ways in which the latter deviates from the original. This analysis serves as a foundation for theorizing a continuum of free translation techniques, which I name after Irinarkh Vvedensky, a prominent translator, whose name remains firmly associated with arbitrary insertions. As presented using examples collected in the process of research, the Vvedensky Continuum of Free Translation Techniques consists of categories such as stylistic shift, overwriting, and amplification. These are fuzzy categories, whose limits blend together. Each technique along the continuum is marked by more freedom and greater deviation from the original.

Keywords: Star Wars, Literary Translation, Free Translation, Translation Theory, Popular Culture, Russian Language

Introduction, or Beyond Free Translation

The debate on the subject of literal versus free translations is probably as old as the art itself. Partisans of the former strive for retaining maximal fidelity to the form and content of the source text, whereas their opponents argue that preserving the spirit of the original justifies the sacrifice of its less important parameters. That said, nowadays both sides of the argument generally agree on the importance of maintaining some kind of equivalence, and prohibit deviating from the original that is dictated not by objective necessity, but translator's will to change a work. Such a claim to coauthorship is considered overstepping the permissible limits of the translator's art. Not only critics and scholars, but also readers, when reaching for a translated work of literature, in most cases expect it to be a proper reconstruction of the original, not a translator's own exercise in creative self-expression.

All things considered, the following essay is inspired by the work of Yana Ashmarina (1963–2015), a prominent Russian translator of over 40 novels, who became famous (or rather infamous) for her excessively untethered renditions of fantasy and sci-fi literature.[1] Her signature method involved introduction of arbitrary insertions, emendations, and other textual changes, which was, to say the least, a rather unusual choice for a professional translator working at the turn of the 21st century. It is telling that the Russian Star Wars fandom even coined a corresponding term for this phenomenon and named it after her. *Ashmarism*, as it is called, refers to a piece of translator's own writing, arbitrarily inserted in the target text. It applies primarily to Russian renditions of sci-fi literature because—as one online user explains sarcastically—"translators of normal books as a rule don't deal with such nonsense" (D.G., 2016). It is seen as a tool for making the target text more interesting and allowing translators to have more significant creative contribution.

From a modern theoretical standpoint, translations conducted in this vein are understandably controversial. However, at the same time, they are highly intriguing on many levels (linguistic, cultural, etc.). Neither Ashmarina's method nor *ashmarisms* have yet been an object of research.[2] Thus, the following essay is intended as a preliminary outline of the problem. It aims to: (1) investigate how exactly Ashmarina's revisions deviate from the original,

(2) analyze her techniques of free translation,[3] and (3) arrange the aforementioned techniques into a continuum.

Method, or In Search of *Ashmarisms*

My study involved three phases. First, I required a piece of literary work and its translation for comparative analysis. I selected *Heir to the Empire* by Timothy Zahn (1991) because it is one of the most important novels in the ever-growing Star Wars franchise. Reason for that being, it is the first installment of the so-called Thrawn Trilogy,[4] which was intended as the original continuation of the story presented in the first three Star Wars movies,[5] long before the acquisition of Lucasfilm by the Walt Disney Company in 2012 and the consequent release of the Sequel Trilogy.[6] The novel is often credited with reviving the Star Wars franchise in the 1990s, after almost a decade of relative dormancy that followed the release of *Return of the Jedi* (1983).

Heir to the Empire was translated into Russian three times.[7] The 2002 rendition was translated by Ashmarina, with a group of unknown collaborators, under the pseudonym T. Karrde.[8] Even though it is a joint effort, the translation prominently features all of the usual traits of Ashmarina's work.

In phase two, I read both language versions of the novel simultaneously. While doing so, I collected hundreds of examples of arbitrary and unwarranted textual changes introduced in the Russian rendition. It needs to be specified, however, that I was not interested in calling attention to unintentional translation errors, most likely caused by the imperfect knowledge of English on the part of Ashmarina's team.[9] I also ignored cuts to the original, since—following the definition of *ashmarisms*—my focus was first and foremost on translators inserting new portions of text, not the opposite. I do recognize, though, that abridgements to this rendition would also constitute an interesting subject of research.

Lastly, in phase three, I organized findings by shared characteristics to inductively determine which translation techniques had led to such deviations from the original. Eventually, I divided them into three fuzzy categories, whose edges blend together.[10] Then, I arranged them into a continuum, which I will now characterize and illustrate.[11]

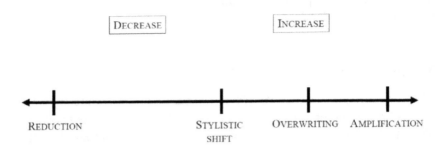

Figure 1. Vvedensky Continuum of Free Translation Techniques

Analysis, or the Vvedensky Continuum of Free Translation Techniques

Stylistic Shift

I decided to name this continuum after another Russian translator, Irinarkh Vvedensky. I will explain the reasoning behind my decision in the latter part of the essay.

The first established set is called Stylistic Shift. When employing this technique, the translator replaces the textual material in the source language with the equivalent textual material in the target language, retaining the original message and imagery; however, they interfere with the language register by using different stylistic measures. Such shifts are unwarranted by the original text, done consistently and intentionally, according to the translator's own artistic vision.

There are instances of regular stylistic errors in Ashmarina's translation of *Heir to the Empire* (later referred to as HTTE–RU, in contrast to HTTE–EN, which is the American original), for example, when Grand Admiral Thrawn, a character known for acting dignified and speaking in a formal manner, suddenly uses an informal phrase "разносить в хлам" (to trash) in place of the rather formal "to obliterate" (see Table 1).

However, there are also instances in which Ashmarina's team changed the register on purpose, as it served her creative vision, and it was consistent with her choice throughout the whole scene or even novel. A perfect example can be found in the middle of chapter two, where Han Solo, a former smuggler and current war hero, engages in a talk with his past colleague Dravis. In the

Table 1. Example of a stylistic error

(HTTE–EN, p. 97)	Remind your gunners once again that the plan is to hurt and frighten, not obliterate.[1]
(HTTE–RU, p. 130)	И напомните, будьте любезны, офицерам, что это акция устрашения, не стоит разносить систему в хлам.
Back Translation	Be so kind and remind the officers that this is an intimidative action, there's no point in trashing the system.[2]

[1] I have underlined words in the citations to emphasize the subject of discussion.
[2] All back-translations from Russian to English of citations from primary and secondary sources are my own, unless stated otherwise.

Table 2. Example of a stylistic shift

(HTTE–EN, p. 26)	Oh, don't give me that hurt look—the simple fact is that you've been out of the business too long to even remember what it's like. Profits are what drives a smuggler, Solo. Profits and excitement.
(HTTE–RU, p. 44)	Не смотри на меня как обиженный жизнью макаут! Факт, что ты так давно не был в деле, что даже забыл, с какой стороны у корабля дюзы. Выгода, вот что заставит контрабандиста оторвать дюзы. Бабки и азарт.
Back Translation	Oh, don't look at me like a hurt makaut! The fact is that you've been legit for so long that you'd forgotten which way ship's nozzles are. Profits will make a smuggler get his nozzles going. Dough and excitement.

English version of the dialogue, the colloquial lexicon is significantly more present than in other parts of the novel, which is understandable, given the background of the characters who are conversing. Meanwhile, the Russian translation (HTTE–RU) sees not only a heavy usage of colloquialisms but also criminal jargon, for example "срубить" (profit through illegal activities) (p. 42), "левак" (someone illicitly working on the side) (p. 43), "быть в деле" (be a criminal) (p. 44), "навариться" (earn money through legal or illegal businesses) (p. 210), "стукач" (informer) (p. 210), "башка" (head) (p. 310), "свалить" (run away) (p. 491).[12] I believe this stylistic shift was employed to make the dialogue more realistic, as Han Solo and Dravis have connections to the crime world. The counterargument could be made, though, that two smugglers, from "a long time ago in a galaxy far, far away," probably should not use vernacular that ties them to a specific group, time, and place in the real world, and thus breaks the illusion of otherworldliness.[13] In other words, Han Solo should not be speaking like a Russian criminal, but he does in this version of the novel. Moreover, he and Lando Calrissian, another former smuggler, are the two main characters who converse in such a manner throughout the whole novel, especially when interacting with each other.

Overwriting

As discussed, a text that underwent a Stylistic Shift stays rather faithful to the original, except for the language register. However, the more the translator changes the text, the more freedom they enjoy and the closer their effort moves to the second technique on the Vvedensky Continuum, which I call overwriting.

There are four basic rules of transformation: amplification, reduction, inversion, and substitution (Krzysztofiak, 1999). The technique of free translation I am going to discuss now bears the most resemblance with substitution. However, in this case, I find the term overwriting more suitable because, first, it implies that a text had been written over, atop of another text, hence replacing it, and second, one of the meanings of the prefix over- is "too much, more than necessary" (as in, for instance, overoptimistic or overpaid). Both meanings describe this technique well. When employing overwriting, a translator follows the sense and thoughts of the original, not so much words, stays faithful to the spirit of an author, while trying to "improve" their work by adding additional, although insignificant and unwarranted, details to the target text, a single word or a sentence, often changing various expressions and imagery.

In the case of translation by Ashmarina's team, overwriting is quite often restricted to introducing an additional adjective, as we see in Table 3.

There are instances, however, in which Ashmarina's team, while staying faithful to the original message, tried to convey it better than the author, most often by using more emotional, hyperbolic, or poetic language. In such instances we can hear the translator's voice creeping in, raising a claim to coauthorship (see Table 4).

The message is clear: droid C3-PO continues to hold a grudge against Lando Calrissian after the events of *The Empire Strikes Back*, in which he

Table 3. Example of a basic overwriting

(HTTE–EN, p. 12)	No, the actual explanation is far more interesting. And far more useful.
(HTTE–RU, p. 24)	– Нет, правильное объяснение гораздо интереснее, важнее и полезнее для нас.
Back Translation	No, the actual explanation is far more interesting, important and useful to us.

Table 4. Example of overwriting in service of expressiveness

(HTTE–EN, p. 17)	"Lando?" Threepio echoed, and there was no missing the disapproval in his voice. Programmed politeness or not, the droid had never really much cared for Lando.
(HTTE–RU, p. 31–32)	– Ландо? – отозвался Ц-3ПО, и в голосе прозвучало явное неодобрение. Программируй вежливость, не программируй, но дроид не слишком жаловал Ландо. Впрочем, удивительно, что Ц-3ПО не плюется, как раскаленный, при одном упоминании Ландо.
Back Translation	"Lando?" said C-3PO with clear disapproval in his voice. Programmed politeness or not, the droid had never really much cared for Lando. Actually, it's surprising that C3-PO doesn't spit in rage whenever Lando's name is even mentioned.

initially double-crossed the main characters. However, the translators used overwriting to enhance expressiveness of this fragment, thus elevating the droid's aversion.

There are also numerous instances in the Russian rendition when overwriting is used in service of worldbuilding, to uphold the illusion of fantastic realism that is so vital to this genre. Consequently, Ashmarina's team creates idioms, phrases, and allonyms that are nowhere to be found in the original but are somewhat fitting to the Star Wars universe—often indecipherable on their own, but clear in the purposely delivered context.[14] By doing so, they stay true to George Lucas's vision.[15] Let us analyze the example from Table 5.

The phrase "blast it" is an old-fashioned informal expression of anger, which is a well-established part of the Star Wars lexicon.[16] Meanwhile, "какого

Table 5. Example of overwriting in service of worldbuilding

(HTTE–EN, p. 5)	"Blast it, Rukh," he snarled. "What do you think you're doing?"
(HTTE–RU, p. 13)	– Екс! Шармута потц!... – грязно выругался Пеллаэон на древнем языке своих предков, – какого ситха, Рукх! – прорычал он уже на общегалактическом. – Вы соображаете, что вы делаете?!
Back Translation	"Ex! Sharmuta potts!", Pellaeon cursed nastily in his ancestors tongue, "What the Sith, Rukh!", he snarled, this time in the universal galactic language. "What do you think you're doing?"

Table 6. Example of overwriting in service of worldbuilding

(HTTE–EN, p. 28)	As far as he was concerned, the only times Wedge didn't stick out like a lump on plate glass was when he was sitting in the cockpit of an X-wing blasting TIE fighters into dust.
(HTTE–RU, p. 46)	Единственно, когда Ведж Антиллес не выделялся из толпы, словно вуки в пустыне, это когда он сидел в кабине «крестокрыла» и надраивал дюзы очередному злосчастному пилоту ДИ-истребителя.
Back Translation	The only times Wedge Antilles didn't stand out like a Wookiee in a desert was when he was sitting in the cockpit of an X-wing whipping another poor TIE fighter pilot's nozzles.

ситха" (what the Sith) is a play on a popular Russian phrase "какого чёрта" (what the devil), used to display extreme confusion, surprise, or aggravation. Ashmarina's team made a rational decision to avoid referencing a Christian concept of "чёрт" (devil), as it would be inappropriately Earthbound in this space novel, action of which takes places in a fictional galaxy.[17] Instead they substituted "чёрт" with "ситх" (Sith)—a name given by Lucas to an evil order of followers of the Dark Side of the Force (see Nowakowski, 2018, p. 69). Arguably, from a worldbuilding standpoint, this was an ingenious, however unwarranted, decision. Moreover, the phrase is repeated throughout the rendition on five separate occasions, which helps normalize it in the eyes of the reader as a common expression in the portrayed reality.[18]

The presented fragment also includes two more textual additions that serve a worldbuilding function. One is an indecipherable, apparently vulgar, exclamation in a fictional language; the other is an insignificant genealogical detail about Captain Pellaeon, one of the novel's supporting characters.[19] Neither of those are present in the source text. They are purely an extension of the translators' creativity.

The number of textual changes and insertions introduced by Ashmarina's team, which serve a worldbuilding function, is vast and deserving a separate study. However, due to restrictions of space, I will limit myself to discussing two examples.

In this example (see Table 6), Ashmarina's team substituted Zahn's metaphorical idiom, "to stick out like a lump on plate glass," with a creation of their own, "выделяться из толпы словно вуки в пустыне" (to stand out like a Wookiee in a desert). Conceptually, this metaphor works very well, as it combines a topographical phenomenon known for being barren, with a fictional species of "shaggy giants" who are "an impressive sight to even the most jaded spacer" (StarWars.com, n.d.). Once again, Ashmarina's idiom sounds natural and believable. Curiously enough, when translated into English, it somewhat brings to mind famous Texas critter colloquialisms.

The presented fragment is interesting for at least two more reasons. First, because of how Ashmarina's team translated allonyms "X-Wing" and "TIE fighter" (as "крестокрыл" and "ДИ-истребитель"), which is another research-worthy subject on its own. Second, because the fragment also includes one more newly coined idiom. "Надрать дюзы" (whip one's nozzles) is a play on a colloquial Russian phrase "надрать задницу" (whip one's butt) but adjusted to a fictional space pilot jargon.

Amplification

We have seen that overwriting can range from inserting a single word, absent in the original, to what is essentially a paraphrase: loose rewriting of a whole portion of the text in a different fashion, in one's own words, while staying faithful to the spirit of the original. Overwriting gives a translator more freedom than stylistic shift, but there is a technique of free translation that results in even more excessive deviations from the source text: amplification.

As already mentioned, amplification is one of four basic rules of transformation. To amplify a text means simply to make it longer. I refer to the technique of amplification when the target text features larger units of translation

Table 7. Example of amplification in service of humor

(HTTE–EN, p. 89)	"Hmm," C'baoth murmured, stroking his long beard, his gaze drifting off to infinity. Pellaeon held his breath … and after a minute the other abruptly nodded. "Very well," he said. "The plan is sound."
(HTTE–RU, p. 121)	– М-м-м, – промычал К'баот, задумчиво поглаживая свою длинную спутанную бороду и глядя куда-то вдаль. Пеллаэон повел носом. Запах форвишского эля казался ему сейчас сладчайшим ароматом по сравнению с духом старого джедая. Какое-то время К'баот размышлял над сказанным. Пеллаэон маялся в ожидании. – Ну, хорошо, – наконец выдал магистр. – Довольно неплохой план.
Back Translation	"Hmm," C'baoth murmured, musingly stroking his long, tangled beard, staring somewhere into the distance. Pellaeon sniffed. The smell of Forvish ale suddenly seemed delightful when compared to the odor of the old Jedi. C'baoth kept pondering what had been said for some time. Pellaeon suffered in anticipation. "Fine," the master finally said. "The plan is quite good."

(sentences or even whole paragraphs) that are absent in the source text, as they are purely translator's invention. Unlike overwriting, which at least stays faithful to the original message, while allowing significant modifications in wording, amplification enables almost-complete disregard of the author, the original text, and even its spirit. One might say that this is the bridge between translation and a piece of literary work based on, but existing independently from, another work (for example, *The Golden Key, or the Adventures of Buratino* by Aleksey Tolstoy, which is based on *The Adventures of Pinocchio* by Carlo Collodi).

There are various reasons why a translator would amplify the target text with arbitrary insertions, such as requirements of aesthetics, ideology, or censorship. Some of these instances I will discuss in the following section of this essay. However, in the case of Ashmarina's rendition, the prime motivation behind using this technique is to add more humor to Zahn's light, but not comedic, novel, possibly to make it more attractive to the presumed target reader, that being a young adult. What supports this presumption is the rather juvenile, or even silly, nature of the inserted jokes.[20] Many of them are made at the expense of the character Joruus C'baoth. Throughout the Russian rendition, he is characterized by scruffiness and bad personal hygiene, as we see in the example presented in Table 7.

I argue that this presented finding is a result of amplification, not overwriting, based on how much text was arbitrarily and unwarrantedly inserted by the translator, but also because of how these additions betray the spirit of the original. This is not a case of a minute biographical detail, casually mentioned to never be brought back again in the story. These are character-shifting moments that break the author's vision.

In the original version of the novel, this scene is sharp, well-paced, and full of tension. Joruus C'baoth is presented with a plan alternative to his own. By this point, the old man had already proven himself to be violent, short-tempered, and unpredictable, hence Captain Pellaeon nervously holds his breath in the wait of C'baoth's response. His eventual agreement comes with a relief. Meanwhile, in Ashmarina's rendition of the novel, the tension is gone. C'baoth is no longer menacing, and Pellaeon seems to be more irritated with him than afraid of him.

In fact, the use of amplification led to several of the novel's characters being slightly reimagined, their fundamental traits often exaggerated.[21] Their comparative portrayal is another topic deserving of separate research. I believe the two most vivid examples of shifts in characterization are the main antagonist, Grand Admiral Thrawn, and his second-in-command, Captain Pellaeon. The two share a Holmes and Watson type of dynamic, which was Zahn's intention. The writer did not want to build his trilogy of books around a grotesquely evil villain but, rather, a cold and cunning, extremely competent adversary whose genius demanded respect. In Zahn's (2011) own words:

> He's competent and capable, enough so that his troops can be assured that they have the best possible chance of winning whatever battle they're being sent into. He cares about his troops, and they know he won't sacrifice them for nothing.
>
> And he's driven by logic and reason, not anger or ego or wounded pride. Throw in the semimystical art thing (through which he can anticipate his enemies' moves), and make him an alien (because the Emperor disliked

aliens and would never give such a rank to one unless he was really, really good) … and when you've done all that, Grand Admiral Thrawn simply falls out of the equation.

I think the greatest compliment Thrawn has ever received came from a US serviceman. (I can't remember if he was a soldier or Marine.) He told me he and his buddies had read the Thrawn Trilogy and had agreed that they would unreservedly follow a commander like Thrawn. (pp. 406–407).

Thrawn was a military commander who fought for the wrong side but was not evil per se, although he could act ruthlessly if necessary. However, much less moral vagueness surrounds the character in the Russian version of the novel, in which he is portrayed as an unapologetic villain. Meanwhile Captain Pellaeon, instead of being Thrawn's faithful protégé, is depicted as a somewhat reluctant follower of the grand admiral, quick to criticize him, albeit only behind his back.[22] The example presented in Table 8 depicts the aforementioned changes in both characters, as well as another variation on the theme of Joruus C'baoth's scruffiness and an additional exercise in comedy.

Thrawn's love of art is established in the first few pages of the novel. He sees it as window to understanding his enemies and then defeating them. In the original version, Pellaeon does not initially share his mentor's dedication to art but understands its usefulness for a tactician. However, in the Russian rendition, Pellaeon mocks Thrawn and sees his fascination as a nuisance. Moreover, a reader of this version of the novel will be aware of Thrawn's cruel treatment of his subordinates. This cruelty is a trait foreign to this character's nature, as he was strict and demanding, but not needlessly cruel.[23] Hence, we see what kind of changes in characterization Ashmarina caused through amplification and not paying respect to the spirit of the source text.

Discussion, or Exploring the Roots

Literary Translation in Russia

Having discussed Ashmarina's approach to translation and the palette of free translation techniques that she employs, I believe the proper way to conclude this essay is to explore the roots of her method. Unfortunately, Ashmarina died at a rather young age in 2015. The number of interviews she had given over the years is scarce, and those are focused on her work as an illustrator. Consequently, finding answers directly from the source is not possible. My

Table 8. Example of amplification in service of humor

(HTTE–EN, p. 47)	"You will now tell me," C'baoth said, gesturing them to low cushions, "how it was you defeated my attack." "Let me first explain our offer," Thrawn said, throwing a casual glance around the room before easing carefully down on one of the cushions. Probably, Pellaeon thought, the Grand Admiral was examining the bits of artwork scattered around.
(HTTE–RU, p. 71)	– Я хочу услышать, как вам удалось отразить мои атаки, – сказал старик, жестом приглашая гостей опуститься на <u>сомнительной чистоты</u> подушки. – Давайте сначала обсудим наше предложение, – сказал Траун, скользя взглядом по комнате, прежде чем занять предложенное место. <u>Потом с подозрением посмотрел на подушку.</u> Опять адмирала заинтересовали произведения искусства, огорчился Пеллаэон. <u>Что можно разглядеть в этой пыли и паутине? У себя на «Химере» он бы вытер подобную грязь последним юнгой, отвечающим за дроидов-уборщиков, но – о вкусах не спорят.</u>
Back Translation	"I want to know, how it was you defeated my attack", said the old man, inviting guests with gesture to sit down on <u>doubtfully clean</u> cushions. "Let me first explain our offer," Thrawn said, throwing a casual glance around the room before taking the offered seat. <u>After that he suspiciously looked at the cushion.</u> <u>"The Admiral got preoccupied with artwork again",</u> Pellaeon thought with frustration. <u>"What can you possibly see through dust and webs? Back aboard Chimaera he would wipe such dirt with the lowest-ranking cabin boy responsible for cleaning droids. Well, to each his own."</u>

attempts to connect with her former colleagues through my contacts in the Union of Russian Writers failed.

However, it is possible to theorize links connecting Ashmarina's method with the Russian tradition of literary translation. Roots of the latter reach back into the early 18th century, when Peter the Great's extensive program of reforms exposed Russia to Western European influences. From there began a steady flow of renditions of secular literature. From that point onward, up until the 1930s, literary translation in Russia can be described as a dance between Neoclassical and Romantic principles of translation, which mostly followed analogous discussions in Western Europe. Maurice Friedberg (1997) explains the two opposite standpoints thusly:

> Theology aside, partisans of free renditions in Western Europe dominated translation during the ascendancy of Neoclassicism when standards of aristocratic decorum were imposed on texts of "barbarian" origin... By contrast, the Romantics showed greater curiosity about other times and customs and displayed less assurance about their own civilization— attitudes conducive to literalism. (p. 16)

Neoclassicists regarded the translator "as a rival of the source text author, with the translated text expected to aspire to higher standards and even to surpass the source text in terms of artistic quality" (Komissarov, 2011, p. 520). This allowed the translator to freely revise the text of the original by introducing arbitrary omissions, additions, and emendations. For instance, Friedberg (1997) discusses attempts made by French translators to "improve" on the works of Homer and William Shakespeare, who were considered overly crude, violent, and vulgar for the public (p. 26). Russian translators followed the steps of their French counterparts. Garbovsky (2004) points out how the 1745 Russian translation of *Hamlet*, completed by Alexander Sumarokov, saw both an introduction of additional characters to the play[24] and an omission of certain scenes, such as the churchyard scene with two arguing gravediggers (p. 511).[25]

The Romantic turn in literary translation brought a more respectful attitude toward the source text, one that encouraged faithful and literal renditions, free from arbitrary liberties in the name of aesthetics or one's need for self-expression. This did not, however, mean that followers of Neoclassical rules of translation resigned from their positions. In fact, throughout the 19th century, literary translation in Russia was in constant flux; sometimes paraphrastic schools of translation would gain the upper hand, while other times favor was on the side of the literalists.

This "dance" stopped in the mid-1930s, under the Soviet regime, when the Socialist Realist translation doctrine, which favored freer forms of translation, became obligatory. The reason for that being, the regime demanded political and ideological censorship. As Friedberg (1997) explains,

> this was done by using the translation as an opportunity to *magnify* whatever elements in the foreign literary work might suggest class struggle, possible admiration for Communism, or any incidents and realia lending support to Communist Party teachings or current Soviet practices. Conversely, whatever did not fit this description was to be minimized or, in extreme cases, blotted out completely. (p. 33)

As a result, translators, seeing themselves as coauthors, flooded the Soviet publishing market with overly free renditions of literature (Friedberg, 1997, pp. 84, 87).

Literal renditions became acceptable in the USSR only in the 1980s. However, half a century of loose attitudes toward source texts left a still-recognizable mark on the tradition of literary translation in modern Russia. It is very likely that Ashmarina, who started working as a translator in the early 1990s, shared this attitude.

Irinarkh Vvedensky

The Soviet translation doctrine might have had an influence on Ashmarina's method, but there was possibly also another factor in play: the legacy of Irinarkh Vvedensky (1813–1855). He was a prominent translator and literary critic, often credited with introducing the Russian reading public to the novels of Charles Dickens and William Thackeray. Although he was not the first translator of their work, his wildly creative renditions made the two writers household names in Russia. Despite competition from other editions, these continued to be republished up until the early 20th century, a mark of the translator's success.

Vvedensky's name quickly became and remains synonymous with what Russians call *otsebiatina* (отсебятина)[26] (that which is added "от себя"— "from oneself"): insertions composed by the translator that are nowhere to be found in the original. Korney Chukovsky (1882–1969), a great theoretician and practitioner of translation himself, had removed about 900 instances of *otsebiatina* when editing Vvedensky's rendition of *David Copperfield* (Chukovsky & Gumilev, 1919, p. 105). The same Chukovsky, however, also had this to say about Vvedensky's method:

Nevertheless, his renditions are wonderful! What does it matter if he is a liar and an ignoramus who distorts nearly every sentence! The fact is that without him we would have no Dickens at all. He alone brought us closer to [Dickens's] work, immersed us in his flavor, infected us with his temper. He did not understand Dickens's words, but he understood Dickens himself… We heard Dickens's real voice, we came to love it. In his translations Vvedensky seems to have dressed himself up in Dickens's costume and mask; he appropriated his gestures and manner of walking… Of course, one cannot tolerate a translator's adding his own words to the text [otsebiatina], but some of Vvedensky's [additions] are so much in the spirit of Dickens, are so much in harmony with his general tone, that one hates to cross them out. Indeed, one wonders whether Dickens would have crossed them out himself, had he chanced upon them! (pp. 47–48, as cited in Friedberg, 1997)

When reading various analyses of Vvedensky's method of translation (see, e.g., Chukovsky, 1936; Levin, 1985; Anufriyeva, 2009), a thought crosses one's mind that his spirit floats above many Russian renditions completed even after the fall of the USSR, those by Ashmarina in particular. I believe she was, intentionally or unintentionally, a continuator of his unusual method, which is quite surprising in the light of Chukovsky's (1936) words: "In our age a figure like Irinarkh Vvedensky is unthinkable. Were he be working now [in 1936], no publishing house would release his translations" (p. 105). Nevertheless, I think it is fitting to name the Continuum of Free Translation Techniques namely after Vvedensky. When discussing excessively untethered Russian translations of fantasy and sci-fi novels, ashmarisms are bound to be mentioned even without Ashmarina's involvement in the translation process. However, it cannot be overlooked that it is Vvedensky's name that is forever linked with this peculiar method and has been ever since the late 1840s.

Conclusion and Further Questions

This essay was intended to be a preliminary outline of the problem, a showcase of an ongoing project.[27] I aimed to discuss several topics: first and foremost, the curious phenomenon of ashmarisms, as seen in Zahn's Heir to the Empire. I then used this analysis to theorize a continuum of free translation techniques. The latter, which I propose to call the Vvedensky Continuum, consists of stylistic shift, overwriting, and amplification.

Finally, the process of developing this chapter has revealed several additional topics worthy of separate studies. I would like to propose them for future research and discussion. They are as follows:

- How much does Ashmarina's rendition of *Heir to the Empire* differ from the other two, by Veselova (1996) and Pleshov (2016), especially the latter, which is believed to be much more faithful to the original?[28]
- Many members of the Russian Star Wars fandom used to be quite critical of Ashmarina's renditions and her deviations from the original. It is understandable, especially since the idea of story canon (the collective belief of the fanbase about the "true" version of events) is vitally important to the intactness of the community. However, what is the reception of her work, when the question of faithfulness is put aside? Does it read better than the more faithful versions?[29]
- What techniques did Ashmarina employ when translating allonyms akin to the Star Wars lore?
- Will analyses of Ashmarina's other renditions help expand the Vvedensky Continuum of Free Translation Techniques?

Acknowledgments

I would like to express deep gratitude to my friends and colleagues at the Department of English (Carpathian State College), School of Communication (East Carolina University), and Chair for Translation Studies (Jagiellonian University). The time we spent together while attending the Across Borders IX conference in May 2022 was the greatest highlight of my 10 years (2012–2022) at Carpathian State College and a perfect conclusion to that phase of my professional life.

I would like to take this opportunity to sincerely thank Aoife Frances Thomas for her most excellent language assistance. It has truly been a privilege to cooperate with her.

I also wish to extend my warm thanks to Patrick Quinn, a fellow listener of the ForceCenter Podcast, for providing me invaluable access to his copy of Timothy Zahn's *Heir to the Empire: The 20th Anniversary Edition*. May the Force be with him.

NOTES

1. Ashmarina rose to fame as an illustrator. She published her solo translations under the pseudonym Y. Keltsky: 19 novels and five short stories released between

2000 and 2016. She also regularly collaborated with a sci-fi writer, Nicolay Yutanov. Their renditions, released under the name Yan Yua, included 19 novels and one short story published between 1992 and 2008. Even though they were a result of a joint effort, all bear her unmistakable imprint. The same is to be said about translations of T. Karrde (Ashmarina with a group of anonymous collaborators): five novels released between 2002 and 2003. Ashmarina's work as an editor of translation publications was extensive as well.

2. To the best of my knowledge, so far, the only scientific attempt to touch on Ashmarina's work as a translator was undertaken by Kabanova and Soina (2018). In their paper, they compared three renditions (including one done by Ashmarina and Yutanov) of Roger Zelazny's fantasy novel *Nine Princes in Amber* from the point of view of translation of onomastic realia.

3. According to Newmark (1995), translation strategies can be applied at the level of the text, whereas translation techniques can be applied to sentences and smaller units of language.

4. Other volumes include *Dark Force Rising* (1992) and *The Last Command* (1993). However, in later years Timothy Zahn revived the character of Grand Admiral Thrawn on several other occasions.

5. The Original Trilogy consists of *A New Hope* (1977), *The Empire Strikes Back* (1980), and *Return of the Jedi* (1983).

6. The (Disney) Sequel Trilogy consists of *The Force Awakens* (2015), *The Last Jedi* (2017), and *The Rise of Skywalker* (2019).

7. The two other Russian translations of *Heir to the Empire* were translated by Irina Veselova (1996) and Kirill Pleshov (2016).

8. Talon Karrde is actually the name of a fictional character created by Zahn and featured in several of his books, including *Heir to the Empire*.

9. For example, it is said that the character of Rukh has a distinct "gravelly voice" (HTTE–EN, 5). In the Russian translation (HTTE–RU), however, this feature of his is described as "замогильный голос" (p. 13), meaning "voice from beyond the grave."

10. In mathematics, as introduced by Lotfi Zadeh, fuzzy sets are sets whose elements have degrees of membership. This concept has also been successfully applied in linguistics as it complements cognitive categorization very well (Antas, 2008).

11. It needs to be mentioned that it was not my goal at the time to count every finding in order to produce statistics and discover the frequency of usage of each translation technique. Suffice to say that every page of the over-500-page-long Russian translation includes at least one.

12. In order to properly identify some of these jargonisms, I used the dictionary of Russian criminal jargon (Zugumov, 2015).

13. The use of modern language by Star Wars characters has been a point of contention among the fandom because the language of Star Wars is known for its

stylized stiffness. Because of that, for example, the line of dialogue spoken by Finn in *The Force Awakens*, "Do you have a boyfriend? A cute boyfriend?" was deemed unfitting by many fans (see, e.g., Scrimshaw & Napzok, 2020). In a similar vein, writer Chris Gore criticized the use of the word "ladder" in the recent *Obi-Wan Kenobi* (2022) series as too mundane, Earthbound, and familiar, and not creative enough (Film Threat, 2022). Also Zahn (2011) mentions how he was chastised for using terms "borg," "corvette," and "hot chocolate" in *Heir to the Empire*. He points out, however, that "those same people apparently weren't bothered by the Millennium *Falcon*, or light*sabers*. It was, though, a reminder that you never know what word or image might jolt someone out of their suspension of disbelief" (pp. 19–20).

14. Allonym is a term coined by Krzysztof M. Maj (2019). It refers to "a neologism that possesses a constitutive worldbuilding function within an allotopy (e.g., hobbit, lightsaber, ansible, imp)" (p. 321).

15. In one of my previous works (Nowakowski, 2018), I praised Lucas's worldbuilding skills by describing one of the very first scenes of *A New Hope* (1977): "The viewer is introduced to a desert planet of TATOOINE, inhabited by species such as the nomadic SAND PEOPLE and robe-wearing JAWAS. The latter are scavengers, who sell discarded or abandoned equipment to the local MOISTURE FARMERS such as OWEN LARS and his nephew LUKE SKYWALKER. Viewers first meet them as Jawas park their SANDCRAWLER in front of Lars' homestead in order to present their used wares. Uncle Owen plans to buy an ASTROMECH DROID and a droid fluent in language of MOISTURE VAPORATORS and BOCCE. In such circumstances Skywalker meets RD-D2 and C-3PO, the story's other main protagonists, and thus his hero's journey commences" (p. 58).

16. The phrase appears three times in *A New Hope* (1977).

17. Such a mistake was not avoided in *The Empire Strikes Back* (1980) that sees Han Solo shouting "Then I will see you in hell!"

18. Table 2 also includes examples of overwriting in service of worldbuilding, for example, "оторвать дюзы" (get the nozzles going), which is a play on a colloquial phrase "оторвать задницу" (get off one's butt). In fact, throughout the novel, the Russian word for butt (задница) gets substituted with the word for nozzles (дюзы) on a couple occasions, thus contributing to the space pilot slang that is unique to Ashmarina's work as a translator. Another example of such wordplay is included in Table 6.

19. As for the topic of insignificant biographical details with a worldbuilding function, it is worth mentioning that Ashmarina's team seems to fixate on the planet Corellia and characters hailing from it. In their rendition (HTTE–RU), Corellians speak with an easily recognizable accent (p. 46), have their own slang (p. 367), are said to possess extraordinary hearing (p. 148), and enter a fight with a signature Corellian battle cry (p. 155). It is very telling that, in the Russian version of the novel,

various forms of the word "Corellia" appear 31 times, while in the original version, only 4 times (exclusively in names of spaceships)!

20. A particularly striking example of an inserted joke is an innuendo on a name of a character Borsk Fey'lya (Борск Фейʌиа). At one point Han Solo refers to him in irritation as Fey'khu… (Фейʹху…) but is cut short, understandably so (HTTE–RU, p. 161). The name happens to rhyme with *khuynya* (хуйня), which is an obscene Russian word for penis. This wordplay is nowhere to be found in the original version of the novel (see HTTE–EN, p. 119).

21. Meanwhile reduction led to one of the novel's subplots, Luke Skywalker's apprehensiveness about becoming a teacher in face of his ill-preparedness, being mostly diminished. The following example shows that much of his self-doubt and insecurity was reduced:

"He wondered why neither Yoda nor Ben had ever told him about this. Wondered what else there was about being a Jedi that he was going to have to discover on his own" (HTTE–EN, p. 147).

"Интересно, почему ни Йода, ни Бен никогда не говорили об этом? Что ж, продолжим самообразование" (HTTE–RU, p. 198).

(Interesting, why did neither Yoda nor Ben had ever talk about this? Well, let's continue self-learning.)

22. According to Zahn (2011), "Pellaeon was named after Pelleas, an idealistic young knight in the King Arthur mythos" (p. 393).

23. On one occasion in the novel, Thrawn does give an order to execute an ensign for his striking incompetence. As he explains: "Anyone can make an error, Ensign. But that error doesn't become a mistake until you refuse to correct it" (HTTE–EN, p. 185). Zahn, in his following work, will make Thrawn more of an antihero, quite a sympathetic one in fact. In contrast, in *The Last Command* (1993) he will spare a life of a general despite his tactical failure.

24. Neoclassical norms demanded every hero or heroine to have a confidante.

25. As comedic in nature, it did not fit the tragic genre, thus overstepping the classical unities.

26. This derogatory term was coined by painter Karl Bryullov. It initially referred to paintings that did not reference reality but were purely a product of artist's imagination (Dal, 2006, p. 758).

27. The idea behind this research was actually born in 2009, when I was looking for the topic of my master's thesis in Russian studies, to be written under the supervision of Professor Vladimir Myakishev of the Jagiellonian University of Cracow. It was back then that I initially noticed how much Ashmarina's renditions differ from the English original. Eventually I decided on a different topic, so this research did not move past the first phase until late 2020.

28. In the final years of the Soviet Union, Mikhail Gasparov (1988) predicted a revival of literalism in Russia, which certainly became true, when it comes to Star Wars novels. As originals became more and more accessible to the reading public, thanks to the growing popularity of the English language and the Star Wars franchise, the excessive freedom of previous renditions was publicized among members of the fandom, thus creating a need for more faithful renditions.

29. Voices can be found on the internet claiming that Ashmarina's renditions are better written and better paced than competing versions, creating a superior reading experience.

REFERENCES

Abrams, J. J. (Director). (2015). *Star wars: The Force awakens* [Film]. Lucasfilm.

Abrams, J. J. (Director). (2019). *Star wars: The rise of Skywalker* [Film]. Lucasfilm.

Antas, J. (2008). *O kłamstwie i kłamaniu* [On lie and lying]. Universitas.

Ануфриева, М. А. [Anufriyeva, M. A.] (2009). *Переводческая деятельность И.И. Введенского как отражение жанрово-стилевого развития русской прозы 1840–1860-х гг.* [The translation work of I.I. Vvedensky as a reflection of genre and stylistic development of the Russian prose of the 1840–1860s] [Doctoral dissertation]. Томский государственный университет.

Чуковский, К. И. [Chukovsky, K. I.] (1936). *Искусство перевода* [The art of translation]. Academia.

Чуковский, К. И., & Гумилев, Н. С. [Chukovsky, K. I., & Gumilev, N. S.] (1919). *Принципы художественного перевода* [The rules of literary translation]. Всемирная литература.

Collodi, C. (1883/2021). *The adventures of Pinocchio* (J. Hooper, & A. Kraczyna, Trans.). Penguin Books.

Даль, В. И. [Dal, V. I.] (2006). *Толковый словарь живого великорусского языка* [Explanatory dictionary of the living Great Russian language] (Том 2). РИПОЛ классик.

D.G. (2016, February 29). Сообщение #104 [Post #104]. Jedi Council. https://www.jcouncil.net/index.html?showtopic=14928&view=findpost&p=10600905

Film Threat. (2022, June 15). *OBI-WAN KENOBI Ep 5 | Hollywood on the Rocks! | Join the Chat!* [Video file]. YouTube. https://www.youtube.com/watch?v=ZKfQsPwrpBQ

Friedberg, M. (1997). *Literary translation in Russia. A cultural history.* Pennsylvania State University Press.

Гарбовский, Н. К. [Garbovsky, N. K.] (2004). *Теория перевода* [The theory of translation]. Издательство Московского университета.

Гаспаров, М. Л. [Gasparov, M. L.] (1988). *Поэтика перевода* [The poetics of translation]. Радуга.

Johnson, R. (Director). (2017). *Star wars: The last Jedi* [Film]. Lucasfilm.

Кабанова, Н. Е., & Соина, А. С. [Kabanova, N. E., & Soina, A. S.] (2018), Проблема перевода реалий-онимов мира фэнтези на примере романа Р. Желязны „Nine Princes in Amber" [The problem of fantasy world onomastic realia translation as exemplified in the novel *Nice princes in amber* by R. Zelazny]. *Ученые заметки ТОГУ, 9*(4), 424–432.

Kershner, I. (Director). (1980). *Star wars: The Empire strikes back* [Film]. Lucasfilm.

Komissarov, V. N. (2011). Russian tradition. In *Routledge encyclopedia of translation studies* (pp. 517–524). Routledge.

Krzysztofiak, M. (1999). *Przekład literacki a translatologia* [Literary translation and translation studies]. Wydawnictwo Naukowe UAM.

Левин, Ю. Д. [Levin, Y. D.] (1985). *Русские переводчики XIX века и развитие художественного перевода* [The Russian translators of the 19th century and the development of literary translation]. Наука.

Lucas, G. (Director). (1977). *Star wars* [Film]. Lucasfilm.

Lucas, G. (Director). (1999). *Star wars: The phantom menace* [Film]. Lucasfilm.

Lucas, G. (Director). (2002). *Star wars: Attack of the clones* [Film]. Lucasfilm.

Lucas, G. (Director). (2005). *Star wars: Revenge of the Sith* [Film]. Lucasfilm.

Maj, K. M. (2019). *Światotwórstwo w fantastyce. Od przedstawienia do zamieszkiwania* [Worldbuilding in fantasy: From depiction to inhabitation]. Universitas.

Marquand, R. (Director). (1983). *Star wars: Return of the Jedi* [Film]. Lucasfilm.

McGregor, E., Kennedy, K., Rejwan, M., & Harold, J. (Executive Producers). (2022). *Obi-Wan Kenobi* [TV series]. Lucasfilm.

Newmark, P. (1995). *A textbook of translation*. Phoenix ELT.

Nowakowski, A. (2018). Translating Jedi and Sith. Proper names in early translations of Star Wars novels to German, Polish and Russian. *Tertium Linguistic Journal, 3*(2), 56–79. https://doi.org/10.1037/ppm0000185

Scrimshaw, J., & Napzok, K. (Hosts). (2020, January 14). Untold tales from *Rise of Skywalker* (Ep. 204) [Audio podcast episode]. In *ForceCenter*. https://podbay.fm/p/forcecenter/e/1579010400

Толстой, А. Н. [Tolstoy, A. N.] (1936/2021). *Золотой ключик, или Приключения Буратино* [The golden key, or the adventures of Buratino]. Проф-Пресс.

StarWars.com. (n.d.). *Wookie*. StarWars.com. https://www.starwars.com/databank/wookiee

Zahn, T. (1991/1992). *Heir to the Empire*. Bantam Books.

Zahn, T. (1992). *Dark force rising*. Bantam Books.

Zahn, T. (1993). *The last command*. Bantam Books.

Зан, Т. [Zahn, T.] (1991/1996). *Наследник Империи* [Heir to the Empire] (I. Veselova, Trans.). Azbooka Publishers.

Зан, Т. [Zahn, T.] (1991/2002). *Наследник Империи* [Heir to the Empire] (T. Karrde, Trans.). Eksmo.

Zahn, T. (2011). *Heir to the Empire: The 20th anniversary edition*. Random House.

Зан, Т. [Zahn, T.] (1991/2016). *Наследник Империи. Трилогия о Трауне. Книга 1* [Heir to the Empire. Thrawn Trilogy. Book 1] (K. Pleshkov, Trans.). Azbooka Publishers.

Зугумов, З. М. [Zugumov, Z. M.] (2015). *Русскоязычный жаргон. Историко-этимологический, толковый словарь преступного мира* [The Russian-language jargon. The historical and etymological, explanatory dictionary of the criminal world]. Книжный мир.

ERIKA K. JOHNSON, SHEENA M. EAGAN, HANNAH GRACE
LANNEAU | East Carolina University, East Carolina University Brody School
of Medicine, University of California, San Diego

Listen to Your Commander

Trust in Health Care Providers Among Veterans and Active
Duty Military

Abstract

Building on the body of literature in the field, this study focuses on
military-connected patients, recognizing their unique position as patients
within a government health system. Not only are military veterans and active
duty military personnel subject to unique health issues, but they are also part
of a unique health system. The research found that trust in news media and
government were lower than trust in science and physicians; there were differences by provider type and rank in terms of physician trust, suggesting that
veterans and active duty military personnel have more trust in those internal
to the military.

Keywords: health care, trust, provider, rank, health communication

Introduction

Trust is an important part of the patient experience and patient–provider relationship; it is because of trust in the collective health care professions that
patients seek care from these experts during their most vulnerable moments
(e.g., Eagan, 2019). However, there has been a trust crisis in the United States—
one that came into clear focus during the COVID-19 pandemic, when many
Americans expressed distrust in government, science, health care providers,
news media, and even in facts or truth (e.g., Gardner et al., 2022). According
to a recent poll, fewer than one in three Americans think that government
officials are credible, and the majority of Americans find it difficult to assess
what is real versus fake news (Edelman Intelligence, 2018). Additionally, over

the past several decades, medical mistrust has emerged as an important and prevalent public health problem (e.g., Izquierdo et al., 2018). According to one survey, only 23% of Americans express a great deal or quite a lot of confidence in the health care system (Richmond, 2021).

Health system distrust is informed by unfavorable expectations or wariness of an organization's competence and values (Hall et al., 2001). Medical mistrust is bad for patient health as it is associated with lack of willingness to seek care, lower adherence to treatment plans, and poorer self-reported health (Armstrong et al., 2006; Yang et al., 2011; Whetten et al., 2006). According to the literature, health system distrust tends to be higher for minority or non-dominant groups: women versus men and Black versus White patients (Armstrong et al., 2008; Griffith et al., 2021). This difference is credited to negative health care encounters, personal experiences of discrimination, the legacy of structural racism and systemic discrimination, as well as the historical legacies of unethical medical experiments and other systems-level abuses perpetrated by the dominant group against the nondominant group (Armstrong et al., 2008; Griffith et al., 2021).

Our research aims to examine distrust, looking at mistrust in a health system or provider, as well as the lack of trust in government (e.g., due to high-profile scandals related to military and Veterans Affairs (VA) health care, we focus on military-connected populations). Building on the body of literature in the field, this study focuses on military-connected patients, recognizing their unique position as patients within a government health system. Not only are military veterans and active duty military personnel subject to unique health issues (Krause-Parello & Morales, 2018), but they are also part of a unique health system.

Veterans and active duty military represent unique populations as opposed to the general population or laypersons in the United States. For instance, veterans and active duty military personnel are subject to health issues that civilians do not face (e.g., burn pit injuries and injuries from chemicals, etc.) (Krause-Parello & Morales, 2018). They also deal with mental health issues that are more prevalent in military populations, such as posttraumatic stress disorder (PTSD) (Lehavot, et al., 2018). While civilians may deal with similar mental health issues, the veteran and military populations experiences are different/unique to their experiences (e.g., Fortney et al., 2016; Lehavot et al., 2018; Liu et al., 2019; Shepardson et al., 2019).

Additionally, the US military is inherently hierarchical and has a collectivistic culture (McGurk et al., 2006). This population is purposefully separate from broader civilian society. When a civilian enters the military population, they are indoctrinated into military culture; this process involves making an individual part of a collective order, which may excise self and self-interested motivations, as well as some individual identity characteristics (McGurk et al., 2006). Scholars have posited that this process originates with basic training in the US Armed Forces (McGurk et al., 2006). Reintegration and integration (i.e., becoming a part of the military culture vs. the general population) may also play roles in military culture in regard to this topic. As noted, military culture is distinct in regard to norms more generally and in terms of communication based on role or rank (Olenick et al., 2015). Those in the military may communicate interpersonally differently from the general population; this takes place via integration engaged with in basic training and beyond, as well as in integration for those no longer in active duty (e.g., veterans) (Olenick et al., 2015).

Beyond that, military-connected populations may have the experience of receiving health care from the institution that has caused the injury or issue for which they are seeking care. The military-connected population takes on significant risks (to life, limb, etc.) for the government it serves, while also relinquishing significant control, both factors that the researchers posit could impact perceived trust in government and health systems. Additionally, the military and veteran health systems have been the focus of scandals that have led this population to question the values of the system itself, likely causing the erosion of trust (see review below). In the next section, we will briefly summarize high-profile scandals related to military and VA health care.

Background—Trust and Scandal in the Military/VA Health System

In early 2007, the *Washington Post* published two articles outlining several cases of patient neglect and substandard living conditions at the famous military hospital Walter Reed in Washington, DC. The reports dated back to 2004 and outlined, "Seventy-five percent of the troops polled by Walter Reed ... said their experience was 'stressful.' Suicide attempts and unintentional overdoses from prescription drugs and alcohol, which is sold on post, are part of the narrative here" (Priest & Hull, 2007). According to the reports, the neglect resulted in at least two preventable deaths and significant suffering for many. More broadly, this scandal prompted public and media attention, which in turn prompted several congressional and executive actions, including the resignations of several high-ranking officers (Bowman, 2011).

In 2014, the Department of Veterans Affairs was at the center of a scandal over massive wait times in its health care system (Jones et al., 2021). Of particular focus in this scandal was one hospital in Phoenix, Arizona. According to reports (Jones et al., 2021), officials at the Phoenix VA hospital kept a secret waitlist of veterans seeking health care. The secret waitlist showed that patients had to wait an average of 115 days to be seen by a primary care provider and was purposefully kept undisclosed to the federal regulators who were responsible for oversight. Instead, official documents vastly underreported wait times for Phoenix-based veterans to see a doctor and as many as 40 veterans died on waitlists at the Phoenix hospital (Jones et al., 2021). The scandal and news coverage fueled ongoing political debate over access to VA care and was one of many factors contributing to the US Congress passing the 2014 Veterans Access, Choice, and Accountability Act (Jones et al., 2021). This legislation expanded veteran eligibility to receive health care purchased by the VA from the private sector (Jones et al., 2021).

While the negative publicity influenced policy and health system changes, the direct impact of this media coverage on veterans' distrust of the VA health care system is largely speculative. However, the past few decades have seen growing literature (see section below) on the connection between trust and health (care) behaviors in military-connected populations. The next section offers a brief overview of existing literature, highlighting how medical mistrust impacts specific populations of military-connected patients.

Mistrust and Specific Populations

Several studies have investigated trust in a variety of specific subsets of military-connected patients. These studies examine minorities such as African American, female, transgender, and gender nonbinary people (e.g., Izquierdo et al., 2018). Research has also explored trust as related to specific conditions, including PTSD, Gulf War Illness, and COVID-19 (e.g., Kopacz et al., 2018).

A 2016 study employed focus group-style workshops to engage with African American veterans living in south Los Angeles and found that "trust in the VA was generally low" (Izquierdo et al., 2018). This study identified various themes related to trust, including: functional barriers to accessing VA health care services; insensitive VA health care environment; lack of trust in the VA health care system; and veteran status as disadvantageous for accessing non-VA community services (Izquierdo et al., 2018). Another study of 32 African American veterans at three VA hospitals assessed HIV conspiracy beliefs and mistrust in physicians providing HIV care (Mattocks et al., 2017). This study employed semistructured interviews designed to allow respondents freedom of expression related to personal history with HIV, and their perceptions of living with HIV, as well as views on HIV conspiracy beliefs and related health care. The study identified major themes related to trust, particularly on veterans' suspicion of HIV treatment regimens, including speculation/beliefs that the government uses HIV to control minority populations and that the Veterans Affairs health care providers may play a role in withholding HIV treatment. Additionally, several participants in this study disclosed an unwillingness to follow the prescribed treatment recommendations related to their beliefs in HIV conspiracy theories (Mattocks et al., 2017). Since this research suggests that patients may avoid or delay seeking health care from a system they do not trust, this military-specific research highlights the unique position of military-connected patients as recipients of health care from a government system that is often at the center of scandal and distrust, based on the studies discussed.

There is growing recognition that military-connected populations from other nondominant groups report low trust, including female, transgender, and gender-diverse populations. In a 2017 study of 37 female Vietnam and post-Vietnam (1975–1998) era veterans, participants highlighted the perception that the VHA's (Veterans Health Administration) environment was unwelcoming; being "surrounded by men" yielded emotions ranging from discomfort and mistrust to severe anxiety (Kehle-Forbes et al., 2017). A 2019 study of 30 transgender or gender diverse veterans, employed semistructured interviews to explore barriers and facilitators to research participation, recommendations for improving outreach and engagement, and overall perspectives about priorities in health services research. Participants cited privacy concerns of being "outed" and potentially having VHA benefits revoked, in addition to a level of distrust in researchers' intentions as barriers to participating in studies (Wolfe et al., 2021).

Another study sought to examine and identify relationships linking general trust with select health outcomes in a mixed sample of 472 veterans and service members with a self-reported history of deployment to a combat theater and PTSD symptomatology. The findings of this work suggest that trust correlates with various health outcomes in veterans and service members affected by combat-related PTSD (Kopacz et al., 2018).

A 2021 qualitative study examined how experiences with institutions influence perceptions of medical care among US military veterans living with Gulf War Illness (GWI) (Bloeser et al., 2021). This illness was selected for study because of broader research showing that patients with medically unexplained symptoms (MUS) often have poor quality of life and health outcomes. Although this study was not explicitly looking at trust, its discussion focuses on trust-adjacent issues. Of particular interest is the concept of "institutional betrayal" (Bloeser et al., 2021). This concept refers to situations in which the institutions people depend on for safety and well-being cause them harm. Experiences of institutional betrayal both during active military service and when first seeking treatment after active duty service appeared to shape perceptions of health care in this sample. Specifically, veterans expressed the belief that the military failed to protect them from environmental exposures (Bloeser et al., 2021). This is a clear breach of trust, and evidently a cause of distrust in military-provided services, such as health care.

The mistrust of military-connected populations was again highlighted throughout the COVID-19 pandemic when mistrust was prevalent among the broader American population (Gardner et al., 2022). In a 2022 survey of Veterans, almost 40% of participants stated that they would not receive the COVID-19 vaccine (Gardner et al., 2022). In-depth interviews revealed several barriers to vaccination, including lack of trust in the government and vaccine manufacturers, concerns about the speed of vaccine development, fear of side effects, and fear the vaccine was a tool of racism (Gardner et al., 2022).

Trust Variables

Researchers have found that members of the military may trust higher-rank physicians more than lower-rank physicians; patient trust in higher rank has additionally been connected to uniformed officers with uniform/dress of the higher-rank officer as a visual cue (Trowbridge & Pearson, 2013). However, this could be different in terms of *health care settings*. Veterans and active duty military members may have a lack of trust in health care and/or government authorities; for example, veterans may be less likely to seek health care/providers (Lee & Begley, 2017), and veterans are hesitant to participate in evidence-based health research that could improve outcomes (e.g., Littman et al., 2018). There is a need for research into trust because research has found that veterans have identified areas of improvement for health care (Flynn et al., 2019). Health care promotion and communication were identified as areas, in addition to several other concerns, such as care and access models (Flynn et al., 2019).

With that, this research measured trust in news media, trust in government, physician trust, and trust in science. The research also specifically examined whether trust in physicians differed by rank.

Research Question 1: Do veterans and active duty personnel trust news media, physicians, science, and government entities?

Research Question 2: Does trust in provider vary by rank of physician (in relation to the patient)?

Method

This study used a survey method to ascertain the relationship between the variables government trust (Song & Lee, 2016), news trust (Kalogeropoulos et al., 2019), rank of provider, trust in science (Agley, 2020), and provider trust (Dong et al., 2014) among veterans and active duty military (i.e., currently serving or a veteran of the US Uniformed Services: Air Force, Army, Coast Guard, Public Health Service, Navy, Marines, or Space Force).

Sample

The sample consisted of veterans and US Armed Forces members; we specified that participants must currently serve or be veterans of the US Uniformed Services: Air Force, Army, Coast Guard, Public Health Service, Navy, Marines, or Space Force. These participants were recruited through snowball and convenience sampling. A total of 52 participants started the survey, and a total of 36 completed the survey.

Of the 36 participants who completed the survey, 66.66% reported as male, 30.56% reported as female, and 2.78% reported as other (1 out of 36 participants who answered the question). Educational background was as follows: some college, 13.89%; 2-year degree, 33.33%; 4-year degree, 30.56%; professional degree, 13.89%; doctoral degree, 8.33%. In terms of race, 66.67% reported as White; Black, 12.82%; American Indian or Alaska Native, 5.13%; Asian, 5.13%; Native Hawaiian or Pacific Islander, 2.56%; Other, 7.69%. The average age was

38.75 years old. In terms of political affiliation, the breakdown was: Republican, 27.78%; Democrat, 27.78%; Other, 44.44%.

Procedure

The survey took 5–10 minutes to complete, and participants kindly volunteered their anonymous participation. Participants were recruited through social media promotions as well as targeted recruitment by way of researcher connections with military populations. Responses were recorded using Qualtrics survey software.

Measures

In regard to the measures, there were three statements for government trust (α = .90; e.g., "I trust the federal government"; Song & Lee, 2016), one for rank of provider ("Is your primary doctor or health care, team/providers, at a higher rank than you are?"), and one for trust in science ("Please report your trust in science/scientists," from 5 = *a great deal* to 1 = *not at all*; Agley, 2020). The research also measured provider trust (α = .94; 10 statements; e.g., "I think my doctor's treatment decisions are best for me," from 1 = *strongly disagree* to 5 = *strongly agree*; Dong et al., 2014), and had three statements for news trust (α = .83; e.g., "I trust the news media," from 1 = *strongly disagree* to 5 = *strongly agree*; Kalogeropoulos et al., 2019).

Results

In terms of the results, the following was found for the variables considered: trust in news media, (M = 2.35; SD = 1.14), government trust (M = 2.70; SD = 1.19), federal (M = 2.62; SD = 1.42), state (M = 2.59; SD = 1.32), local (M = 2.89; SD = 1.17); all had values that fell below 3 on the scale from 1 = *strongly disagree*; 5 = *strongly agree*. Trust in science (M = 4.16; SD = 0.76) and physician trust (M = 3.75; SD = 0.96) were higher than the middle point of 3 from 1 = *strongly disagree* to 5 = *strongly agree*.

In regard to rank of provider, 23.32% reported "Yes," 5.41% reported "No," 67.57% reported "My doctor or provider(s) are NON-military (e.g., VA, civilian, etc.)," and 2.70% reported "Other." In regard to differences in means of doctor trust by rank, the results were as follows (in response to "Is your primary doctor or health care team/providers at a higher rank than you are?"):

Yes, $N = 9$, $M = 3.98$, $SD = 0.57$; No, $N = 2$, $M = 4.50$, $SD = 0.71$; Nonmilitary provider/doctor, $N = 25$, $M = 3.58$, $SD = 1.07$; Other, $N = 1$, $M = 4.42$; Total, $N = 37$, $M = 3.75$, $SD = 0.96$.

Discussion

Trust was generally low among all participants in news media and government. Respondents reported high levels of distrust in the federal government, ranking local government as more trustworthy and consistently ranking the federal government as the least trustworthy. Conversely, trust in science was higher, as was general physician trust. Respondents reported high levels of trust in their providers with the majority of respondents reporting high levels of trust in the credentials/skills of providers and trusting that they have their best interest in mind. Also, there were high levels of trust in the confidentiality of the patient–provider relationship with the majority of respondents strongly disagreeing with the statement, "I believe that my provider will have my information with unauthorized parties."

This was of particular interest, as a perceived lack of patient–provider confidentiality has been previously cited as a barrier to care (Eagan, 2019). Since trust may be higher in future/prospective research in the dominant group (White/male) when compared to the nondominant (non-White/nonmale), the high levels of trust rated in our study could be a function of the predominantly White male sample. Future research should target minority populations for comparison.

Our research also specifically examined whether trust in physicians differed by rank. There were subtle differences between higher- and lower-rank doctors in terms of trust, while military providers were generally more trusted than nonmilitary providers. Although the differentiation (military vs. nonmilitary provider) may not adequately capture the nuance of nonmilitary providers within military/VA health systems, the fact that the participants had higher trust toward any type of military doctor, as opposed to nonmilitary, warrants further study. This indicated to the researchers that military culture strongly buttresses internal military trust and that this finding may have a connection to military integration and indoctrination, discussed in the literature (e.g., McGurk et al., 2006).

Since the majority of respondents did not use military health care (over 67%), the preliminary findings from this study offer a greater understanding of those who do not engage with military/VA health systems and offers a more nuanced understanding of trust in the VA. According to the VA's most recent trust report, a majority of veterans trust the VA. Internal data from April 2022 to June 2022 on VA trust indicates that more than 76% of veterans trust the VA (Department of Veteran Affairs, n.d.). This VA-wide trust score is compiled by surveying approximately 257,000 randomly selected veterans with recent interactions with VA products and services. However, this data does not fully capture those veterans who seek care outside of the VA, either by choice or because of a lack of access.

Future Research and Limitations

One limitation of the research was sample size. It was difficult to generate statistical inferences due to this and so this work became quite exploratory and based on descriptive statistics. This study originally aimed to probe the following question: Do members of the military trust higher-rank physicians more than lower-rank physicians (as a follow-up to Trowbridge & Pearson, 2013)? The research team will work to improve sample size and expand the study so inferential stats can be performed (e.g., the question of whether rank and other salient variables statistically relate to provider and science information trust). This population or sample is difficult to access because of veteran protections, unlike the college student population or other convenience samples. Military or veteran participants may also not trust those external to the military culture and may be hesitant to participate in research in general (e.g., evidence-based health care research; Littman et al., 2018).

Future research should also examine reintegration theory and explore indoctrination; according to reintegration theory (Elnitsky et al., 2017), military members might feel closer to their military counterparts than family, friends, colleagues, etc. In terms of indoctrination, an individual presumably becomes a part of a collective and in many cases a hierarchy (McGurk et al., 2006). There are opportunities for exploring media and expression applications like examining military culture on social media, such as TikTok.

Future research may also want to consider veterans and active duty military members separately. It is also worth considering that all doctors in the military are officers rather than enlisted, and hold a minimum rank of 0-3 (Trowbridge & Pearson, 2013; Military Officer Training, 2022) Other military populations in other cultures or countries may also be considered, as well as specific populations (e.g., women in the military, transgender/nonbinary populations, LGBT populations, etc.). Trust and adjacent variables could differ within these populations taken separately. More self-identifying items or variables (e.g., sea time or deployment type, officer or enlisted) may also clarify the locus of mistrust (if any). There may also be opportunities to differentiate between trust in providers for physical health care versus mental health care. A methodological change may also be considered as a future research opportunity. Qualitative methods, like in-depth interviews and focus groups, with help from informants can help researchers identify other informants/participants (unless the military population is uncomfortable). Qualitative methods may also help researchers uncover more information that may not be gleaned from the survey or other quantitative methods (e.g., reasoning behind trust opinions and military culture).

REFERENCES

Agley, J. (2020). Assessing changes in US public trust in science amid the COVID-19 pandemic. *Public Health, 183*, 122–125. https://doi.org/10.1016/j.puhe.2020.05.004

Armstrong, K., McMurphy, S., Dean, L. T., Micco, E., Putt, M., Halbert, C. H., ... & Shea, J. A. (2008). Differences in the patterns of health care system distrust between blacks and whites. *Journal of General Internal Medicine, 23*(6), 827–833.

Armstrong, K., Rose, A., Peters, N., Long, J. A., McMurphy, S., & Shea, J. A. (2006). Distrust of the health care system and self-reported health in the United States. *Journal of General Internal Medicine, 21*(4), 292–297.

Bloeser, K., McCarron, K. K., Merker, V. L., Hyde, J., Bolton, R. E., Anastasides, N., ... & McAndrew, L. M. (2021). "Because the country, it seems though, has turned their back on me": Experiences of institutional betrayal among veterans living with Gulf War Illness. *Social Science & Medicine, 284*, 114211.

Bowman, T. (2011, August 31). Walter Reed was the Army's wake-up call in 2007. *NPR.* https://www.npr.org/2011/08/31/139641856/in-2007-walter-reed-was-the-armys-wakeup-call

Department of Veteran Affairs. (n.d.). *Veteran trust in VA.* Department of Veterans Affairs. https://www.va.gov/initiatives/veteran-trust-in-va/

Dong, E., Liang, Y., Liu, W., Du, X., Bao, Y., Du, Z., & Ma, J. (2014). Construction and validation of a preliminary Chinese version of the Wake Forest Physician Trust Scale. *Medical Science Monitor: International Medical Journal of Experimental and Clinical Research, 20*, 1142–1150. https://doi.org/10.12659/MSM.889992

Eagan, S. M. (2019). Menstrual suppression for military women: Barriers to care in the United States. *Obstetrics & Gynecology, 134*(1), 72–76.

Edelman Intelligence. (2018). *Edelman trust barometer.* Edelman Intelligence. https://www.edelman.com/sites/g/files/aatuss191/files/2018-10/2018 _Edelman_TrustBarometer_Executive_Summary_Jan.pdf

Elnitsky, C. A., Blevins, C. L., Fisher, M. P., & Magruder, K. (2017). Military service member and veteran reintegration: A critical review and adapted ecological model. *American Journal of Orthopsychiatry, 87*(2), 114.

Falvo, M. J., Bradley, M., & Brooks, S. M. (2014). Is deployment an "exposure" in military personnel? *Journal of Occupational and Environmental Medicine, 56*(11), e139–e140.

Flynn, L., Krause-Parello, C., Chase, S., Connelly, C., Decker, J., Duffy, S., ... & Weglicki, L. (2019). Toward veteran-centered research: A veteran-focused community engagement project. *Journal of Veterans Studies, 4*(2), 265–277.

Fortney, J. C., Curran, G. M., Hunt, J. B., Cheney, A. M., Lu, L., Valenstein, M., & Eisenberg, D. (2016). Prevalence of probable mental disorders and help-seeking behaviors among veteran and non-veteran community college students. *General Hospital Psychiatry, 38*, 99–104.

Gardner, J., Brown, G., Vargas-Correa, J., Weaver, F., Rubinstein, I., & Gordon, H. S. (2022). An assessment of veterans attitudes and willingness to receiving the COVID-19 vaccine: A mixed methods study. *BMC Infectious Diseases, 22*(1), 1–10.

Griffith, D. M., Bergner, E. M., Fair, A. S., & Wilkins, C. H. (2021). Using mistrust, distrust, and low trust precisely in medical care and medical research advances health equity. *American Journal of Preventive Medicine, 60*(3), 442–445.

Hall, M. A., Dugan, E., Zheng, B., & Mishra, A. K. (2001). Trust in physicians and medical institutions: What is it, can it be measured, and does it matter? *The Milbank Quarterly, 79*(4), 613–639.

Izquierdo, A., Ong, M., Jones, F., Jones, L., Ganz, D., & Rubenstein, L. (2018). Engaging African American veterans with health care access challenges in a community partnered care coordination initiative: a qualitative needs assessment. *Ethnicity & Disease, 28*(Suppl. 2), 475.

Jones, A. L., Fine, M. J., Taber, P. A., Hausmann, L. R., Burkitt, K. H., Stone, R. A., & Zickmund, S. L. (2021). National media coverage of the Veterans Affairs waitlist scandal: effects on veterans' distrust of the VA health care system. *Medical Care, 59*(6 Suppl. 3), S322.

Kalogeropoulos, A., Suiter, J., Udris, L., & Eisenegger, M. (2019). News media trust and news consumption: Factors related to trust in news in 35 countries. *International Journal of Communication (Online)*, 3672.

Kehle-Forbes, S. M., Harwood, E. M., Spoont, M. R., Sayer, N. A., Gerould, H., & Murdoch, M. (2017). Experiences with VHA care: A qualitative study of US women veterans with self-reported trauma histories. *BMC Women's Health*, *17*(1), 1–8.

Kopacz, M. S., Ames, D., & Koenig, H. G. (2018). Association between trust and mental, social, and physical health outcomes in veterans and active duty service members with combat-related PTSD symptomatology. *Frontiers in Psychiatry, 9*, 408.

Krause-Parello, C. A., & Morales, K. A. (2018). Military veterans and service dogs: A qualitative inquiry using interpretive phenomenological analysis. *Anthrozoös*, *31*(1), 61–75.

Lee, D., & Begley, C. E. (2017). Delays in seeking health care: comparison of veterans and the general population. *Journal of Public Health Management and Practice, 23*(2), 160–168.

Lehavot, K., Katon, J. G., Chen, J. A., Fortney, J. C., & Simpson, T. L. (2018). Post-traumatic stress disorder by gender and veteran status. *American Journal of Preventive Medicine, 54*(1), e1–e9.

Littman, A. J., True, G., Ashmore, E., Wellens, T., & Smith, N. L. (2018). How can we get Iraq-and Afghanistan-deployed US Veterans to participate in health -related research? Findings from a national focus group study. *BMC Medical Research Methodology, 18*(1), 1–10.

Liu, Y., Collins, C., Wang, K., Xie, X., & Bie, R. (2019). The prevalence and trend of depression among veterans in the United States. *Journal of Affective Disorders, 245*, 724–727.

Mattocks, K. M., Gibert, C., Fiellin, D., Fiellin, L. E., Jamison, A., Brown, A., & Justice, A. C. (2017). Mistrust and endorsement of human immunodeficiency virus conspiracy theories among human immunodeficiency virus–infected African American veterans. *Military Medicine, 182*(11–12), e2073–e2079.

McGurk, D., Cotting, D. I., Britt, T. W., & Adler, A. B. (2006). Joining the ranks: The role of indoctrination in transforming civilians to service members. In A. B. Adler, C. A. Castro, & T. W. Britt (Eds.), *Military life: The psychology of serving in peace and combat: Operational stress* (pp. 13–31). Praeger Security International.

Military Officer Training (2022). *Medicine and the Military.* https://www .medicineandthemilitary.com/education-and-training/military-officer-training

Olenick, M., Flowers, M., & Diaz, V. J. (2015). US veterans and their unique issues: enhancing health care professional awareness. *Advances in medical education and practice, 6*, 635- 639. doi: 10.2147/AMEP.S89479

Ozawa, S., & Sripad, P. (2013). How do you measure trust in the health system? A systematic review of the literature. *Social Science & Medicine, 91*, 10–14.

Priest, D., and Hall, A. (2007, February 18). Soldiers face neglect, frustration at Army's top medical facility. *The Washington Post*. https://www.washingtonpost.com/archive/politics/2007/02/18/soldiers-face-neglect-frustration-at-armys-top-medical-facility/c0c4b3e4-fb22-4df6-9ac9-c602d41c5bda/

Richmond, J. (2021). *What can we do about medical mistrust harming Americans' health?* Interdisciplinary Association for Population Health Science. https://iaphs.org/can-medical-mistrust-harming-americans-health/

Shepardson, R. L., Kosiba, J. D., Bernstein, L. I., & Funderburk, J. S. (2019). Suicide risk among Veteran primary care patients with current anxiety symptoms. *Family Practice, 36*(1), 91–95.

Song, C., & Lee, J. (2016). Citizens' use of social media in government, perceived transparency, and trust in government. *Public Performance & Management Review, 39*(2), 430–453. https://doi.org/10.1080/15309576.2015.1108798

Trowbridge, R. E., & Pearson, R. (2013). Impact of military physician rank and appearance on patient perceptions of clinical competency in a primary care setting. *Military Medicine, 178*(9), 994–1001.

Whetten, K., Leserman, J., Whetten, R., Ostermann, J., Thielman, N., Swartz, M., & Stangl, D. (2006). Exploring lack of trust in care providers and the government as a barrier to health service use. *American Journal of Public Health, 96*(4), 716–721.

Wolfe, H. L., Boyer, T. L., Rodriguez, K. L., Klima, G. J., Shipherd, J. C., Kauth, M. R., & Blosnich, J. R. (2021). Exploring research engagement and priorities of transgender and gender diverse veterans. *Military Medicine, 188*(5–6), e1224–e1231.

Yang, T. C., Matthews, S. A., & Shoff, C. (2011). Individual health care system distrust and neighborhood social environment: how are they jointly associated with self-rated health? *Journal of Urban Health, 88*(5), 945–958.

LINDA G. KEAN, LAURA C. PRIVIDERA | East Carolina University

Examining the *Essence* Advertising Landscape

A Content Analysis of Advertisements in *Essence* Magazine
From July/August 2020 to July/August 2022

Abstract

Essence magazine has been the leading lifestyle magazine for African American women for more than 50 years. During this time, researchers have analyzed the advertising and editorial content of the magazine on a variety of topics including advertising imagery and appeals, and editorial content related to health, spirituality, politics, and more. This essay examines the results of a content analysis of 296 full-page ads in 13 issues of *Essence* magazine from July/August 2020 through July/August 2022. Results showed that the most frequently advertised products included skin creams/lotions/soaps, pharmaceuticals/over-the-counter medications, hair products, and media content. Typical product claims focused on health and beauty, and most advertisements used information as a persuasive tactic. Several ads also included messages of empowerment and a focus on culture.

Keywords: *Essence*, advertising, Black/African American women, media content, magazines, persuasive appeals

For decades, the power and prevalence of advertising in the United States has become a normative part of everyday culture. In fact, Guttmann (2022) states that the United States spent approximately $285 billion on advertising in 2021—making it the largest advertising industry in the modern world. Advertisers are inherently strategic communicators and have increasingly sought to capture niche markets and their consumers. One of these niche markets is the Black[1] female audience. A media outlet that has become expert in reaching this audience is *Essence* magazine. According to the company's website:

Essence is the premiere lifestyle, fashion and beauty magazine for African-American women. With its motivating message, intimate girlfriend-to-girlfriend tone, compelling and engaging editorial lineup and vibrant modern design, *Essence* is the definitive voice of today's African American woman. *Essence* speaks directly to Black woman's spirit, her heart and her unique concerns.

Essence magazine, which began circulation in 1970, is one of the first magazines aimed specifically at African American women. Its long-standing presence, growth, and continued mission of support and empowerment to African American women makes it a rich site for analysis. Given the growth of the African American female population as well as advertisers' attention coupled with African American women's historical marginalization and lack of representation, this is an imperative group to examine (Madadi et al., 2022).

Prior to 1970, advertising aimed at African American women was virtually nonexistent (Hollerbach, 2009). In Timeka Tounsel's (2022) text, *Branding Black Womanhood*, she situates the emergence of *Essence* magazine as a media outlet designed to speak specifically to the newly empowered Black woman. She further describes in her historical review how *Essence* was created alongside the Seven Sisters magazines, a group of magazines aimed at the "typical" married woman in the United States, that included *Better Homes and Gardens, Family Circle, Good Housekeeping, Ladies Home Journal, McCall's, Redbook* and *Woman's Day*. However, unlike these other magazines, which were often geared for a White audience, *Essence* was focused on a niche market—the Black woman. Tounsel (2022) explains that it was Marcia Gillespie, the first female editor-in-chief in 1971, that strengthened the legacy of *Essence* magazine and its efforts to support self-empowered and race-conscious Black women as readers and consumers. From 1970 through 2007, under Gillespie's leadership from 1971 to 1980 and later Susan Taylor`s editorship from 1981 to 2007, *Essence* grew in subscriptions, prestige, and profitability. Tounsel (2022) describes and examines a magazine and organization focused on honoring and empowering Black women and their identity through media content. Tounsel (2022) reviews how in 2000, the original owners of *Essence* sold 49% of the company's shares to Time, Inc. with the final 51% going to the media giant in 2005. Hill's (2016) research specifically examined this timeframe to determine if feature articles in *Essence* magazine continued to support the lives, voices, and experiences of Black women before and after acquisition. What

Hill (2016) describes in their critical analysis of editorial content in *Essence* prior to the 2000 acquisition, is that the magazine content was firmly rooted in African American women's culture, identity, and empowerment. Hill found that postacquisition, empowerment messages remained present but to a lesser degree. In 2020, Richelieu Dennis purchased *Essence* magazine, which put the media outlet back in the hands of Black ownership (Tounsel, 2022). At this time, *Essence* went from monthly publications to bimonthly publications with enhanced editorial content making this media outlet a strong site for continued analysis.

Woven throughout the pages of editorial content for *Essence* magazine, are visual, mediated, and discursive advertisements and messages framed for this niche market. Kean et al.'s (2014) research discusses how "magazines have the power to influence, confirm, and create opinions, health practices, and decisions among African-American women" (p. 3). In step with the editorial content, the message of empowerment for Black women can be reflected in advertising content. In Madadi et al.'s (2022) research, they found that "African American consumers' consumption of brands is related more strongly to psychological and symbolic causes than to functional or practical ones" (p. 366). Hence, identifying one's culture with products matters with respect to consumption.

This essay investigates the advertising content of *Essence* magazine since its return to Black ownership in 2020 to examine the products advertised and messages associated with those products. This research considers the connection between the editorial goals of *Essence* magazine and the advertising content asking whether they are aligned in supporting and empowering today's Black woman. We acknowledge that there are multiple forms and definitions of empowerment. While Black women have been historically marginalized in media and society (see Collins, 1990), we also recognize that representation is one route to empowerment. Tounsel (2022) presents multiple forms of empowerment in her research and argues that:

> Consumption is a crucial act Black women perform to assert and elevate our identity ... for Black women in particular, shopping, watching, spending, and engaging are some of the mechanisms we use to be seen, to appear legible in contexts where we might otherwise go unregistered. (p. 2)

The power of advertising is profound in today's media saturated culture. Collins (1990) notes in her watershed text *Black Feminist Thought* that

"African-American women have long struggled to find alternative locations and techniques for articulating our own standpoint" (p. 236). Woodard and Mastin (2005) argue that studies on *Essence* and advertising content remain critical and needed to advance our understandings of this important population of women. Next, we turn to an examination of past research on Black women and advertising.

Black Women and Advertising Content

Over the past five decades, there have been several research articles written on the advertising and editorial content of *Essence* magazine. Hill's (2016) review of literature found that much of the scholarship on *Essence* has focused on health messaging, stereotypes, and/or sexuality. Other studies compare *Essence* magazine's content to that of a largely White readership to identify and describe potential differences in advertising as well as the impact on the African American consumer (Campo & Mastin, 2007; Kean & Prividera, 2007).

One avenue of research concerned the advertising of unhealthy products such as cigarettes, alcohol, and high-calorie foods to African American consumers. These studies revealed that magazines aimed at Black readers were more likely than those aimed at White readers to advertise cigarettes (Basil et al., 1991), alcohol (Cui, 2000), and calorie-rich, nutrient-poor foods (Campo & Mastin, 2007; Kean & Prividera, 2007), thus potentially impacting positive health behaviors and wellness. More specifically, Campo and Mastin (2007) found that much of the advertising content in *Ebony, Essence,* and *Jet* magazines over a 21-year period focused on high-calorie, low-nutrition products. Like print media, Henderson and Kelly (2005) found that television programs targeting African Americans contained advertisements that were more likely to be for "fast food, candy, soda or meat and were less likely to be for cereals, grains and pasta, fruits and vegetables, dessert or alcohol," compared to programs aimed at a general market (p. 191). In fact, Kean and Prividera (2007) found that fast food was a commonly advertised product in *Essence* magazine in 2004, making up about 15% of ads.

Gender and racial stereotypes have also been examined in a variety of media including magazines. Hollerbach's (2009) analysis of 358 prime time advertisements—one aimed at general audiences, and one aimed at African American audiences—found that representations of African Americans has increased from prior research. While that is positive progress, Hollerbach

(2009) also found that African Americans were limited in their standing with said advertisements. The author states that "products with less social status, such as food, alcohol, and discount department stores, were more likely featured in African American" media whereas "products with more social status, such as automobiles, medicine, and finance, were more likely featured in General Audience" advertisements (p. 612). The author concludes that although African Americans have increased in representation in ads, their status remains subordinate to the dominant paradigm. Mastin et al. (2004) found in their analysis of more than 14,000 advertisements in *Essence* and *Ladies Home Journal* that women from both magazines were portrayed as fulfilling traditional and stereotypical female gender roles. This included purchasing products that focused on appearance, cleaning, childcare, and the domestic sphere rather than in areas that represented the unique and complicated lives of contemporary women. Advertisements on financial services and products as well as technology were relatively limited. Almost a decade later, Reviere and Byerly (2013) state that "women's magazines both reinforce traditional gender roles and reflect the changes in women's lives" (p. 680). Their research specifically examined "women's sexual freedom" and liberation through performing a critical discourse analysis of advice columns in *Essence* and *Cosmo* magazines. Ultimately, the authors found that both magazines spoke to tenets of feminist thinking and empowerment to include freedom, pleasure, and voice; however, *Essence* presented their readership with more empowered thinking and action. Reviere and Byerly stated that "*Essence* columnists affirm Black women's authority over their sexuality and over their relationships to the point of telling the fella goodbye when he strays" (p. 687). Additionally, "[T]he sexual discourse in *Essence* contrasts starkly with the hypersexualized images and accompanying messages of Black women that dominate today's popular culture" (p. 687). This is certainly progress from earlier representations of Black women in media.

While messages sent to Black women remain differing and complex, we embrace Tounsel's (2022) perspective on Black female empowerment as she notes that

> Black Girl Magic matters because it is one process through which a constrained public can access media citizenship. Despite its limitations as a form of enfranchisement bound to certain affirming images ... this framework offers Black women a pathway to a kind of everyday empowerment. (p. 126)

It is in this vein that we delve into an examination of advertisements in *Essence* and their corresponding messages from 2020 to 2022 when *Essence* magazine returned to African American ownership.

Methodology

Essence is the top-rated lifestyle magazine aimed at Black women, and it is "the place 31 million Black women call home" (*Essence*, 2022, p. 2). According to the 2022 *Essence* media kit, *Essence* has more than one million paid subscribers, with an average monthly print readership of 6.5 million. The median age of print readers is 48 and for digital readers 41. The median household income is $75,455 with 35% of readers having a college or postgraduate degree and 64% with some college. Fifty-three percent of readers are employed and 71% own a home. Fifty-one percent report being married and 36% of readers have children.

This research reviews product advertisements in *Essence* magazine from the July/August 2020 issues through the July/August 2022 issues. In addition to examining products advertised, we also investigate the messages constructed to entice *Essence* readers on product purchases as well as why said products should be purchases. Thus, this research is guided by three research questions:

Research Question 1: What types of products are advertised to *Essence* readers between 2020 and 2022 and in what frequency?

Research Question 2: What claims and appeals are used to entice *Essence* readers to purchase products?

Research Question 3: What are the implications of products advertised, appeals used, and claims made in *Essence* during 2020–2022?

Coding Scheme

This coding scheme included three broad variables—product type, claims made (statements about product characteristics), and appeals (strategies used to sell the products). All full-page advertisements were selected from each *Essence* magazine issue from July/August 2020 through July/August 2022 for a total of 13 issues. If an advertisement ran for more than one page, it was coded once. Based on previous research (Hollerbach, 2009; Kean & Prividera, 2007; Mastin et al., 2004; Reviere & Byerly, 2013), and in an effort to cover all potential advertised products, the coding scheme included 30 unique product categories: skin lotions/creams/soaps, hair products, nail products, cosmetics, fashion/apparel (clothing/accessories—nonathletic), athletic clothing, shoes (nonathletic), shoes (athletic), jewelry, athletic products/equipment, pharmaceuticals (prescription/over-the-counter (OTC) drugs), sexual health products, fast food/restaurants, food, alcoholic beverages, non-alcoholic beverages, cigarettes/tobacco products, travel/tourism, consumer electronics, cleaning, child related, pet related, telecommunication products/services, automobiles, media, cooking, home goods, hygiene, financial/insurance, and other.

Beyond what products were advertised, we were also interested in what claims were made about each product. Essentially, what were the characteristics of the product being touted to the consumer? What was being promised by the product if purchased? Each ad was coded for the presence of each of the following claims about the product: beauty, financial, relational, professional, weight loss, health, and empowerment/activism. A beauty claim was coded as present if the advertisement copy used words such as beauty/beautiful/handsome/attractive or words and phrases that generally implied improved appearance such as radiant, glowing, reduced wrinkles/spots, and/or smoother skin. Financial claims were coded as present if the product itself was going to save the buyer money in some way. A coupon code was not coded as a financial claim because it was not considered a quality of the product but rather a tactic used to attract the buyer. Relational claims were coded as present if images and language referenced family, friends, relationships, and/or gatherings as being developed through product use. If a mother and a daughter were pictured using a skin cream, this was not coded as relational. However, if an ad implied that a certain product would bring families together, this would be coded as a relational claim. The advertisement, in this case, is making the claim that the product produces a relational benefit. Products were coded as having a professional claim if words like career, workplace, and/or profession were in the text and associated with the product. Weight loss claims were coded as present if the text addressed weight loss specifically as an outcome of product use and this outcome was seen as beneficial. A health claim was considered present if terms such as health/healthy were used, but also nourish, protect, safe, clean, vitamins, minerals, and other terms associated with health or healthy products. The argument for including a wide variety of terms here is that the reader could assume that the product is making a health claim, not necessarily that the product is healthy. By their nature, all prescription medications would be coded as having a health claim. Other OTC medications that addressed specific issues such as heart burn, bladder control, and so on would also be coded as having a health claim. Phrases like no sugar and low fat were coded as health claims but not as weight loss claims. Empowerment or activism would be coded as present if the message was about lifting up/serving the community, addressing bias/racism, or using terms such as amplifying voices, speaking out, standing up, and other language associated with the concepts of empowerment and activism. We chose to code each claim as an individual variable using a series of yes/no response items because products could have multiple claims. For instance, many advertisements for lotion talked about glowing and soft skin that would fall into the beauty claim but would also use terms like repair and nourish, which would be considered health-related claims.

In addition to the claim being made about the product, we also wanted to consider what type of appeal was being used to make these claims. Again, we coded for the presence of each appeal. The appeals we coded for were emotional, informational, celebrity, testimonial, and cultural. Emotional appeals were present when using terms such as concern, trust, courage, and love, but also if the advertisement was attempting to use humor or fear as a motivator. If the advertisement contained information about the product ingredients, guidelines for product use, or effects, then an information appeal was coded as present. If a celebrity endorsed a product or was seen using the product, celebrity appeal would be coded. Testimonial appeals would be present if a non-celebrity indicated having used the product and was endorsing it. Products that were "dermatologist recommended," for example, would also be coded as having testimonial appeal present. Finally, a cultural appeal was present if culture was being used to sell the product or provide validity to the product such as "Black girl magic" or "created by Black scientists."

Results

Advertised Products

In total, there were 296 product advertisements in the 13 *Essence* magazine issues analyzed in this research.

The most advertised products were skin lotions/creams/soaps with 46 advertisements (16% of all ads), pharmaceuticals/OTC medications with 37 ads (13%), hair products with 34 ads (12%), media content with 30 ads (10%),

Table 1. Numbers of Advertisements in Each Essence Issue

Issue	Number of Advertisements
July/August 2020	23
September/October 2020	28
November/December 2020	26
January/February 2021	11
March/April 2021	18
May/June 2021	19
July/August 2021	25
September/October 2021	19
November/December 2021	26
January/February 2022	17
March/April 2022	25
May/June 2022	32
July/August 2022	27

nonalcoholic beverages with 20 ads (7%), and hygiene products with 17 ads (6%). See Table 2 for full list of products advertised.

There are a few important items to note here. The media category was exclusively filled with *Essence* products. These included advertisements with minimal content for *Essence* and its digital platform, detail-rich advertisements for video programming and podcasts that are part of *Essence* Inc., and large multipage ads for the *Essence* culture festival that occurs annually in New Orleans. In terms of advertisements in the pharmaceutical/OTC category, 34 out of 37 were for prescription medications. Medications were for various health issues including psoriasis, metastatic breast cancer, HIV, sickle cell, and others. Nonprescription OTC products advertised were for fiber supplements and pain relievers. Hygiene products fell into two categories—deodorant and bladder control pads. Hair and skin products included a variety of different items by different companies.

One area of interest for the researchers in addition to the products that *were* advertised, is the products that were never or rarely advertised. Two products entirely absent from the pages of *Essence* were cigarettes and alcoholic beverages. Past research has criticized advertisers for specifically targeting Black

Table 2. Number of Occurrences of Each Product Type

Product	Number
Skin lotions/creams/oils/soaps	46
Pharmaceuticals – prescription/OTC (nonsexual health)	37
Hair products	34
Media (music, videos, movies, books)	30
Non-alcoholic beverages	20
Hygiene (pads, deodorant, tooth)	17
Financial/insurance	16
Other:	16
Food	10
Automobiles (including light trucks and SUVs)	10
Fashion/apparel/accessories (nonathletic)	9
Travel/tourism (hotels, resorts, airlines)	9
Shoes (athletic)—all for sketchers	8
Cosmetics	7
Jewelry	5
Pet related	5
Cooking products	5
Home furnishing	4
Cleaning	4
Nail products	2
Fast food/restaurants	1
Telecommunication products/services	1
Athletic clothing	0
Shoes (nonathletic)	0
Athletic products/equipment	0
Sexual health products	0
Alcoholic beverages	0
Cigarettes/tobacco products	0
Consumer electronics	0
Child related	0

media outlets with products that can be seen as unhealthy (Basil et al., 1991; Cui, 2000). *Essence* seems to have made a clear choice about focusing on the health of the consumers or, at the very least, not promoting unhealthy behaviors. Regarding those products present but limited in the sample, we can consider the data for food and beverages. In the 13 issues reviewed in this current study, only 30 advertisements (10%) were for food and beverages. However, Kean and Prividera (2007) conducted a content analysis specifically of food and beverage products advertised in *Essence* in 2004 and found different results. In the 12 issues published that year, a total of 134 advertisements were found relating to food and beverage products. In the 2007 study, three of the most advertised consumption products were nonalcoholic beverages with 37 ads, alcoholic beverage with 16 ads, and fast food with 13 of the total 134 consumption product advertisements. In the data reported in the current study, there were no advertisements for alcoholic beverages over a two-year period, 20 for nonalcoholic beverages, and only one ad represented a fast food company—McDonald's. However, the message in the McDonald's ad was not about food but rather about the empowerment of Black women. The text reads as follows:

> Yes, Black women. We are strength defined. Expressive by intent and powerful in voice. We are love learned. Magical in design and tenacious by choice. We are bold, Black and beautifully golden in very way. Thank you for showing us our essence each and every day.

The tagline for the ad reads, "Black and Positively Golden," followed by the McDonald's golden arches. This would seem to indicate a shift in the focus of advertising in *Essence* since 2004 away from food products, particularly those that would be considered unhealthy such as fast food and alcoholic beverages, to products more in keeping with self-care. Overall, *Essence* has clearly distanced itself from less healthy products as there were no coded advertisements for cigarettes and alcoholic beverages and very few for less healthy products such as fast food.

Surprisingly, there were also no advertisements coded as child related even though almost 40% of readers indicated having children. There was one advertisement for dinosaur-shaped chicken nuggets, which was clearly meant for children but was primarily a food product and so was coded in that category. An additional advertisement for IKEA furniture featured an image of a sleeping child but is not a store in which only children's items can be found. This was coded as an advertisement for home goods. Even when considering these products primarily as child related, there were only three in total, making up just 1% of advertised goods. Some advertisements did refer to keeping family "safe" or "healthy," but they were not for products specifically to be used by children such as children's shampoos, soaps, books, toys, or medications.

Advertising Claims

In alignment with products focusing on empowering the *Essence* woman, we found that the claims made and appeals used followed suit. The most typical claim used to sell a product in the advertisements reviewed for this study was health, followed by beauty, relationship, empowerment/activism, financial, then professional claims. There were no advertisements associated with weight loss claims. One hundred thirty-one (44%) of the advertisements coded used some language that connected the product with a health outcome. These products included prescription medications, deodorant, skin lotions, and more. We do not argue here that all products that were coded as having a health claim do affect the readers' health. Rather we take the view that the language used in the text infers that the product can be positively related to one's health. For example, skin lotion and body wash ads said, "visibly healthier skin" or "helps stop dry; infuse your skin with moisture." In fact, 72% of advertisements for skin-related products were coded for the presence of a health claim. Descriptions of the product ingredients related to a health claim as well. For example, "Infused with collagen and vitamin B3 complex; 5 skin-conditioning ingredients; 20% pure vitamin C serum." These references to vitamins and nutrients read as a health claim. Forty-one percent of the hair products referenced health in some way. For example, hair products "strengthen and protect your hair from within," "provide deep moisture to penetrate hair shaft," and are "formulated with aloe vera and soy protein to lock in hydration, protect and nourish hair." This language indicates that hair will be healthier with product use. Hygiene products were also highly likely to have a health claim. For example, deodorants would focus on what was *not* in the product and would advertise as "aluminum free" with the implication that aluminum can be unhealthy and therefore is not included. The athletic shoes advertised in the 13 issues reviewed were all for Skechers® arch fit. The ads claim that the benefits of this shoe are a "podiatrist designed shape and comfort arch support." Referencing the physician design connects the shoe with being a healthy product. Pharmaceuticals were coded to have a health claim in 100% of the advertised products. In addition to ads for prescription medication, over the counter medications claimed to "lower cholesterol, kill germs and promote heart health." The final category in which 100% of the ads made a health claim were products for pets. Our pets are very important to us, and making healthy decisions for them is central to being a good pet parent. The readers of *Essence* want to make good choices and that includes healthy choices. Connecting products to health is a common claim in the advertisements in *Essence* and can be read as empowering the reader.

The next most typical claim was a beauty claim. Fifty-two (18%) of the products made a claim that indicated product use would be tied to enhanced beauty. This is not surprising when more that 25% of the products being advertised are skin lotion/wash and hair care products. Terms like "radiant, glowing, long-lasting softness," all speak to components of beauty.

Forty-three (15%) of the advertisements in the issues coded made a relational claim for the product. Advertisements for media were very likely to make relational claims. This is due to the number of multipage advertisements for the *Essence* culture fest. The ads laid out all the events for the weekend, which included workshops on developing relationships, financial growth, and other topics. Other products indicating improved relationships with product use included travel, automobiles, nonalcoholic beverages, and pharmaceuticals. In ads for a medication used to treat HIV-1, text copy reads, "Keep connecting, because HIV doesn't change who you are." The message here is that one can still develop relationships even when living with HIV. An advertisement for the National Crime Prevention Council also addressed relationships when it encouraged communities to reach out to the police and vice versa. The ad stated, "Listen to each other, build partnerships, build trust … that is how we get to where we all can finally Celebrate Safe Communities®." Coca-Cola® teamed up with *Essence* for the digital content, "If Not for My Girls," which provided stories "of women who support, uplift and cheer each other on through it all." Another Coca-Cola ad tells readers, "This season, celebrate what it means to be together." Developing and maintaining relationships is a theme that has long been central to the *Essence* brand (Kean & Prividera, 2007).

Thirty-four (12%) advertisements in this study focused on empowerment or activism to support a product or service. An example of this comes from the National Fair Housing Alliance with a message focused on discrimination against the LGBTQ+ community. Copy reads, "Did you know that HUD can help you fight housing discrimination?" The ad gives details about how to file a fair housing complaint. This information and the knowledge that a government office is there to help in addressing discrimination can be seen as empowering to the reader. An ad that uses a message of empowerment for a commercial product is for Smart Water®. This copy reads, "putting radical self-care first so you can own the way you show up to the people and things you love most." In advertisements for the *Essence* culture fest, we see images of raised fists along with copy that reads, "Celebrating the resilience of our community." An ad for the Girls United Summit talks about creating a forum for activism. One insurance ad addressed what it is doing for its labor force with the headline, "Empowering employees professionally and personally," and then providing details about implicit bias training in the workplace and community outreach. Coca Cola reminds the reader that:

> Together we shimmer a radiant light of joy and beauty
> Together we remind ourselves who we are and what we can be
> Together we reaffirm the power of our possibilities
> Together we uplift and inspire a nation
> Together we raise hope for our future
> Together we are a community making history.

In sum, many of the advertisements in *Essence* use an explicit connection to the notion of empowerment that is key to the *Essence* reader's identity.

Twenty-one (7%) advertisements in this study used a financial claim. Not surprisingly, most of these were for products coded as financial or insurance products. AARP® addressed financial issues by stating, "You Make Money. Now Make It Work for You," and provided a link to a retirement savings website. The other category that made up most of the ads with financial claims was the media category. This category was exclusively filled with *Essence* products, which were mostly large multipage ads for the *Essence* festival. Again, these ads would lay out details of the days-long event including content of workshops, socials, etc., including those with a financial focus. Although only 7% of ads used financial claims, this is an increase from research about a decade ago.

Sixteen (5%) ads include a professional claim in their text. This was the least often used claim in the advertisements in this study, other than weight loss for which there were no ads in any of the 13 issues. An example of a professional claim can be found in one of the advertisements for cosmetics. Members of the sales team gave testimonies regarding the benefits of working for the company. Insurance and investment companies also spoke to professional goals. Advertisements gave advice on how to "Pave your new path." Ads for medications for metastatic breast cancer indicated that you could "Be in your career moment," even when battling cancer with the help of this medication.

Advertising Appeals

In terms of appeals, this research coded for the presence of emotional, information, celebrity, testimony, and cultural appeals. The most used appeal was informational, followed by emotional, then cultural, celebrity, and finally, testimonial appeals. Two hundred twenty-five ads (76%) used an informational appeal. Often this included product ingredients for a wide range of items including body wash, deodorant, dog treats, hair care products, and medications. "Waterproof and smudge resistant" and "Serum with vitamin B3 and SPF 50" served as information about cosmetics, while "unlimited talk and text and data $45/month no contract" laid out the details of a telecommunications plan. Hair care advertisements provided information that the product was "alcohol free." Those advertisements lacking information tended to fall into the clothing and jewelry category in which the ad simply includes a picture of the item.

Ninety-seven advertisements (33%) had an emotional component used as a strategy to sell their products. In this category, some products used fear to get readers to pay attention. "Could this be the moment that helps you face cancer?" was one headline that calls out to the reader regarding a pharmaceutical that may address a particular type of lung cancer. While ultimately the message is reassuring that the product can help, it is expected that the word cancer will create fear initially. The fear is then expected to dissipate knowing that there is a medication available to help. Other advertisements used fear but to a lesser degree. "When it counts, trust Clorox®" is the tag line for an advertisement that tells us that if we want to make sure we keep germs and bacteria from our homes, we should use their product. Another appeal to the reader's role as one charged with the health of the family is for laundry detergent, "certified safer for you and your family." The implicit message is that some things are not safe and thus creating that same fear that one must use this product to keep the family safe. Another product that calls to readers' drive to provide a safe and healthy environment for their families is Reynolds Wrap®. In one ad the text tells the reader, "1 in 9 Americans don't have access to a meal, which means dinnertime desperately needs our help. Reynolds is joining

Feeding America in the fight against hunger by helping provide two million meals to families across the country." The reader may feel the emotional pull of knowing some families do not have enough food. This negative feeling is then turned positive by reading that the product they buy can help families in need. Some additional positive emotional components can also be found in the advertisements for nonalcoholic beverages. Coca-Cola has a series of ads about "History Shakers" in which individuals are honored for their contributions to science, sports, media, and nonprofits that serve children and other marginalized or disadvantage individuals. Images of happy families, couples, and friends smiling as they gather create positive emotional responses, and advertisers hope these connect with the products whether it be home goods, nonalcoholic beverages, or skin lotion. Many of the advertisements for pharmaceuticals, in addition to containing a great deal of information about the drug and its effects, also have an emotional component. Telling the stories of individuals overcoming physical obstacles, making personal connections, and feeling confident generates positive emotional responses. Some emotional appeals come from a place of happiness and self-love. Dove uses a quote from Dominique who claims, "Watching my daughter grow has made me more proud of my stretch marks." This tugs at readers who both have children and know the joy of parenthood but who also may have judged their bodies. This copy reminds readers to love themselves top to bottom.

Not surprisingly, a connection to culture and race was often a part of the advertisements found in *Essence*. Forty-seven (16%) ads referenced culture or race in some way. In an ad for Ford®, readers can find the phrases such as "Black Girls Run!," "Black Girls Do Bike," and "Outdoor Afro." Ford is appealing specifically to the magazine's demographics of Black women. An ad for Maui moisture vegan hair care included a Q&A with Kennedy Jones, a digital content creator and influencer. Jones explains, "[B]eing a Black woman is one of God's greatest gifts, and now more than ever sisters need to own this." Not only does this ad reference Black culture, but it also uses an empowering and emotional message as part of the strategy. All the advertisements for media products included some reference to culture. *Essence* podcasts network advertised its program, Yes, Girl! "It's a Black girl magic happy hour filling your glasses with celeb interviews, pop culture, politics and more." By nature of the event, the *Essence* festival of culture included images and text that focused on culture. Phrases included "raise your voice" and "unstoppable" with details about workshops and sessions related specially to Black women and men on topics such as wellness, finances, music, and more. Cosmetics also included cultural references such as: "Skincare for your shade of amazing. We believe that melanin-rich skin is unique and fabulous." This text not only references culture but celebrates and empowers Black women, which is the central tenet of *Essence, Inc.* An advertisement for Charleston, South Carolina, encourages readers to "Explore centuries of African and African American influence in one of the world's most captivating destinations. Discover Charleston's rich history, culture and authenticity." The ad copy is written with the specific audience in mind.

Regarding the use of celebrity appeals, thirty-six (12%) advertisements included this strategy. Cedric, the Entertainer, was one of the celebrities found in the advertisements advocating that people diagnosed with cancer learn more about clinical trials in a standuptocancer.org advertisement. Brook Burke and Martha Stewart both appeared in ads for Skechers ArchFit. In terms of celebrity appeals, these were associated with athletic shoes, hair care, financial products, and more.

Finally, 29 (10%) advertisements included testimony as a strategy to sell products. Examples include, "My skin glows, I feel moisturized and beautiful" and "dermatologist recommended brand." In an advertisement encouraging people to "Go RVing®," the Frazier family provided testimony about their trip to Oregon. "We put down our phones to get outdoors with the family and simply enjoy the journey." The ad includes photos of the Frazier family together in several different outdoor locations. In a sobering message from the National Fair Housing Alliance, readers are given testimony from an individual who was denied an apartment because he was Black, illustrating the continued discrimination that exists in contemporary society.

Discussion

Overall, the advertisements in *Essence* appear to align with the magazine's vision of honoring and empowering Black women. The advertisements maintain the focus on the *Essence* Black woman. For this reason, we see ads specifically related to the woman herself and her needs. These can be related to beauty or external image such as skin creams, cosmetics, hair products; physical health/confidence with advertisements for feminine hygiene and prescription drugs; and financial wellness including insurance products and credit cards. Products not receiving much focus in the pages were those mostly related to potentially unhealthy products and choices such as the consumption of fast food, alcohol, and cigarettes. This is a positive direction for the *Essence* consumer.

The most common advertising claim focused on the health of the *Essence* woman followed by claims associated with beauty, relationships, empowerment, financial, and professional topics. Many of the health claims focused on products that helped a woman be her best self—a claim that could help women relax and feel good while maintaining healthy choices. As Gilbert et al. (2021) state, "[H]ealth and wellness are at the very core of consumer well-being," which is a relatively unexplored area of scholarly focus in today's complex world (p. 499). Beauty, another common claim, allows women to look and subsequently feel like their best selves. Claims focused on positive relationships were common as was female empowerment and activism—topics of great interest to Black women (Tounsel, 2022). Finally, although in lesser quantities, both financial and professional advertising claims appeared throughout *Essence*, thus appealing to working women who have complex decisions to make with finances and their professions. Prior research has suggested that these topics were less visible in ads framed toward Black women, so this visibility in advertisements represents a positive direction in potential topics of importance to today's Black woman.

With respect to appeals, it is not surprising that an informational appeal was the most used appeal followed by emotional, cultural, celebrity, and testimonial appeals. Today's diverse *Essence* woman understands the importance of information to make decisions that impact her life. Such messaging appeals to the educated female consumer, which is consistent with the *Essence* demographic.

We are encouraged by the results of this study that advertising in *Essence* is presenting women with a variety of products and choices showing value for diversity, culture, and Black women's voices. Many products speak to women's health, and while some focus on appearance, the claim is focused on female empowerment rather than beauty for male pleasure. Advertisements frame women's lives as complex with diverse needs. Perhaps, most importantly, Black women are framed as having agency in their lives with varied depictions of choice and success. It is also important to note that some media genres, including advertising, may sometimes work against such important empowering messages.

Advertising is an ever-expanding industry. Mediated venues evolve daily and remain a critical context for analysis. Research on the impact of advertising involving Black women in its multiple platforms must continue. Advertising is merely one venue out of many where Black women can experience empowerment. We recognize that this study presents a snapshot of data and analysis in one media venue. We also acknowledge that there are multiple ways in which messages can be consumed and interpreted and that the context of current societal times matter for message construction and consumption. Research that would help develop the conclusions of this current work could investigate the multiple components of *Essence Inc.* such as digital advertising and the *Essence* cultural festival as well as other outlets aimed at Black consumers.

NOTE

1. Readers will note that the terms Black and African American both appear in this text. These terms are used by the authors of this essay as well as those authors being cited. We recognize that individuals may experience these terms differently, and it is our goal to be inclusive and respectful in our use of both terms.

REFERENCES

Basil, M. D., Schooler, C., Altman, D. G., Slater, M., Albright, C. L., & Maccoby, N. (1991). How cigarettes are advertised in magazines: Special messages for special markets. *Health Communication, 3*(2), 75–91. https://doi.org/10.1207 /s15327027hc0302_1

Campo, S., & Mastin, T. (2007). Placing the burden on the individual: Overweight and obesity in African American and mainstream women's magazines. *Health Communication, 22*(3), 229–240. https://doi.org/10.1080/10410230701626885

Collins, P. H. (1990). *Black feminist thought: Knowledge, consciousness and the politics of empowerment.* Routledge.

Cui, G. (2000). Advertising of alcoholic beverages in African-American and women's magazines: Implications for health communication. *The Howard Journal of Communications, 11,* 279–293. https://doi.org/10.1080/10646170050204563

Essence. (2022). *Essence media kit.* Essence Inc. https://www.essence.com/wp -content/uploads/2022/01/2022-ESSENCE-MEDIAKIT.pdf

Gilbert, J., Stafford, M., Sheinen, D., & Pounders, K. (2021). The dance between darkness and light: A systematic review of advertising's role in consumer well -being (1980–2020). *International Journal of Advertising, 40*(4), 491–528. https://doi.org/10.1080/02650487.2020.1863048

Guttmann, A. (2022). *U.S. advertising industry—statistics and facts.* Statista. https:// www.statista.com/topics/979/advertising-in-the-us/#dossierKeyfigures

Henderson, V., & Kelly, B. (2005). Food advertising in the age of obesity: Content analysis of food advertising on general market and African American television. *Journal of Nutrition Education & Behavior, 37*(4), 191–196. https://doi.org /10.1016/S1499-4046(06)60245-5

Hill, M. (2016). Do Black women still come first? Examining *Essence* magazine post Time Warner. *Critical Studies in Media Communication, 33*(4), 366–380. http://dx/doi.org/10.1080/15295036.2016.1225968

Hollerbach, K. (2009). The impact of market segmentation on African American frequency, centrality, and status in television advertising. *Journal of Broadcasting & Electronic Media, 53*(4), 599–614. https://doi.org/10.1080 /08838150903324014

Kean, L., & Prividera, L. (2007). Communicating about race and health: A content analysis of print advertisements and general readership magazines. *Health Communication, 21*(3), 289–297. https://doi.org/10.1080/10410230701428720

Kean, L., Prividera, L., Howard, J., & Gates, D. (2014). Health, weight, and fitness messages in *Ebony* and *Essence*: A framing analysis of articles in African American women's magazines. *Journal of Magazine & New Media Research, 15*(1), 1–25. https://doi.org/10.1353/jmm.2014.0015

Madadi, R., Torres, I., Fazli-Salehi, R., & Zuniga, M. (2022). Brand love and ethnic identification: The mediating role of brand attachment among African American consumers. *Journal of Consumer Marketing, 39*(4), 358–370. https://doi.org /10.1108/JCM-06-2020-3922

Mastin, T., & Campo, S. (2006). Conflicting messages: Overweight and obesity advertisements and articles in Black magazines. *The Howard Journal of Communications, 17*, 265–285. https://doi.org/10.1080/10646170600966527

Mastin, T., Coe, A., Hamilton, S., & Tarr, S. (2004). Product purchase decision-making behavior and gender role stereotypes: A content analysis of advertisements in *Essence* and *Ladies' Home Journal*, 1990–1999. *The Howard Journal of Communications, 15*, 229–243. https://doi.org/10.1080/10646170490521167

Reviere, R., & Byerly, C. (2013). Sexual messages in Black and White: A discourse analysis of *Essence* and *Cosmo*. *Feminist Media Studies, 13*(4), 676–692. https://doi.org/10.1080/14680777.2012.680195

Tounsel, T. (2022). *Branding Black womanhood: Media citizenship from Black power to Black girl magic*. Rutgers.

Woodward, J., & Mastin, T. (2005). Black womanhood: *Essence* and its treatment of stereotypical images of Black women. *Journal of Black Studies, 36*(2), 264–281. https://doi.org/10.1177/0021934704273152

Władysław Chłopicki is a professor at the Jagiellonian University in Kraków, Poland, and in the State Academy of Applied Sciences in Krosno, where he teaches linguistic and translation courses. He is the precursor of humor studies in Poland with his book *O humorze poważnie* (Humour taken seriously, PAN, 1995). He is a co-editor of e.g. *Cognition in Language* (Tertium, 2007). *Culture's Software: Communication Styles* (Cambridge Scholars, 2015), *Humorous Discourse* (De Gruyter, 2017) *Handbook of Humor Research* (forthcoming with De Gruyter, 2024). Most recently his main focus has been humor in the public sphere: he has led and participated in a number of related European grants (the research results of these are systematically published on the website humorinpublic.eu). He is the past president of the International Society of Humor Studies and long-term president of the Cracow Tertium Society for Language Studies, and editor of The European Journal of Humour Research and Tertium Linguistic Journal.

Sheena M. Eagan, Ph.D. (University of Texas Medical Branch) is an associate professor with the Department of Bioethics and Interdisciplinary Studies in the Brody School of Medicine at East Carolina University. Her research and teaching have focused on medical ethics and the history of medicine, with a subspecialized focus on military medicine. Dr. Eagan is co-director of ECU's Veteran to Scholar Boot Camp, a program supported by grant funding from the National Endowment for the Humanities. Dr. Eagan has published articles in peer-reviewed journals, military-specific journals, and contributed to edited books on a variety of topics in military medicine. She has also given talks and lectures on her work in North America, Asia, Europe, and the Middle East. Her research interests include: Military Medical Ethics; Military Women's Health; The History Of PTSD; Veteran Re-Integration; Moral Injury; Research Ethics; Medicine During The Holocaust; The History Of Military Medicine.

Hamdi Echkaou is an Assistant Professor of Communications Media and PR at Al Akhawayn University in Ifrane (AUI) in Morocco. His work has been published in the Journal of North African Studies and authored a number of edited book chapters on the youth movement and cyberspace, online newspapers, and internal migration. He has also collaborated with a number of universities in Germany, the United States, and China on field projects that involved both research and teaching. In 2018, Dr. Echkaou earned his first Ph.D. in Humanities from Mohamed V University in Rabat. He studied Cyberspace Discourses of the Youth Movement. This academic year Dr. Echkaou is finalizing his 2nd dissertation in

Communications Media and Instructional Technology doctoral program at Indiana University of Pennsylvania (IUP) where he also was working as a Teaching Associate in the Communications Media Department. Hamdi has taught both graduate and undergraduate students at Mohamed V University in Rabat, IUP, and AUI.

Erika Johnson, Ph.D. (Missouri) is an associate professor at East Carolina University in the School of Communication. Her internationally recognized research in various journals and conference venues addresses interactive, social, and entertainment media effects (e.g., Communication Research, International Communication Association). Erika Johnson approaches her research agenda from various methodological perspectives, also delving into social media trends and pedagogy. While much of her research explores source in regard to communication persuasiveness from a social science perspective, she also endeavors qualitative research. She teaches a variety of courses in the realm of persuasion and mass media research and application, including capstone, research methods, strategic communication, and social influence.

Linda Kean is a professor of communication and Dean of the College of Fine Arts and Communication at East Carolina University. Her research area concerns images of gender, race, and ethnicity in media and the impact of these representations on the perceptions, attitudes, and behaviors of media consumers. Her work has been published in *Communication Research, Media Psychology, Health Communication,* and the *Howard Journal of Communications.* She is on the editorial board of *Women and Language* and *Health Communication.* Kean has taught at the graduate and undergraduate levels in the areas of Media Effects, Public Relations, Communication Theory, and Health Communication. She also works in the area of international scholarship and education, designing programs to facilitate the global exchange of ideas related to communication and arts.

Justin Tyler King obtained an undergraduate in Graphic Design at Mercer University and currently is a graduate student at East Carolina University. King strives for lively and empathetic design that encourages connectivity and has designed for health clinics, non-profit organizations, local apparel stores, and others.

Hannah Grace Lanneau received her Ph.D. from the University of California San Diego (2022). She engages in collaborative scholarship, pedagogy, and advocacy specializing in equitable access to education and healthcare at universities across the U.S. Hannah Grace has served as a key member of the research team evaluating the pedagogical methods of one of UCSD's undergraduate writing programs. She also co-presented at ECU oncology grand rounds in April 2022 with the Chief of Gynecologic Oncology (ECU Health) on interdisciplinary approaches to fostering open communication between physician and patient to develop satisfactory treatment plans in the event of uterine cancer recurrence. Her dissertation (2022) examines the influence of book subscription programs and the post-WWII GI Bill in her analysis of the intersections between access to housing, healthcare, and higher education in the mid-20th century. Her research interests include 20th-century American literary and cultural studies and the health humanities.

Adam Nowakowski holds Master's Degrees both in Russian Studies and in Polish Linguistics, with a doctorate in Russian Literature (all from the Jagiellonian University). He published over twenty papers in three languages and one book. His research interests include nonverbal communication, translation studies, and language teaching. He worked at Carpathian State College in Krosno (Poland), Jagiellonian University in Cracow (Poland), and East Carolina University in Greenville, NC (USA). As a visiting lecturer, he taught classes at Dalarna University in Falun (Sweden), University of Bologna (Italy), Istanbul University (Turkey), St Mary's University College in Belfast (Northern Ireland), "1 Decembrie 1918" University in Alba Iulia (Romania), Suleyman Demirel University in Almaty (Kazakhstan). He currently works at the International Centre of Education (an inter-faculty unit of the Cracow University of Technology), where he teaches Polish as a foreign language to students from over a hundred different countries.

Mariusz Marczak is an associate professor in the Chair for Translation Studies at the Jagiellonian University in Kraków, Poland. He has taught in both undergraduate and graduate programs in EFL teacher training and translation studies, including a European Master's in Translation (EMT) program, accredited by the European Commission's Directorate-General for Translation. He has also worked for the British Council in Poland and the Educational Research Institute (IBE) in Warsaw. He has published his research in numerous book chapters and academic journals, including *The Interpreter and Translator Trainer, International Journal of Continuing Engineering Education and Language Learning, Angles – New Perspectives on the Anglophone World* and *Teaching English with Technology*. He has also written the monograph entitled *Communication and Information Technology in (Intercultural) Language Teaching* (CSP, 2013) and *Telecollaboration in Translator Education* (forthcoming with Routledge, 2023), and co-edited *Contemporary English Language Teaching Research* (CSP, 2015) and *CALL for Openness* (Peter Lang, 2016). His major research interests comprise computer-assisted translation, telecollaborative learning, and the development of intercultural competence.

Chra R Mahmud is a Ph.D. researcher in Applied Linguistics and Sessional Academic at the Centre for Language and Linguistics, Faculty of Arts, Humanities, and Education, Canterbury Christ Church University. She holds an MA in Linguistics and BA in English Language and Communication. She has taught linguistic and communication-related modules in the undergraduate and foundation degree programs, including intercultural communication, sociolinguistics, and social sciences at the Centre for Language and Linguistics. She is interested in examining the relationship between people and objects concerning identity. In her Ph.D. project, she took the multidisciplinary and multimodal approach to explore the lived experiences of Kurdish migrants in the UK, focusing on identity negotiation and navigation among Iraqi Kurds in Southeast England by implementing the postcolonial, nonessential, and posthuman standpoints. Apart from her Ph.D., she is working on a Ukraine Project with colleagues in her department.

Mariella Olivos Ph.D. is an associate professor at the School of Economics and Management and Director of International Affairs for Bachelor Programs at Universidad ESAN in Lima, Perú. She is since 2001 the Executive Coordinator of CLADEA (The Latin American Council of Management Schools). She is a founder member of REDIPERU, the Network for the internationalization of Peruvian universities, and is a board member in international networks as GPE and NIBES. Her research interest focus on the field of internationalization of Higher Education, virtual teams, cross-cultural studies, COIL, and teaching methods in Entrepreneurship. Is visiting professor at ISCTE BS in Lisbon Portugal, Krakow University of Economics in Poland, Audiencia BS in France, and Nottingham Trent University in the United Kingdom. She holds a Ph.D. in Information Management at Tilburg University in The Netherlands, an MBA from UQAM in Montreal, Canada, a Ms.Sc in Economics from UNALM, is Economist from PUCP -Pontifica Universidad Católica in Perú.

Laura C. Prividera is a professor of Communication and Director of the School of Communication at East Carolina University. She has taught in both the undergraduate and graduate programs in the School of Communication. Her research examines the social constructions of gender, race and/or power in mediated contexts. Her research studies have been published in *Women's Studies in Communication*, *Women & Language*, *Journal of Magazine & New Media Research*, *Health Communication*, and *The Howard Journal of Communications*.

Kenneth Reeds is an associate professor in the Department of World Languages and Cultures at Salem State University in Massachusetts, USA. He has taught both undergraduate and graduate courses in Spanish and English on literature, culture, and language. He is the author of *What is Magical Realism?: An Explanation of a Literary Style*, co-editor of *Women Taking Risks in Contemporary Autobiographical Novels*, and translator to English of *Caras B de la historia del video arte en España*. He has a Ph.D. in Comparative Literature from University College London.

Ewa Rusek is a lecturer at the State University of Applied Sciences in Krosno, Poland. She holds a Ph.D. in ethnolinguistics (research into linguistic worldview) but her interests also comprise intercultural communication, ethnicity and European studies. She is the Departmental Coordinator of Erasmus + programme. She published a book on the picture of Europe as seen by Turkish students as well as several articles on intercultural communication and working with multilingual and multicultural groups. She has been a guest lecturer in Eger Foiskola, St Mary's College in Belfast, and taught intercultural communication in the School of Communication at East Carolina University. She also holds joint international virtual exchange classes with an American partner there.

Dorota Rygiel is a lecturer at the Department of English at the State Academy of Applied Sciences in Krosno, Poland. She has taught undergraduate courses on English literature and history of Great Britain. She holds a Ph.D. in identity dilemmas of South Asian immigrants in contemporary British literature. Her major research interests include British Asian fiction, immigrant identity, intercultural communication and migration. She has authored several articles and book chapters on immigrant writing in Britain, quest for identity, notions of home, food and foodways in an immigrant context. She has been a guest lecturer at several universities in Europe.

Sachiyo M. Shearman is a professor in the School of Communication at East Carolina University. She has taught in both the undergraduate and graduate programs in the School of Communication as well as in the International Studies Master's Program. Her research studies have been published in *Communication Teacher, Communication Quarterly, Human Communication Research, Journal of Family Research, Journal of Family Communication, and the Howard Journal of Communication*. She has written an electronic textbook, *Communication Across Cultures*, and has authored several book chapters on topics where communication and culture *intersect*. She has employed experiential learning methods in several courses, including project-based service learning and international virtual exchange. For international virtual exchange sessions, she has collaborated with partners in Japan, Peru, and Poland in the past, and she hopes to continue working with diverse international partners and prepare students to thrive across borders.

Brittany Thompson received her Bachelor of Science in Animal Science from North Carolina State University in 2001. In 2007, Brittany completed an Associate in Photographic Technology from Randolph Community College. In May 2014, she received a master's in communication from East Carolina University. She currently is a senior teaching instructor at East Carolina University in the School of Communication. Ms. Thompson's teaching and creative interest centers around professional readiness in college students. In Spring 2019, Brittany received ECU's Robert L. Jones Teaching Award for excellence in engaged teaching. In the Fall of

2018, she received the first Faculty Impact Award from ECU Career Services for her dedicated work in preparing students for careers after college. In Spring 2021, Brittany received the Board of Governor's Distinguished Professor of Teaching Award.

Mary Tucker-McLaughlin is a professor, undergraduate studies coordinator, and graduate faculty member at East Carolina University's School of Communication. Her research centers on the use of media tools to find solutions to health problems. Much of her work is with cross-disciplinary teams on grant-funded studies implementing technology and community engagement tools to disseminate critical health messages, but she has also published articles about gender representations in media. She has a strong interest in global studies and has pursued this by teaching for the ECU Global Education Partners and leading two study abroad programs. Her work has been published in *The Journal of Rural Health, Journal of Community Health, Journal of Public Health Management Practice, Electronic News*, and more.

Alicja Witalisz is a professor of linguistics at the Institute of English Studies at the Pedagogical University of Krakow, and in the State Academy of Applied Sciences in Krosno, Poland. She holds a Ph.D. from the Jagiellonian University in Krakow. Her research areas include language contact, linguistic borrowing, contact-induced language change, and neology. She has authored three monographs on English linguistic influence on Polish and published widely on linguistic borrowing-related issues, covert loans, pseudo-Anglicisms, formal and lexicosemantic variance in loans, and the perception of foreign words by the recipient language speakers. She is a member of Polish and international academic associations and research groups and a member of the Editorial Board of the *Polish Linguistic Society Journal*. She lectures on English linguistics.

Władysław Witalisz is a professor of English literature at the Institute of English Studies of the Jagiellonian University. His research covers Medieval and Renaissance authors focusing on drama and theatre, religious and mystical literature, as well as the reception of classical texts in the Middle Ages. His book, *The Trojan Mirror: Middle English Narratives of Troy as Books of Princely Advice* (Peter Lang, 2011), is a widely quoted monograph on the subject. Witalisz teaches early English literature and stages Shakespeare with his students. For most of his career, he worked in university administration in the capacity of Vice-Rector of Krosno State College (2004-2012), Vice-Dean of the Faculty of Philology at the Jagiellonian University (2012-2020), and currently as Dean of the same Faculty. As an educational administrator, he has always promoted international cooperation and student mobility.

Printed in the USA
CPSIA information can be obtained
at www.ICGtesting.com
LVHW020518121023
760822LV00002B/79